D1156506

THE PSYCHOLOGY OF SERIAL KILLER INVESTIGATIONS

The Grisly Business Unit

THE PSYCHOLOGY
OF SERIAL KILLER
INVESTIGATIONS

The Grisly Business Unit

ROBERT D. KEPPEL

Sam Houston State University
Huntsville, Texas

WILLIAM J. BIRNES

Shadow Lawn Press
Los Angeles, California

ACADEMIC PRESS

An imprint of Elsevier Science

Amsterdam Boston Heidelberg London New York Oxford
Paris San Diego San Francisco Sigapore Sydney Tokyo

The sponsoring editor for this book was Nikki Levy, the senior developmental editor
was Barbara Makinster, and the senior project manager was Paul Gottehrer. The
cover was designed by Cathy Reynolds. Composition was done by SNP Best-set Typesetter
Limited, Hong Kong and the book was printed and bound by Maple-Vail,
York, PA.

This book is printed on acid-free paper.

Academic Press
An imprint of Elsevier
525 B Street, Suite 1900, San Diego, California 92101-4495, USA
http://www.academicpress.com

Academic Press
84 Theobald's Road, London WC1X 8RR, UK
http://www.academicpress.com

Library of Congress Catalog Card Number: 2003109041

International Standard Book Number: 0-12-404260-0

PRINTED IN THE UNITED STATES OF AMERICA
03   04   05   06   07   9   8   7   6   5   4   3   2   1

CONTENTS

1

RECOGNITION AND ACKNOWLEDGMENT OF SERIAL MURDER

2

THE ARCHETYPAL SERIAL KILLER TASK FORCE INVESTIGATION: THE YORKSHIRE RIPPER CASE

3

ANATOMY OF AN INVESTIGATION

4

THE CONSULTING DETECTIVE

5

THE PAUL BERNARDO CASE

6

PROFILING THE SERIAL KILLER: THE EFFICACY OF PROFILING

7

TAKING CONTROL OF DENIAL AND DEFEAT

8

THE PLAYBOOK

9

BEST PRACTICES

BIOGRAPHIES

Robert D. Keppel, Ph.D., is an Associate Professor of Criminal Justice at Sam Houston State University and the Director of the Center for Crime Assessment and Profiling. He has over 29 years of homicide investigation experience, having participated in more than 2000 murder cases and including 17 years as the Chief Criminal Investigator with the Washington State Attorney General's Office. He has been a consultant to the Atlanta Police on the Missing and Murdered Children's Cases; a member of the national planning committee for the Violent Criminal Apprehension Program (VICAP); the primary investigator for the King County Sheriff's Department in the Ted Bundy murder cases in the Pacific Northwest; and was a consultant to the Green River Murders Task Force in Seattle, Washington.

Dr. Keppel is the author of a number of articles and four books on serial murder and has lectured extensively to police officers at national seminars on homicide investigation. He has testified in trials as an expert on the method of operation of serial killers, the "signature aspects" of murder investigations, and police investigations. He is the founder of the Washington State Homicide Investigation and Tracking System (HITS), and has been the project director for several federal grants on investigative technologies, case management, and the apprehension of murderers.

Dr. Keppel received his Doctor of Philosophy Degree in Criminal Justice from the University of Washington (1992), a Bachelor of Science Degree in Police Science and Administration from Washington State University (1966), and a Master of Arts Degree in Police Science and Administration (1967). He also holds a Master of Education Degree from Seattle University (1979).

William J. Birnes, Ph.D., obtained his doctorate from New York University and is currently completing his J.D. at Concord University School of Law. Dr. Birnes was responsible for evaluating the use of computers in homicide task force investigations as part of a grant from the Bureau of Justice Administration for the Institute of Forensics. He has also acted as a consultant to the Sentinel Corporation on international anti-money laundering compliance training. Dr. Birnes has been a National Endowment for the Humanities Fellow, a Lily Fellow, and a grants award judge for the National Endowment for the Arts.

Dr. Birnes is a *New York Times* best-selling author and has written over 20 books, as well as a literary agent. He has worked with the Drug Enforcement Administration on the development of a motion picture, and is currently producing a cable television feature and a reality series for Hearst Television. Dr. Birnes lives in New York and Los Angeles with his wife, novelist, Nancy Hayfield.

Introduction: the Study of Serial Murder Investigations

Serial murder has become part of the public consciousness even though most people are not really sure what it is, why it happens, and much less how to investigate it. This ignorance is as much a part of the professional circles as the lay public. Federal and local law-enforcement officers have a common interest in how to investigate serial murder cases, but no authority has perfected an answer to investigating these most troublesome cases. When the acts of a serial murderer are discovered, these very law-enforcement officers only share the vaguest of ideas on how to solve them.

My study of serial murder began in 1974. It was not prompted by any great design, but out of the futility I encountered investigating the murders of eight female coeds later attributed to Theodore Robert Bundy. It was this lack of investigative know-how in this and the subsequent 50 serial murder investigations that I have been involved in, as an investigator or a consultant, that forced me to continue studying for the last 25 years. The pursuit of successful procedures in the investigation of the serial killer is what drove me to continue.

As I studied, first techniques of homicide investigation and then the crime of serial murder itself, I was struck with how remote the reality I saw was from the rhetoric I heard. The most potent example was from the early 1980s at a homicide investigation seminar in Atlanta, GA. A detective from Florida, who investigated the 40-plus murders of Gerald Stano, was giving a lecture about the unique use of sodium pentathol in interviewing a serial killer. His presentation was well received, but I detected a tinge of shame in his voice. After the presentation, I introduced myself to him. Immediately, he took on the role of a subservient and humble person. He claimed he had come to hear me speak about methods for investigating serial killers. At first I was dismayed, and then started recognizing and commending him for his presentation to the group of over 300 investigators. But it wasn't long before his true emotions were laid out on his sleeve. He hung his head as though he possessed a heavy burden. He was a combination of the psychologically stressed victim of a serial killer and the investigator undergoing the political and administrative lack of support within his own law-enforcement agency. His main complaint was that his work was unappreciated. What a contrast; he went from the experienced and proud investigator-presenter to the emotionally whipped person standing before me.

This psychological dichotomy has stuck with me for years. What happened to cause this hard-working detective to finish his career without the respect of his co-workers? This perspective is not easily stated, but I begin by pointing out what serial murder investigation is and isn't all about. By the end of this book, the reader will appreciate how these cases psychologically affect the personnel involved in those investigations.

Few offenses involve a sole operator. Instead, they often consist of groups or teams of individuals that, to a greater or lesser extent, have to interact to make the offense possible and make it beneficial for the criminals. This is most obvious in what is known as "organized" crime. To understand how these crimes are possible, the implicit and formal organizational networks of which they are a part, have to be understood (Canter and Allison, 1999). We know more about solving cases in which there are perpetrators acting in concert, and the research in this area is abundant.

But how can serial murders be understood and solved when most of the cases are committed by one person, and not a member acting in concert with other members of the group? Canter's point is that examining the profile of the criminal entrepreneur is not sufficient unless one also has a grasp of the entrepreneurial landscape. What is so troublesome about serial murder investigations is that no formal research has ever taken place that aids police in understanding the serial killer's landscape and how to solve these types of cases. Worse yet, the social fabric between the investigative team and the serial killers is often intertwined—they do, after all, have some overlapping social concerns. Predatory crime does not merely victimize individuals, it impedes and, in the extreme case, even prevents the formation and maintenance of community (Wilson, 1975).

When a disturbed man kills his girlfriend at her home in a rage of jealousy and in a blizzard of bullets, the murder investigation is solved quickly. The boyfriend is present when police officers arrive, possibly more afraid of what he's done than of the punishment he may be facing. He hands over the gun while he tries to explain the circumstances of the shooting before the police can stop him so they can read him his rights first. However, when a nude female is found raped, stabbed, and strangled in a remote wooded area, the case takes on a complexity far from the norm. The solution is not imminent. Not only do the investigating officers have a "who done it," worse yet, they have a "who is it." Even further complicating this case is that the victim may be one of others by the same killer. This book focuses on the psychological behavior of detectives and the effects of investigating the grisly business of serial murder cases by members of law-enforcement agencies.

In my study of the UK's longest running serial killer case, outlined in Chapter 2, a complex serial murder investigation is examined. It is proto-typical in the sense that the killer was active for a number of years, killing more than ten prostitutes and assaulting others, before the police discovered his identity as Peter Sutcliffe. The Yorkshire Ripper Task force experienced all the typical ills of investigating an ongoing serial killer case: numerous victims, thousands of suspects, poor control and coordination of incoming leads, inexperienced personnel to investigate or supervise, improper media relations, investigations conducted on tangents, ill-conceived procedures in prioritizing investigative leads, and inadequate filing procedures of case materials. The Yorkshire Ripper cases are atypical because the British Parliament conducted a major review critical of the investigative procedures; a procedure unprecedented in U.S. criminal investigations. The product of the review was the discovery of a multitude of investigative errors and the establishment of the HOLMES system, a central repository of case information in major cases. That kind of database, along with the ability of investigators to draw on the data contained therein, goes a long way to solve many of the information disconnects that plague interagency task force investigations, particularly the cases involving serial offenders such as killers and sex offenders.

But what have we learned from all of this? Just this past year, in October 2002, a shooting spree inside one of the most policed areas of our country defied a joint task force comprised not only of highly trained police officers from local agencies but the FBI, ATF, and perhaps even other federal agencies that we don't even know about. My brief review of the DC Beltway sniper case will show that not only did the individuals charged with these crimes, but not as of this writing either tried or convicted, manage to elude a massive manhunt including military aircraft, but they left a visible trail across the very areas the police were patrolling. Police in at least six different states along with federal authorities are only now beginning to put together the pieces of one of the most troubling coast-to-coast murder and felony murder sprees in American history. This was a shooting spree that took place in the months before the DC Beltway shootings actually began, and it took place right under the noses of police in local jurisdictions who couldn't put the pieces together until after weapons were retrieved and ballistics identified them as the murder weapons.

The primary suspects in the DC Beltway shootings have been charged with some of the shootings in other states. The investigation, now beginning to come together, is already revealing disturbing aspects about how warning signs were laid out and simply missed, how leads were not followed, and how similar patterns of crimes, because they were outside the immediate jurisdictions impacted during the DC Beltway shootings, were not considered by a narrowly focused task force. This points to the heart of what I intend to show in my study: The exclusivity of data in task force investigations and the reliance on superficial modus operandi (MO) profiles not only doesn't further a task force serial homicide investigation, but actually distracts investigators and detracts from the overall effectiveness of the task force. The exclusivity and profiling in the DC Beltway shootings, as we will see, actually might have eliminated potential evidence that needed to be evaluated and which might have resulted in an earlier resolution of the case. This case, and others like it, will enable us to show, as a general rule, that inclusiveness rather than exclusivity is a better methodology of data management for serial homicide task force investigations.

Serial homicide investigations succeed or fail on whether the police *know* what they have on their hands, how they accept the truth, and how they manage it once they've accepted it. Accordingly, I will explore thoroughly how task forces deal with the key factors of recognition, acknowledgement, and control. In other words, it will be shown that the psychological forces of denial and defeat can easily creep into a task force investigation and do so because agencies fail to recognize what they have on their hands, fail to acknowledge it to themselves and to their constituents even after they know what they're chasing down, and fail to exercise control over their own data in the case.

Failure to recognize, to acknowledge, and to manage often leads to a collective sense of denial and defeat as you will see this in the Yorkshire Ripper case. This prevents police from putting together even the most obvious of clues. In the study of how bureaucratic or administrative denial operates, the elements involved in recognizing that there is a serial killer in operation will be shown to come in two phases. You may not recognize the series due to skepticism, but the killer goes on anyway. Those skeptics do not share the instincts of some experienced detectives, and because there are no hard facts, the case is believed to be a single event. But the detectives have to be salesmen to those unbelievers. Secondly, the utility of homicide information systems monitoring the frequency and types of murders will be discussed. The conclusion is that a more thorough and comprehensive analysis by an information system may detect the workings of a serial killer much earlier, therefore, helping prevent future murders by catching the killer.

Once recognition is confirmed, then comes the problem: Are the members of the police agency willing to tell others that a serial killer is on the loose? You will see in our examination of acknowledgement and media relations that by acknowledging this, the investigation can create its own luck. The DC Beltway sniper case showed that by releasing information judiciously, even though the authorities in this case might have released too much information, a member of the public looking for the suspicious car discovered the suspects in a parking area and alerted police who made the arrest without any violence (Chapter 9).

Ultimately, I will deal with the issue of administrative and bureaucratic control. Control refers to who runs the investigation. One person must be in charge. There have been instances when there have been co-commanders of a task force. For example, in the William Scott Smith serial murders in Oregon there was a city police department, a sheriff's department, and the state police who simultaneously commanded the case. The cases were solved eventually, but not due to the efforts of having three commanders at the same time. Whatever the case, there must be a working agreement about who is going to run the show. If there is not one leader, all that gets accomplished are meetings that try to placate everyone. Dealing with egos, politics, and differing investigative philosophies places a great strain on all aspects of the investigation. Even though a request to have a joint investigation looks good on paper, it is very inefficient and delays any meaningful investigation.

Negative and conflicting operational procedures affect control. As was apparent in the Atlanta child murders, each agency will have its own agenda and interfere with control. Most investigations were solved from the bottom up not from the top down. One person is necessary to buffer detectives and lead the charge. There must be someone to put things in perspective even if that person's most important function as a supervisor is to sit, listen, and nod.

All other problems associated with serial murder investigations are secondary to recognition, acknowledgement, and control. If you cannot handle these first, all else will fail.

Seven years after the Atlanta cases, I again became involved in a high-profile task force investigation into a major serial killer case. The formation of the Green River Murders Task Force, too, created a lot of interagency turbulence, became one of the most infamous cases of its time, and suffered from the psychology of denial and defeat. Finally, today, a suspect is in custody for some of the homicides associated with this case, but this happened almost 18 years later after the accumulation of thousands of leads, tips, clues, and other evidence. Because of my relationship with the agencies and the lead investigators, my career became almost inextricably involved with this investigation.

Like the Bundy case and the Atlanta child murders, the Green River Task Force at times stumbled over itself in its attempts to coordinate the activities of all of its investigators. It still solved other violent crimes along the way and the Green River Killer still managed to elude justice. It will turn out that our suspect had been arrested in the course of the investigation. As the King County affidavit shows, the suspect's name has been in our computer files since 1983, buried on a long strip of Mylar in a sealed room. Perhaps, if the suspect is ultimately found guilty and sentenced to death, he will wait until it's close to the end to make a death-row confession right before his last appeals run out, just like Bundy did. Maybe.

What I gleaned from these three task forces was a common denominator that I discovered about the investigators who had to work the case day after day no matter how cold the leads became. I discovered that no one, not the detectives working the case, not their commanders, and not the heads of the agencies involved wanted to be involved with the case. Why? It was simple. The case was a loser by anyone's definition. The investigators couldn't find the killer, and if they ever did find the killer they were afraid that the clues that led them there were so obvious they'd look like fools because they missed them. They were also afraid that more victims were taken while they were stumbling over themselves to sort out the evidence.

How can this be? Why would investigators not want to close out a case with a solid arrest leading to a conviction, even though they might have neglected obvious clues along the way? The answer is as simple as something one might find in a Psychology 101 textbook—avoidance reaction. People, and cops are no different from any other group of people, if given the choice tend to avoid those things which cause them pain, create anxiety, make them uncomfortable, or make them look anything less than successful. In the case of a serial murder investigation most detectives are made to look inept by the killer, especially when he's eventually picked up for running a red light, making an illegal U-turn, or even for driving a stolen car and then confesses to the first uniformed cop he sees. Even catching the killer turns out to be a revelation of all the mistakes the police made during the course of the investigation. Therefore, when they ultimately succeed, they have to face exactly what they did wrong. It's no wonder that many police agencies typically put themselves into denial about the existence of a serial killer. Then, after the task force is formed and plays catch-up with the unknown, the members of the task force find themselves faced with daily frustration as leads grow cold, and they actually have to wait for the next homicide in order to pick up new clues. It often can be a demoralizing situation.

As the psychology of defeat pervades the investigation, even the small successes that the police might achieve are not perceived as successes. Maybe the killer was forced out of one comfortable pattern into an unfamiliar one because he sensed the police were on to him. Maybe because a television station's helicopter spotted police surveillance at the river, the Green River killer was forced away from the river and into the woods.

Maybe that's where he left a valuable clue or a body before it completely decomposed on the river bottom and the police might have been able to get closer to the killer. But if you don't know how to manage successes, such as initiating a wise surveillance practice, they're as invisible as the killer and valuable effort is wasted. Equally important, the psychological value that the investigators might have derived from a feeling of achievement might be misinterpreted as another failure, and the pattern of self-defeat is allowed to continue.

As the self-esteem of each investigator on a task force flags, the unit itself seems to suffer from a collective loss of confidence breeding mistakes, infighting, defensive behavior, and, ultimately, bureaucratic paralysis. In a multiagency task force, such as the Atlanta child murders, the paralysis ran so deep that different agencies actually distorted facts in order to protect themselves from the recriminations everyone believed would come. This, obviously, benefits the killer who is often only a few steps away, reading about the dissension in the newspaper or hearing it in the news, and realizing that each change of his MO throws the entire police machine off the track.

We will also explore the investigative process of following leads. What we call "red herrings, information overload, and the needle in the haystack," will cover the gamut of the problems involved in pursuing the real killer. As the serial killer strikes more victims and adds more clues to the already overwhelming stockpile, individual members of the police task force become overloaded. They look at the four walls, see their own failure day after day, and actually long for a reassignment. Collectively, this tends to drag down the task force as an institution as each member's frustration feeds the others. Even management reinforcement or cheerleading doesn't always help, because the managers themselves have to explain both to the higher echelons in the police command and to the media why they haven't caught the killer. Ultimately, supervisors and investigators surround themselves by walls of frustration everywhere they turn, clouding any possibilities of success, and wearing down the resiliency of the task force even as the killer continues to prey on his victims. This was one of the factors that stymied the multijurisdictional task force formed in response to the ongoing Atlanta child murders.

Before I was a consultant to the Green River case, I was called in to consult on the Atlanta child murders. As body after body turned up in the Chattahoochee River outside of Atlanta, members of the Atlanta Police Department, the Georgia Bureau of Investigation, and local sheriff's offices kept butting heads over the best ways to pursue the killer. Between the jurisdictional disputes and the political forces at work in what many believed at first to be racially motivated crimes, little progress was made in the case. Even the FBI couldn't come up with a workable predictive investigative model that would allow the homicide detectives to make assumptions based on what the killer would do next. All that they thought they knew was that they had a perpetrator or perpetrators whose focus was on abducting and then killing young African-American children from in and around Atlanta.

I became a member of the second group of national consultants to the investigators on the case, helping to develop proactive measures that might end the reign of terror and bring peace to the grieving families of missing and murdered children. We reviewed the work of the first group of consultants and those investigative reports the agencies involved in the case elected to share with us. What we found, and what I, in particular, discovered was a case rife with political issues among the different law-enforcement agencies that reflected the politics of Atlanta and its suburbs.

What I also discovered, and which has stayed with me throughout my career, was the level of distaste the investigators in Atlanta had for pursuing leads in a case which, despite some obvious clues, in their minds held out little hope of ever being solved. Like other members of serial murder task forces, they lacked the insight and knowledge of how to prioritize incoming leads. The impact of conducting tangential investigations, methods of prioritizing incoming leads, and strategies for finding that needle in the haystack is discussed in the context of keeping personnel focused on the central mission of the case—finding the serial killer. Personnel must stay focused even when that mission takes them down blind alleys and forces them to look at leads that are exciting at 7:00 in the morning when the coffee's fresh and they're full of enthusiasm, but turn out to be as stale as yesterday's lunch by 6:00 in the evening when they're worn out after a frustrating day.

The section about how the serial killer hides and what he knows is the focus of our characterization of a serial killer's natural camouflage and his instinct for survival. Many times, police do have to track serial killers who have been, in Bundy's words, "out there," for so long that the killer is for all practical purposes invisible to police investigators but in plain sight to others. We know that was the case with the Green River killer just as it was the case with Wayne Williams in Atlanta, Jeffrey Dahmer in Milwaukee, and Arthur Shawcross in Rochester.

A confident, long-term, control-type serial killer can become so much a part of the landscape you'd expect to find that he can even interact with the police investigating the case and still not be looked at as a suspect. Ted Bundy sat at a phone bank in a rape crisis center; Arthur Shawcross, the Genesee River killer, had his early morning doughnuts and coffee with Rochester police coming off shift after having searched for the Genesee River killer all night; Wayne Williams was a photographer making the acquaintances of young African-American boys in their schools while police were searching for missing children; our suspect in four of the Green River homicides was cruising the street and chatting up the prostitutes out tricking while the police were conducting sting operations for johns; and Jeffrey Dahmer was even serving time in jail during the night while he was working at Ambrosia Chocolates during the day and looking for victims. Dahmer actually killed out on the streets while he was serving part of his jail sentence. And most recently, DC Beltway sniper suspect John Mohammed allegedly told at least one person in Tacoma exactly what he planned to do and why he thought it would wreak terror on his victims. And this informant allegedly told police what he said Mohammed told him. As bizarre as this seems, it is exactly how serial killers work. That's why most police departments don't want to admit they have a serial killer case to investigate even when its obvious, and that's why they can exhibit an extreme reluctance to pursue the case even as it's going forward.

In a prototypical serial homicide task force investigation, the killer keeps on striking and more bodies are discovered as the chronology of the case proceeds. By this time the police usually have to provide daily briefings to the press. If the case has bizarre aspects to it or if it involves special victims such as children, a frenzy created by the media builds. As the presence of the media creates more pressure for the police to perform according to some kind of schedule, the frustration and failure investigators feel usually goes from bad to worse. This often can become the next critical stage for the task force because it's here that mistakes begin to compound.

As most of the investigators who worked the Atlanta child murders or Green River murder cases found out first hand—and as could be seen from the Beltway sniper shootings—there is a relentlessness that stalks high-profile cases. The more bodies that keep popping up the more incompetent the police look. Even if you've deployed your entire force of uniformed officers on overtime shifts in an effort to stake out every possible location the serial killer might visit, you're probably not going to find him overnight. And the murderer, because he's part of the landscape blending in completely with the community he's preying on, moves right through the police surveillance without being spotted and kills with impunity. At a certain point in most major serial killer cases the victims are visible and the killer is invisible.

When a major serial killer case is finally solved and all the paperwork completed, police are sometimes amazed at how obvious the killer was and how they were unable to see what was right before their noses. Even during a case, there is sometimes a feeling that the killer is right there only you can't see him. During the Green River murders, I often had the feeling that the killer was on the street watching the Seattle and King County units drive right by as he looked for his next victim. The cops might have been looking for a driver in a particular car or a van while the killer was pulling up to his victim in a pickup truck. The conclusion of our evaluation of a serial killer's survival mechanism covers how the inability of the police to see their case with a clear vision that only comes with hindsight adds significantly to their frustrations.

This book takes a close look at what serial killers know about the police investigation and how they know it. For part of my research into the nature of the psychology of a serial killer on the loose, I've interviewed serial killers and studied others who've revealed their own experiences eluding the police. During the time I interviewed Ted Bundy on death row in Florida, I learned about the paranoia and grandiosity that drove Bundy each and every day of his existence. He described to me the feelings of superiority killers like him experience when they know they've successfully cloaked themselves in a mantle of invisibility so securely that they can actually stand near a crime scene in the presence of the police without fear of detection. He also told me how he followed the progress of the investigation into the missing and murdered women cases that we conducted even as he was abducting more women. He knew the police were on the trail, but he also knew that by traveling outside our circle of jurisdiction, he could commit crimes that other departments wouldn't connect with our cases. I knew how true this was and remembered that the first indication we had that this killer was different from more conventional killers was his extraordinary wide range of trolling. He killed whenever the opportunity presented itself, and thought nothing about traveling hundreds of miles away to find a victim. This presents an enormous and frustrating obstacle to members of a serial killer task force who have to remain wide open to similarities between their case and cases in other jurisdictions, even if it seems impossible that a killer can be in more than one place at the same time.

Because most serial killers are sex offenders who live or work in the very neighborhoods where they are killing, they blend in and are hard to detect. However, because they live where they kill, they also establish subtle relationships with their victims. Our Ted Task Force, for example, looked at the Lynda Healy case again and again for clues to her abduction. It was only after we had identified Bundy that we were able to find out that not only did Bundy possibly know Healy, but he may have had a relationship with her through his cousin. If we had known about this information and that Healy's disappearance was connected to the Lake Sammamish murders, Bundy may have had a much shorter career.

We also describe how killers become locked into the psychology of flight. As they move from a kind of equilibrium in their daily lives—always trying to appear normal while they look for opportunities to kill—into a dream state when the sexual fantasies surrounding the kill propel them toward the next victim, and ultimately into the frenzy of sexual anticipation and gratification. With their lust expended, they quickly lapsed into a kind of panic, a fugue state within which they were almost primordial in their ability to camouflage and flee the area. They hid until they thought it safe to come out, relived their sexual gratification from seeing stories about their victims in the newspapers, and got even greater thrills by hearing how the police had been stymied yet again.

In other words, the serial killer's gratification and sexual experience was actually heightened, in some cases, by the activities of the police task forces on their trail. Just knowing that a name had popped up on a missing person list, a name associated with a victim who was buried in a secret location or dumped off into the river at the killer's special place, was enough to excite the killer out of a sensible and nonviolent equilibrium into a killing mode.

The analysis of the serial killer's methodology in pursuing his crimes is dealt with in a discussion of the killer's psychological crime scene calling cards. Many experienced homicide detectives have gut instincts when it comes to how a killer leaves his crime scene. If a scene has been scrubbed too clean or if there are indicators of a killer who's acting out some fantasy-driven drama on his victim, a detective can make a fair guess that this is probably not the first murder the offender has committed. It's also probably an accurate guess that this killer will strike again. But to go from that gut instinct to a formal task force requires more than guesses. It requires clear and convincing evidence for the detective's superiors to take the next step and form a task force.

The best evidence that a particular crime is linked to a series comes from an analysis of crime scene characteristics and information. If an investigator is fortunate enough, the way my partner and I were at Lake Sammamish, he or she may have a number of witnesses who were approached by the killer and can provide a description of a suspect. When Denise Naslund and Janice Ott disappeared from Lake Sammamish State Park in 1974 my partner Roger Dunn and I were able to interview several witnesses who not only had seen the suspect but upon whom Ted actually made some moves. The girls described what we would eventually come to understand as one of his MOs, the broken-wing plea he would give to his potential victim to lure her into his power just before he sprang the trap. We would look for this MO in other cases.

Using gut instincts and adding information about the killer's signature, detectives may discover that a person probably has killed before or is on a trajectory to kill again. The hard evidence of the killer's signature may require an expert's evaluation of the evidence. This can be done through signature analysis, one of the several outcomes of a formal crime scene assessment. As a look at crime scene signatures reveals, the MO of a killer includes only those actions necessary to perpetrate the murder. Many serial murderers are not satisfied with just committing the murder but feel compelled to go further. Actions beyond those necessary to commit the killing demonstrate behavior unique to that particular killer. The killer's personal expression is called his signature. Unlike the MO, the signature remains constant. We provide examples of previous cases in which signature analysis has been performed and the usefulness of that analysis to the investigation and prosecution of the killer. We also introduce our own specific type of profiling based on what type of signature police can glean from the crime scene to show how MO profiling not only doesn't work, but can wear investigators down by setting them along the wrong paths.

Ultimately, we address the arc of the serial killer task force in order to understand the way serial killer investigations work. Whether these investigations are multiagency task forces or the more typical investigations confined within a single department, the entire arc of the process has to be examined from the first stirrings among police commanders that a series of sexual homicides have been perpetrated by the same individual to a task force being necessary. Then the process of organizing a task force should be looked at:, who should be on the task force, how leads are prioritized, how those leads are investigated, and what strategies most likely will catch the killer.

In the final chapters we look specifically at the DC Beltway sniper case to see how a high-profile task force worked in the glare of media lights. We also look at the best practices of managing information to examine the ways in which it can be an ally rather than an enemy. We look at Washington State's HITS system, the FBI's VICAP, Orange County's TracKERS and other computerized data management systems to see what ways are effective to keep task forces from falling into the twin foes of denial and defeat.

The formation of a task force officially represents a police consensus that a serial killer is on the loose. That is an important psychological hurdle and establishes that the arc of the serial murder investigation is well under way. Once everyone agrees on the nature of the problem, far less time is wasted on extraneous investigation not germane to the "task" implicit in the term "task force." (Aynesworth and Michaud, 1989).

When you diagram the prototypical arc of a serial murder investigation, it begins with the first body discovery through the emotional highs and lows of hot leads that turn out to be dead ends. Along the way the frenzy of media involvement and pressure as each local news reporter decides to solve the case on the air contaminates the investigation. Maybe a final realization is that you're locked into a siege mentality and that the case may take years to complete. You can understand how conflict and denial can often creep in, creating a sense of futility, that pervades the investigation after the serial killer task force has been formed and is at work.

The beginning of an arc is best exemplified in the Green River murders investigation. Two boys biking over the Peck Bridge in King County saw a body floating among the tall grass along the Green River shore. This victim was later identified as Wendy Coffield. By the time the police arrived on the scene and realized some weeks later that Coffield wasn't the only dead victim dumped into the river by a phantom killer, a headline-making case had begun.

In the Bundy case, we never discovered the deceased victims until we found one of Ted's mountainside burial grounds. In the George Russell murders in Bellevue, WA, Mary Ann Pohlreich, the first victim, was posed alongside a dumpster in an alley where she was certain to be discovered by anyone collecting trash that morning. Green River, Ted Bundy, and George Russell were three different cases, but they all had one thing in common— the killer had taken some care with the disposal of the body. George Russell wanted his victim discovered. The Green River killer and Ted Bundy did not.

If you're a seasoned homicide detective, you can tell from the way the body has been left if you're dealing with a killer who's left his signature at the scene. The seasoned detective will expect that this killer will strike again or that he's killed before, maybe in a different jurisdiction. But unless more bodies turn up that can be connected through the same type of killer MO or signature to this particular crime, most police agencies will not look for a serial killer. In fact, many agencies will be downright exclusive in what they consider related crime scene patterns, because they don't want to create a serial killer case when there isn't one. Therefore, the arc is broken before it begins.

What's also at work in the minds of these investigators, unfortunately, is a sense of denial, a sure-fire way to break the arc once again. They're usually too exclusive in how they parse and relate crime scene evidence because they don't want to start looking for a serial killer. So they prolong a process which, had they jumped into it right way, might have yielded some results. In the first few days of what might be a serial investigation a good team of investigators can sort through enough information to develop a few solid leads. However, once the separate homicide investigations in the case begin to stack up, evidence gets forgotten or lost, leads that might have been meaningful turn cold and become discarded, and witnesses tend to disappear. Because the sense of denial has pervaded the investigation, the investigation itself slows down from the very start and police lose a valuable ally—time—which sometimes starts out on their side but turns against them as the killer gets more confident of his ability to elude the police.

While the police are sifting through evidence in what they think might be, but hope it's not, a serial murder case, the killer himself may be watching. If he's inexperienced and just broke through the psychological barrier of having committed his first sexual homicide, his thrill is punctuated by a real fear that the police might know who he is. It's only after time has passed without being caught and a few successful kills that the killer develops the confidence to stride right by the police wearing his mask of invisibility.

But the police many times don't realize the advantage they have when they're looking into the first murder, which may have psychological overtones to it.

In examining the prototypical arc of the serial killer task force investigation, two competing psychologies will be explained: the killer's deviant psychology that often reveals itself with calling cards at every crime scene, and the institutional or collective psychology of the police serial killer task force that may alternate between exuberance with any new clue or lead and deep depression when the leads dribble away into dead ends. These psychologies forge their own dynamic of perseverance as the killer may feel compelled to take greater risks to enhance the sexual thrill he experiences with each successful kill. Meanwhile the police, wrapped within their own collective siege mentality, doggedly pursue the offender and try to develop proactive or alternative strategies to uncover more information about the case.

As our archetypal case progresses and the killer's reputation grows, the police, under even greater pressure, may actually abandon case logic and be forced to spend time on clues or leads generated in the media and foisted upon them by senior management. Even the most seasoned of detectives in this environment can make procedural errors, mistakes in allocating time and resources which may send investigators down blind alleys or into cul-de-sacs that draw them away from the valuable leads which might have pointed them to a real solution in the case. As the investigation itself flounders and its mistakes are documented, a clever killer may realize that he has the opportunity to develop a new victim pool somewhere else. At the very least, he may find a new body dumpsite in a jurisdiction outside the borders of the task force on his trail, a place where his victims are less likely to be found, or he may strike at victims in another jurisdiction.

Through the eyes of the task force, once the body discoveries stop, the urgency is relieved, the pressure to solve the case instantly is reduced, and detectives can return to background investigations of previous disappearances that may yield results. Also, other detectives may seek reassignment elsewhere. If this happens, the task force may slow down or allow another agency to join in the pursuit. Seeing this, a long-term killer can gradually set up shop elsewhere and keep on avoiding detection for years, as Bundy did, or, like the Zodiac Killer, never be identified.

Our study of task forces concludes with the institutional psychology that says: Because the police know this, they can defeat themselves from the very start by looking at the hopelessness of the task in front of them. It is a type of institutional psychology deriving from a collective frustration and perception of defeat that is a singular phenomenon of many types of crime-solving task forces. But, which will become clear, this institutional psychology is intimately connected with the psychology of the killer. His own complete lack of self-worth and perception of himself as a hopeless failure drives him from crime to crime. Each entity, the killer and the police on his trail, is probably unaware of the psychological advantage the one has over the other at the same exact time. And the way the investigation plays out may be, at the very end, simply the result of chance, a traffic stop for an illegal U turn, or the identification of a license tag on a stolen car. Thus, what was the result of chance becomes the explanation of solution to an entire case. This, then, is how the two psychologies interact to define the arc of serial murder investigations into what is, still, the most perplexing of crimes and the most difficult of investigations to pursue.

The goal of any serial murder investigation is to find the killer before he kills again. For the police task force, one of the most critical breaks they can get is to locate and interview a living witness, a victim of a serial killer who got away. In our exploration of the solution to serial killer cases through the discovery of living witnesses, we show how the identification of the killer lifts the psychological spirits of the investigators involved in the cases. In the Green River killer affidavit, which documents the interview process, we demonstrate that even though the police could not make an immediate arrest as a result of one of the interviews they conducted with a SeaTac strip prostitute, the information she provided led them to interview a suspect who they later arrested in four of the Green River homicide cases.

The cases of Ted Bundy, Wayne Williams, John Gacy, and Larry Eyler also had living witnesses who testified against them. For reasons known only to the killer, the circumstances were inopportune for these living witnesses to become homicide victims. The presence of living witnesses in these cases remains a favorable implication for future serial murder investigations. These witnesses provided the necessary facts of similar offenses to strengthen search warrant affidavits and the probable cause for arrest (Keppel, 2000; Keppel and Birnes, 1995). The search for these witnesses will be a focus of Chapter 9.

In addition, our study highlights how serial killers are caught by normal, routine police procedures. As elusive and intelligent as serial killers appear to be, the fact remains that the routine work conducted by uniformed patrol officers is a frequent way they are caught. On two occasions, uniformed officers from Utah and Florida stopped Ted Bundy for driving violations. The circumstances surrounding those stops were the beginning of his identification as a serial killer. Further investigation of Bundy's behavior revealed he was a traveling serial killer.

In 1986, a California Highway Patrol officer stopped a man driving while intoxicated. This stop was the beginning of the end for one of the longest and most prolific serial killing cases in American history. During the stop, the patrolman noticed that the passenger was not passed out, but was in fact a homicide victim. Randy Kraft, the Scorecard Killer, is on death row and is suspected of killing 63 victims in California, Oregon, and Michigan since 1970.

Our look at the standard police procedures that produce results concludes with the use of computer applications and technology to manage large amounts of data and help in the apprehension of serial killers. In several cases, such as Ted Bundy and Randy Kraft, the computer was used to collate large amounts of information and literally locate that needle in the haystack. The strategies behind the gathering of certain information in the investigation and the types of computer applications employed will be covered.

In our examination of the serial murder investigation manual, recommendations for investigating serial murder cases are covered. Up to this point the book deals with the problems associated with investigating complex serial murders. This concluding overview summarizes the investigative suggestions from three major sources: The Multiagency Investigative Team Manual produced by a Department of Justice Committee, the Major Incident Response Procedures of the Royal Canadian Mounted Police (RCMP), and the Murder Investigation Manual of a consortium of members of police agencies in the UK.

Investigating high-profile serial murder cases was the highlight of a conference sponsored by the U.S. Department of Justice in August 1986. For two weeks in the 115 degree heat of Phoenix, AZ, over 20 detectives responsible for the investigations of the country's most famous serial killers discussed the proper methods of investigation and pitfalls of dealing with those very difficult serial murder cases. The idea was to arrive at a consensus about the best practices used to investigate and apprehend a serial killer or, more appropriately, what not to do. Investigators who were members of task forces in the Ted Bundy cases, the Green River murders, the Hillside Strangler cases, the John Gacy murder cases, the Atlanta child murders, the Zebra Killer, and the Calavaras County Lake and Ng murder cases presented the bad and good investigative strategies in their individual serial murder cases. What was curious about the presentations was that each began in similar fashion by being organized into a multiagency investigative task force. (Brooks, Devine, Green, Hart, and Moore, 1998).

The Canadian Police authorities have been severely criticized by the public, the media, and from within their own organizations for the handling of the investigations into the murders of Clifford Olson and Paul Bernardo. It is from these highly visible cases that the members of the RCMP developed the Major Incident Response Procedures. This comprehensive procedural manual contains everything from soup to nuts about organizing and managing major investigations for Canadian law-enforcement agencies. The most important procedures from this manual will be highlighted in Chapter 8.

The UK has not been without it notorious murder cases. Police authorities throughout England have taken much criticism in cases like the Yorkshire Ripper, documented in Chapter 3, serial killer Frederic West, the Stephen Lawrence inquiry, and the investigation into the murder of Rachael Nichole. A product from these various inquiries was the development of the Murder Investigation Manual. This manual provides a structure for homicide investigation in the UK. The consultant list is quite extensive resulting in a very thorough and comprehensive manual of procedures for homicide detectives.

As Chief Constable John D. Phillips most aptly put: "Murder most foul!" This rather melodramatic Edwardian Phrase nonetheless captures the public perception of homicide. Chilling, ultimate, and full of menace with the dark suspicion that nobody is safe until the killer is apprehended; murder calls out like no other crime.

Ironically, almost no other crime has created more controversy when suspects have been brought to trial. Has the sheer horror of the crime prejudiced investigation and the court alike? Has the urgency to clear the case brought about too hasty inferences? And of course, in the modern justice system, no other kind of prosecution will receive the scrutiny a murder case will in the turbid search for a means to undermine the case.

We can fairly presume the investigation of homicide represents the supreme test for the detective. It is akin to managing a drama; often alive in media interest and, sometimes, political intrigue, while bringing to bear every professional skill in policing and many other disciplines too (ACPO Crime Committee, 1998).

What we have sought to do in preparing this book is to learn from the combined experiences of investigators on major task forces and murder cases and couple their wisdom with the great new opportunities emerging from the analytical capacity of modern technology. Perhaps more undauntedly, within this book is a theory of serial murder investigation and the beginnings of more formulated doctrine covering the subject.

REFERENCES

ACPO Crime Committee (1998). *Murder Investigation Manual.* Kent, England.

Aynesworth, H., and Michaud, S. G. (1989). *Ted Bundy: Conversations with a Killer.* New York: Signet Books.

Brooks, P., Devine, M., Green, T., Hart, B., and Moore, M. (1988). Multi-Agency Investigative Team Manual, U.S. Department of Justice.

Canter, D., and Allison, L. (1999). *The Social Psychology of Crime: Groups, Teams, and Networks.* Aldershot, Burlington, VT: Ashgate Publishing.

Keppel, R. D., and Birnes, W. J. (1995). *The Riverman: Ted Bundy and I Hunt the Green River Killer.* New York: Pocket Books.

Keppel, R. D. (2000). Serial Murder: Future Implications for Police Investigations, Authorlink. com.

Wilson, J. Q. (1975). *Thinking About Crime.* New York: Basic Books.

1

RECOGNITION AND ACKNOWLEDGMENT OF SERIAL MURDER

Recognition
    When Recognition is Impossible
Finding Similar Cases
    Characteristics of Serial Murder
Information Sources
    The Violent Criminal Apprehension Program (VICAP)
    TracKERS
    HITS
Scott William Cox
Acknowledgment
References

How investigators survive the psychological rigors of investigating serial murder cases depends on the three main factors of recognition, acknowledgment, and control: (1) a quick and valid interpretation that one murder is related to another, (2) a reliable admission to others that a serial killer is in operation, and (3) a strategy that properly commands, staffs, and funds the investigative effort. These factors were first publicly set forth in a professional forum by retired Lieutenant Ray Biondi of the Sacramento Sheriff's Department in his presentation on the Investigation of Serial Murders at the Fifth National Conference on Homicide, Unidentified Bodies, and Missing Persons in Nashville, TN (Biondi, 1987).

Among the issues most troublesome for Lt. Biondi was that he discovered problems routinely associated with recognition, acknowledgment, and control throughout the country. He explained why serial murders are the worst scenario for the allocation of resources to solve a case and argued that because most departments knew this and were aware of the costs associated with previous serial murder cases, there is often a lot of resistance to the acknowledgment that a homicide might properly belong to a larger serial murder investigation. This resistance engenders a collective denial that ultimately can pervade the entire investigative staff. Therefore, Biondi emphasized that because the primary goal of supervisors and management personnel is to catch the killer before he kills again, they must create an atmosphere in the organization where there is less bureaucratic wheel-spinning and allow the persons who will solve the case, the detectives—those "who do the spade-work"–the resources and freedom to investigate.

For investigators, realizing that their department has a serial case can be extremely difficult, even in the best of circumstances. A police agency investigating one victim may not know from what they immediately see at a crime scene whether that victim is the beginning or just one case in a series of murders. The case at hand may be in the middle of a killer's series. Unless the agency is or has been made aware of a series of crimes with victims who fit the same profile as the victim at their crime scene, the police may know nothing more about the homicide than what they can figure out from what they see. So the investigation may, right from the outset, lag behind the ongoing events of the case, with investigators unaware that there have been previous victims of the same killer.

This happened in the Ted Bundy cases in the Pacific Northwest in 1974. Two young women went missing from Lake Sammamish State Park in July. These cases were within the King County Sheriff's jurisdiction. In actuality, a string of six disappearances and killings had already begun as early as January of that same year in Oregon and Washington prior to any involvement from the King County Sheriff's detectives, or at least before a positive connection had been made among any of the law enforcement agencies in the area. It wasn't until bones identifying three victims were found just east of Lake Sammamish State Park and skull parts from four more victims were discovered about 6 months later 11 miles further east in the Taylor Mountain area of the foothills of the Cascades that anyone linked the missing coeds to the same killer.

So in the Ted Bundy cases, interagency recognition and acknowledgment that a new kind of killer was on the loose, murdering young, pretty, white college-aged women, didn't take place until two body recovery sites were discovered, and after the discovery of the human remains at the sites, it was confirmed by the homicide investigators that at least seven of the victims died at the hands of the same person. Prior to this time, the investigation was not headed in the direction of investigating all eight victims as victims of the same killer. Each jurisdiction was operating independently and not pursuing any leads that would have lead to Theodore Robert Bundy. Whatever frustration the individual departments might have felt at their inability to solve the mysterious murders of young women or the missing persons cases in their jurisdictions suddenly became, on the one hand, compounded by the recognition that the same killer might be operating in a 300-mile radius across two states, but relieved, on the other hand, by the understanding that the individual agencies were not alone, and that there might be a solution in a joint task force investigation.

The inability of officers to link murders or missing persons to the same offender is referred to as "linkage blindness" (Egger, 1984, 1990). Specifically, linkage blindness occurs when police administrators and investigators refuse to admit or do not know that a serial killer is operating. The reason for this blindness has been attributed to officers not recognizing the characteristics of a serial victim, and more importantly, not having the ability to track murders in a central repository of information. At worst, you cannot tell until the killer tells you. We will see more of how devastating linkage blindness can be in our examination of the Yorkshire Ripper cases in England when police in unrelated agencies, but part of the same large task force, could not identify a serial killer during his 4-year skein of murders, even though they were actively interviewing him from the perspective of their separate points of entry into the case.

As we will see, even though a series of murders is linked to the same killer, a homicide may not fit the pattern of facts the police have established for their series. Therefore, the killer is investigated separately in the different homicides, and important clues or leads to the rest of the cases may go unnoticed. This also happened during the Arthur Shawcross investigation in Rochester when one woman didn't fit the profile the police established for the victims. Her murder was not considered part of the case until Shawcross himself confessed to it after he was in custody.

RECOGNITION

Recognition is the single most important concept in serial murder investigations, primarily because it is the beginning of a required sequence in the understanding of the serial murder investigative process along with acknowledgment and control. Without it, the realization that a serial killer is operating is nonexistent, the probability of solving cases diminishes, and, worse yet, the likelihood someone else being killed rises. A recurring theme throughout our study of the psychology of a serial murder investigation is the mismanagement of information; either problems with collecting, storing, analyzing, and prioritizing incoming information or the inability of recognizing information that is useful to the investigation. That management or mismanagement directly relates to the sense of individual and institutional frustration which can impede the work of the task force and ultimately paralyze it, all the while the killer is adding new victims to the list. This is what happened in the Atlanta child murders investigation when police overlooked vital information they had at their fingertips because of a collective mismanagement of clues, tips, and leads. The mismanagement of information, and resulting paralysis of a case, often occurs at the beginning of an agency's involvement, resulting from its failure to recognize the kind of crime it is investigating. Therefore, in serial murder cases, the root of those problems begins with the concept of recognition: How are victims identified as one in a series of killings committed by the same offender?

There are three main methods used to link murders prior to a killer's apprehension. They are (1) physical evidence, (2) offender description, and (3) crime scene behavior. Each method has its strengths and weaknesses. It is not uncommon for a series of crimes to be connected through a combination of these means (Rossmo, 2000).

The first question that immediately arises is: Why should investigators care to link cases? Police investigators and prosecutors need cases linked for their own purposes. From an investigative standpoint, the linking of crimes enables investigators to pursue the same suspect instead of operating without the knowledge that the cases are linked. Prosecutors want similar cases linked so the defendant can be tried on multiple charges in the same trial (Keppel, 1995, 2000; Keppel and Birnes, 1997).

But what happens when there is both an administrative and a psychological denial of the recognition process, when connections may not want to be made in the first place? I discovered that some homicide departments were reluctant to declare a serial murder case because the investigations were expensive, sometimes futile, and ultimately frustrating endeavors that, more often than not, made the members of a task force look confused and inept. In other words, the very act of taking the first step to solving the case is also, in the minds of police commanders, the first step in encountering failure, a resulting loss of morale, and, perhaps, even public humiliation. Therefore, denial sets in at the very beginning to protect the institution from the possibility of failure.

For example, my partner and I were looking for similar murdered and missing women cases because we were not having much success solving the murders later attributed to Theodore Robert Bundy. Our hope was to find a similar murder in another jurisdiction and use suspect information from that murder to help solve our cases. We assembled numerous characteristics of our murders so we could compare them with the characteristics of murders from outside agencies. The assumption was that we were looking for someone familiar with the university atmosphere. Therefore, any coed types of killings or murders on or near university campuses were of primary interest. Since July 1974 when the Bundy murders began, it took us a year and a half to discover over 90 similar cases in western states over the previous 5-year period. In his confessions prior to his execution, Bundy admitted to some of those killings from our list.

Not far from Seattle, we discovered the case of a murdered coed from an Oregon university whose body had been found in the woods near that school. The factors of disappearance and death in that coed murder resembled the modus operandi (MO) in our cases. I visited the sheriff's office responsible for the investigation with the idea that I would examine the case file and interview detectives in order to determine if there were any suspects developed that could have ties to the Seattle area. Astonishingly, the sheriff wanted nothing to do with investigating whether or not his Oregon case was linked to the victims found in Washington State. His reasoning was that the Washington cases had generated far too much publicity. Publicizing any link between the Lake Sammamish murders and the Oregon murder would cause too much disruption in their daily routine. Even though we previously linked Roberta Parks from Oregon State University to our series because her skull was found with three others on Taylor Mountain, and had received the utmost cooperation from Parks' missing person investigators from the Corvallis Police Department and Oregon State University Police, this sheriff denied access to this other, possibly related, case files. Undoubtedly, this uncooperative contact stymies any linkage analysis and possible solution, and it confirms the public's suspicion that the police don't do everything possible to investigate cases.

But what can happen when the actions of the killer himself prevent the police from recognizing the extent of the series? The Green River murder cases are a prime example. By September 1982, investigators in King County, WA, had linked five victims found in or near the Green River. They had also found reports of six missing women which detectives felt could be linked to the series if they were found murdered. By March 1983 when the King County police commissioned me to analyze the entire Green River investigative effort after no suspect responsible for these murders had been discovered, there were two additional victims found, one of which was mostly bones and remained unidentified until over a year later. Postmortem examination revealed that the unidentified victim had been there for at least several months.

Thereafter, no other bodies were discovered, but detectives had found a total of 13 missing women from July 1982 through March 1983 who could be linked if they were found murdered. And they would find more and more missing women every month. Police officials were under extreme pressure to demonstrate that they were doing everything they could to solve these cases. Based on my recommendations and those of others, King County officials formed the enhanced Green River Task Force in January 1984. A total of 50 personnel were assigned to the investigation. That total far exceeded the three officers the investigation had dwindled to by March 1983. With all

TABLE 1   The Number of Murders that were Known by
Police for Each Year and the Number of Murders Actually
Committed by the Green River Killer(s)

Year known	Murders	Actual murders
1982	6	16
1983	8	27
1984	14	2
1985	7	0

From Evans, R. Interview with Captain Robert Evans,
Green River Task Force Commander, March 1989.

this, an unprecedented murder investigation for King County law enforcement officials was under way.

Those who predicted the size of the force and resources needed greatly
underestimated the number of murders that had been committed up to that
point. Unbeknownst to law enforcement and by the time the enhanced task
force was formed, there were 14 known deaths attributed to the Green
River Killer. As Table 1 shows, the killer(s) had actually murdered at least
45 women, 27 of which were yet to be discovered at their graves in the succeeding years. The task force was understaffed at 50 members, it should
have been started with 150. For the two years subsequent to forming the
task force, investigators ran from one crime scene or bone find to another.
There was no let up. Every time someone ventured into the woods to hike
or harvest mushrooms and moss, another body was located. It was as if the
only function the task force performed was that of an archeological processing team digging up old bones.

The task force members soon became experts in processing outside
crime scenes, but that function alone didn't catch the killer. It was almost
like the killer had intentionally dispersed the bodies in remote locations
so those investigating him couldn't recognize the extent of the series of
murders. Underestimating the number of murders and, therefore, only
placing 50 officers on the task force and limiting the resources that were
dedicated to the problem, may have placed the investigators so far behind
the killer that the Green River cases might never have been solved.

WHEN RECOGNITION IS IMPOSSIBLE

There have been more than a few unbelievable instances where law
enforcement officials were totally blindsided by a killer, never recognizing
that a serial killer was operating over a long duration in their jurisdiction,
murdering many victims out of sight. From an agency's perspective, this is
serial murder recognition at its worst. An example of this was the murder

series committed by John Wayne Gacy in the Chicago area. This series ended with his arrest for 33 murders in the latter part of December 1978. However, the investigation of his final victim was actually the first time the police found even a trace of evidence that a large series of murders had occurred. It was an investigation that started with a missing person report filed by the mother of Robert Piest beginning the the worst serial murder investigation in the Chicago history. The official police reports say it all.

> **From the Des Plaines Police Report:** Mrs. Piest related she went to pick up her son from work at Nisson's, 1920 Touchy, at 2100 hours.
>
> Her son requested she wait a few minutes while he speaks to a subject about attempting to get a summer job with a construction contractor.
>
> Mrs. Piest related she waited over 30 minutes in the store and then began calling a few of her son's friends to find out if they knew where he might be. Mrs. Piest also spoke of Phil Torf, her son's employer, who related he may have heard him speaking to a John Gacy of P.D.M. Construction Co., Chicago, about Mr. Gacy possibly hiring high school students for summer work. Mr. Torf attempted to call Mr. Gacy to find out if he had seen Robert Piest, but was only able to leave a message at Mr. Gacy's telephone number (457–1014).
>
> Mr. Torf related if he could be of any other assistance, he could be contacted at home or at night at the store. (Des Plains Police Missing Persons Report, 1978)

What made this missing person report different from the many thousands of others was that there was information in the body of the report that the police could follow up. In this case, investigators began immediately to reach John Gacy. After midnight on December 12, 1978, Lt. Joseph Kozenczak attempted to contact John Gacy and left a message that he wanted to see him. That morning Gacy contacted the police station.

> **From Officer Loconsole's report:** At 0050 hours, Lt. J. Kozenczak advised the reporting officer (R/O) that he had been expecting a Mr. John Gacy to come into the station and talk with him, but Mr. Gacy was late. Lt. Kozenczak stated he could not wait any longer and advised the R/O that if Mr. Gacy showed up, the R/O was to tell Mr. Gacy to come back first thing in the morning.
>
> At 0320 hours, December 13, 1978, a man identifying himself as Mr. John Gacy entered the station. The R/O told Mr. Gacy that Lt. Kozenczak could not wait and had to leave, and that he, Mr. Gacy, was to come back first thing in the morning. Mr. Gacy appeared somewhat apprehensive and asked the R/O what Lt. Kozenczak wanted to see him about. The R/O told Mr. Gacy that the R/O had no information. Mr. Gacy then told the R/O that the reason he was late was because he had been involved in some sort of automobile accident. Mr. Gacy then left the station.
>
> The R/O observed that Mr. Gacy's eyes were glassy, and he had fresh mud on his pants and shoes (Field Supplementary Report, 1978).

As the police followed up on that report, they were led to the Gacy residence and eventually discovered 28 bodies of male boys in the crawl space of his house and five more were found in or near the Chicago River. Even though the cases have been solved by Gacy's conviction, 11 bodies from his crawl space remain unidentified to this day. The fact that Gacy chose victims who were runaways or homeless—and the fact that some law enforcement agencies do not routinely follow up on these types of reports anyway—contributed to the inability of the police community around Chicago to recognize that a very brutal and efficient serial killer was operating. There was no hint that John Gacy had murdered 33 people over a period of time until Des Plaines Police Department investigators followed up on the missing person report of Robert Piest (*People v. Gacy*, 1984; Keppel, 2000).

Another bizarre series of murders was uncovered in Pasadena, TX, in 1973. Three suspects, Elmer Wayne Henley, Dean Corll, and David Owen Brooks, were involved in murdering at least 17 teenage boys. No information about these murders was known until the police investigated Elmer Wayne Henley in the shooting death of Dean Corll. In that death investigation, police interviewed Henley and Brooks. In Brooks' appeal, the Supreme Court of Texas wrote the following information in its decision in to affirm the trial court's conviction of Brooks (*David Owen Brooks v. The State of Texas*, 1979).

Detective Jim Tucker testified that he took an oral statement from appellant on the morning of August 9, 1973. On August 8, Elmer Wayne Henley, Jr., had shot and killed Dean Corll in Pasadena and had subsequently led police officers to a boathouse in Houston where 8 bodies had been found buried. In his statement, appellant told Tucker that Corll had told him that he, Corll, had killed two boys and buried them at the boathouse. Appellant also told Tucker of his discovery, during a visit to Corll's apartment, of two nude boys tied to Corll's bed. Finally, appellant told Tucker that he had met Corll when he was in the sixth grade (appellant was 18 at the time he gave the statement), that Corll had engaged in homosexual activities with many boys, including appellant, that he had introduced Henley to Corll, and that he had lived with Corll intermittently. In this statement to Tucker, appellant said nothing to indicate that he had been present at any murders committed by Corll or Henley.

On August 10, 1973, appellant executed two written confessions, both of which were admitted in evidence.

The first confession reads, in pertinent part: "I came to the police station on August 9th in order to make a witness statement about what I know about Dean Corll. I came down of my own free will and I gave that statement to Det. Tucker. In the statement what I said was partially the truth but I left out the fact that I was present when most of the killings happened. I was in the room when they happened and was supposed to help if something went wrong.

"The first killing that I remember happened when Dean was living at the Yorktown Townhouses. There were two boys there and I left before they were killed but Dean told me that he had killed them afterwards. I don't know where they were buried or what their names were. The first few that Dean killed were supposed to have been sent off somewhere in California.

"The first killing that I remember being present at was on 6363 San Felipe. That boy was Ruben Haney. Dean and I were the only people involved in that one but Dean did the killing and I just was present when it happened.

"I also remember two boys who were killed at the Place One Apartments on Mangum. They were brothers and their father worked next door where they were building some more apartments. I was present when Dean killed them by strangling them, but again I didn't participate. I believe that I was present when they were buried, but I don't remember where they were buried. The youngest of these two boys is the youngest that was killed I think.

"A boy by the name of Glass was killed at the Columbia address. I had taken him home one time but he wouldn't get out because he wanted to go back to Dean's. I took him back and Dean ended up killing him. Now that I think about it I'm not sure whether it was Glass that I took home or another boy, but I believe it was Glass.

"It was during the time that we were living on Columbia that Wayne Henley got involved. Wayne took part in getting the boys at first and then later he took an active part in the killings. Most of the killings that occurred after Wayne came into the picture involved all three of us.

"There was another boy killed at the Schuller house, actually there were two at this time; a boy named Billy Balsch and one named Johnny and I think that his last name was Malone. Wayne strangled Billy and he said 'Hey Johnny' and when Johnny looked up Wayne shot him in the forehead with a .25 automatic. The bullet came out of his ear and he raised up and about three minutes later he said, 'Wayne please don't.' Then Wayne strangled him, and Dean helped.

"Dean moved to the Frencesa Apartments on Wirt. At that time I was using Dean's car so I was in and out all of the time.

"After the Frencesa apartments Dean moved to Pasadena. I know of two that were killed there. One was from Baton Rouge and one was a small blond boy from South Houston. I saw the boy from South Houston for about 45 minutes. I took him for a pizza and then I left, and he wanted me to come back. I wasn't there when either of these boys was killed. I did come in just after Dean had killed the boy from Baton Rouge; that was on a different day from the blond boy.

"In all I guess there were between 25 and 30 boys killed and they were buried in three different places. I was present and helped bury many of them but not all of them. Most of them were buried at the boat stall. There were three or four buried at Sam Rayburn, I think, I am sure that there are two up there. On the first one at Sam Rayburn I helped bury them, and then the next one we took to Sam Rayburn. When he got there Dean and Wayne found that the first one had come to the surface and either a foot or a hand was above the ground. When they buried this one the second time they put some type of rock sheet on top of him to keep him down.

"The third place that they were buried was on the beach at High Island. This was right off of the Winnie Exit, where that road goes to the beach. You turn east on the beach road and go till the pavement changes, which is about a quarter or half a mile and the bodies are on the right-hand side of the highway about 15 or 20 yards off of the road. I never actually buried one here but I always drove the car. I know that one of the graves had a large rock on top of it. I think that there were five or more bodies buried at this location. The bodies at the beach are in a row down the beach for perhaps a half a mile or so. I am willing to show officers where this location is and will try to locate as many of the graves as possible."

The second confession reads, in pertinent part: "I want to give this statement about Billy Ray Lawrence.

"About July 10th, 1973, I tried to call Dean's house, Dean Corll, and it was a long time before I could get him or anyone to answer. Finally, Wayne answered and I asked him if they had anyone there and he said yes. I asked him 'It's not a friend, is it?' and he said 'sort of.' He wouldn't tell me who it was so I went over there just to see who it was. He was still alive when I got there but he was tied to the bed. I recognized him only as a friend of Wayne's.

"The boy wasn't doing anything but lying there when I got there. He didn't have any clothes on. I don't remember them calling him by name but I have just now been shown a picture of him, which I will initial with this date and time, and it is the same boy I have been talking about. In fact, I have seen this same picture before at Dean's house.

"I was tired so I went to bed in the opposite bedroom. Before I did go to bed I took Wayne home. Then I went back to Dean's house and went to bed. The boy was still alive but Dean was awake because I remember he let me in. The next morning I went back to get Wayne and Dean was supposed to pay me $10.00 for doing this but he never did. That is, the $10.00 was for taking Wayne home the night before.

"I'm not sure about the time but I think it was the next evening when Wayne's mother called. She was drunk and insisting Wayne come home but he told her no, that he was going to the lake for a couple of days. The boy was still alive. We left about 6:00 p.m. to go to the lake and I know he was dead and in a box when we left so he must have been there when he was killed because I didn't leave to go anywhere before we left for the lake. [However, I do not remember how he was killed. I don't know if I saw it or not.] It didn't bother me to see it. I saw it done many times. [I just wouldn't do it myself. And I never did do it myself.]

"We left for the lake about 6:00 p.m., and got there about 9:30 or quarter to ten. We then went fishing, Wayne and me. This was after we slept. We fished from about 6:30 A.M. to 10:00 A.M. Dean told us he had already picked a spot and started digging, but he actually hadn't done very much.

"When Wayne and I got back from fishing, we ate and I went to sleep. I slept until about 5:00 p.m. and then Dean and I dug the grave. Wayne was keeping lookout in the van. The spot was by a trench near a dirt road. It was probably a few miles from Lake Sam Rayburn itself.

"We took the body out of the box, that is, Dean did, and I held the boy's feet about half way to the grave. The body was already wrapped in plastic. I went back to the van to get the carpet and a flashlight. The carpet is to shovel extra dirt on and take it some place else so there wouldn't be a mound showing.

"I almost took too much dirt off and Dean griped at me for it."

The photograph referred to in the second confession was admitted in evidence. It was found by police in Corll's bedroom and identified at the trial by James Lawrence as a photograph of his son, the deceased.

In his first confession, appellant specifically refers to eight murders with which he was familiar: Ruben Haney, two brothers killed at the Place One Apartments, a boy named Glass, Billy Balch, Johnny Malone, a boy from Baton Rouge, and a small blond boy from South Houston. Except for the last two, appellant admitted being present when each of these murders was committed. What follows is a brief summary of further evidence concerning these murders offered by the State and admitted at the trial.

The body of Ruben Haney, 19, was found buried in a Houston boathouse rented by Dean Corll; the cause of death was strangulation. Haney's mother testified that her last conversation with her son was a telephone call in which he told her he was going to spend the night with appellant.

The bodies of Donald and Jerry Waldrop, 13 and 15, were found buried in the boathouse; the cause of death in each case was strangulation.

The body of James Glass was found buried in the boathouse; the cause of death was strangulation.

The body of Billy Balch, 17, was found buried on the beach near High Island; the cause of death was strangulation.

The body of Johnny Delone, 18, was found buried at High Island; the cause of death was strangulation and a .25 caliber gunshot.

The body of Stanley Blackburn, 20, from Baton Rouge, LA, was found buried near Lake Sam Rayburn; the cause of death was strangulation. Blackburn's Louisiana driver's license was found in Corll's house and identified at the trial by his mother.

The body of James Dreymala, 13, was found buried at the boathouse; the cause of death was strangulation. A bicycle registered to Dreymala and identified at the trial by his father was also found in the boathouse. Dreymala's father testified that his son had blond hair, and at the time of his disappearance the family lived in South Houston.

In each case, the body was nude, wrapped in plastic sheeting, and covered with lime. In most cases, the cord used to strangle the victim was still tied around the neck of the body.

In addition to this testimony, several police officers described in general terms the search for and recovery of bodies at the three burial sites. Although there was no testimony concerning the identity or cause of death of any other victims, all were young males and had been buried in a similar manner (*Brooks v. State*, 1979).

It wasn't until the confessions of Henley and Brooks led police to the first eight bodies in the boathouse before the serial was discovered, and authorities were informed the three serial killers, acting in concert, were in operation all along.

The series of murders committed by Gacy, Henley, Corll, and Brooks highlight times when police investigators were unaware that a serial killer was operating. The ability of police investigators to recognize that a serial killer was operating under those circumstances was next to impossible, even though one would think that with so many people involved in the Pasadena, TX, cases that someone would have found out earlier and reported it to police. One wonders, though, if the coordination and follow-up investigations of missing, runaway, and throwaway persons were thoroughly conducted, maybe some of these cases would have been linked, and the investigations would have occurred much sooner, possibly preventing some of the murders.

Similarly, the more recent case of Jeffrey Dahmer revealed the same blind spot on the part of police after they discovered from the complaint of an escaped victim that a series of grotesque murders had taken place in a nearby apartment. As a result of the ensuing investigation, police realized that a long series of murders of gay men had been taking place in Milwaukee for almost a decade right under their noses. Families of the victims had been filing missing persons reports, complaining to police, and fomenting among themselves about the lack of progress or even interest on the part of the police in the cases of their family members. Only after police searched Dahmer's apartment where they found skulls and bones and the severed heads of Dahmer's victims, along with grim photos of his drugged and murdered victims, did they realize the extent of his crimes. In some ways this was a pattern familiar to the Gacy case in which recognition was forced upon the police by the final case in the series.

FINDING SIMILAR CASES

Finding similar cases is just for investigative purposes, enabling detectives to network about their cases; getting them assembled to discuss similar cases to determine if investigating them in concert will lead to a killer sooner. It is not an attempt by detectives to conclusively link two or more cases together as in the case of signature analysis. Linking cases through crime scene and psychological signature analysis will be discussed in detail in Chapter 6.

When detectives finally do realize that a murder might be the work of a serial killer, what drives these investigators to search for similar murder cases? Call it gut instinct or, perhaps, a sixth sense. Experienced detectives look for other cases because they hope that information from those distant cases may hold the key to solving their own. But at exactly what point does an investigator turn the switch and actively search for similar case(s)? And how is linking one case to another actually accomplished?

The ability to recognize that another case is related depends on two factors. First, there are individual characteristics of murder that should reveal (1) signs of prior killing and/or (2) that the killer will strike again. Secondly, the information sources available to detectives govern whether or not they will discover similar murders. I will deal with the characteristics of murder first.

CHARACTERISTICS OF SERIAL MURDER

How do detectives recognize that the apparent single victim murder they have just responded to is the work of a serial killer? What are the differences between those killers who choose to kill one person versus those who choose to kill multiple victims over a period of weeks or longer? Certain signs at the crime scene tell detectives what kind of a killer they have. Those signs have been referred to as characteristics of symbolism or ritualism—not ritualistic in the satanic sense or indicative of a specific kind of religious or cult ceremony—but a kind of psychological ritualism or internal psychodrama directly related to an attempt to fulfill the killer's perverted fantasies. This is a ritual the killer may carry out every time he kills. In this ritual he's acting out or working out the elements of a script in his own mind, which gratify his immediate lust at the kill and follow-up and satisfy his recurring psychosexual compulsion that drives him from victim to victim.

Consider this scenario. The scene was riveting. Every police officer arriving to secure the crime location stared at the single, grim, motionless female stretched out upon the pavement in an outlandishly bizarre position after being severely beaten. The police had never seen anything like it before. Clearly, her body had been deliberately posed. There was no question in anyone's mind that whoever committed this terrible atrocity hadn't worried about spending considerable time with her corpse. The body had been displayed in a busy area—the killer obviously wanted his work to be discovered quickly—nude and arranged to bear an unmistakable message of sexual degradation. The victim was left lying on her back, with her left foot crossed over the instep of her right ankle. Her head was turned to the left and a Frito-Lay dip container lid rested on top of her right eye. Her arms were bent at the elbow and crossed over her abdomen with her hands gently touching, one inside the other. In one hand, detectives found a startling piece of evidence: a Douglas fir cone. What did this clue represent? What kind of message was being sent, and to whom? Only the killer knew.

The victim's gold watch on her left wrist and her gold choker chain with a crescent-shaped white pendant around her neck were the only personal items left on the otherwise nude corpse. Noting that the especially aggressive predator had been meticulous in removing all of the victim's clothing, police figured that he was either too pressed for time to strip her of her jewelry, or he didn't see any value in the pieces and deliberately left them as adornments to the body. The postmortem examination revealed that the victim had been raped anally with a foreign object. Semen was also found in the victim's vagina (Keppel and Birnes, 1997).

The questions are: Can certain case characteristics such as those above reveal an intensely perverted fantasy life and, at the same time, alert investigators that a serial killer is in operation? If there is more than one case, it is possible to link those cases by examining physical evidence, such as through DNA comparisons?

What happens when investigators do not have another case to compare it to until the killer strikes again? The signal to detectives in the above example was that the killer was not finished. Rarely do killers fulfill their ultimate fantasy, and that is the very reason that other killings are occur unless the killer is caught.

Let's break down the significant characteristics in the above example that are indicators that a serial killer is in operation. First of all, one must look at each characteristic individually and, secondly, in combination with other characteristics. For example, it may not be particularly significant that the victim was left out in the open for someone to intentionally find the body, because that occurs in about 10% of all murders. That characteristic along with posing and foreign object insertion are extremely rare in combination and were significant markers of a killer's intent to kill again. When those three characteristics were analyzed in the Homicide Investigation and Tracking System's database of 2115 murders, it was discovered that no cases possessed all of the characteristics simultaneously. As expected, the killer struck again and murdered two females in which the characteristics noted here were exactly the same (Keppel, 1995). As Roy Hazelwood (1999), the former FBI profiler, has said, "You can say that cases are linked when the number of MO characteristics and ritualistic characteristics reach a point that you have never seen in combination before."

INFORMATION SOURCES

Assuming that detectives need to know whether the homicides they are trying to solve share characteristics with homicides in other jurisdictions, how do the investigators go about getting that information? Most detectives rely on traditional means, such as the teletype, telephone calls, bulletins, letters, and discussions at seminars or meetings. In 1974, using these same antiquated techniques, it took my partner and I over a year to accumulate 90 murder victims from western states that might be connected to the Bundy cases in Seattle. Finding murders in that fashion was far too inefficient and slow. As it turned out, seven victims from that list were eventually connected to the Ted Bundy murders. We needed to know that information as soon as possible. The same problem cropped up in 1984 during the investigation of the Green River murders when we tried to locate similar murders in other jurisdictions. Unfortunately, ten years later the process of finding similar murders had not changed; there was still no central repository of homicide information to query.

County, state, regional, and federal violent crime information systems are beginning to crop up and be extremely useful in linking similar crimes for investigative purposes. There are several noted examples, such as the FBI's Violent Crime Apprehension Program (VICAP), the Washington State Attorney General's Homicide Investigation Tracking System (HITS), and the Orange County District Attorney's TracKERS project, the contributions of each will be highlighted in Chapter 9.

These important database storage, query, and retrieval programs are investigative decision support systems. They help investigators search along user-defined fields to identify similar cases. They were created based on ideas suggested by Pierce Brooks, a retired captain with the Los Angeles Police Department's elite Robbery Homicide Division. As early as the 1950s and 1960s, Brooks was a visionary who realized that to solve some of his most bizarre and perplexing homicides he had to search for similar cases outside the insular confines of Los Angeles. One method he used was to go to a library and search the newspaper stacks for stories about similar murders. He noted that because the track of similarly committed violent crimes often spanned across jurisdictional lines, it was important for detectives to be informed of similar cases in other jurisdictions in order to improve solvability. In the early 1980s, Brooks was asked to become a member of the planning committee for the FBI's VICAP program.

The sole and initial purpose of VICAP was to provide homicide detectives with information on the possibility of murder cases being linked to the same offender. It was a well-known fact that certain types of serial offenders trolled for their victims and often felt compelled to travel outside their immediate neighborhoods when their comfort zones became unstable due to police presence. Bundy, for example, traveled for victims over a radius of 300 miles and across state lines. Pierce Brooks discovered evidence as far back as the 1960s that the patterns of similar crimes were so strong, they sometimes indicated that the same offender was committing crimes in different jurisdictions. But police agencies were often reluctant to ask even neighboring jurisdictions for help locating similar types of crimes, because agencies sometimes jealously guard their respective turfs. Therefore, in order to formalize the possibility of searches for similar offender patterns across jurisdictions, the FBI created VICAP.

Critics of the VICAP procedures complain about the reliability of some questions on the VICAP form and the value of any linkage produced by that analysis (Godwin, 2000). What these critics don't realize is that VICAP was not intended to provide any sort of expert linkage or sophisticated statistical analysis. Its main function is that of a pointer system to help detectives find similar cases so they can communicate with each other one-on-one about the "possibility" that cases are linked. Then, those informed detectives decide whether or not to pursue a cooperative investigation to find the same killer. The VICAP system and its data were conceived by homicide detectives for the use of homicide detectives, not as an information source for academic research, self-proclaimed profilers, or talking heads frequently seen on television documentaries.

THE VIOLENT CRIMINAL APPREHENSION PROGRAM (VICAP)

VICAP, a national data center housed at the FBI Academy, Quantico, VA, is designed to collect, collate, and analyze information regarding the following:

- Solved or unsolved homicides or attempted homicides, especially those that involve an abduction, are apparently random, motiveless, or sexually motivated, or are known to be part of a series.

- Missing persons, where the circumstances indicate a strong possibility of foul play and the victim is still missing.
- Unidentified dead bodies where the manner of death is known or suspected to be homicide.
- Cases in which the offender has been arrested or identified should be submitted to the National Center to permit unsolved cases in the VICAP system to be evaluated for possible linkages with known offenders.

VICAP staff determines if similarities exist among the individual cases newly reported and those already in the VICAP database. The recognition of patterns of murders is made by analyzing similarities or changes in MO, victimology, physical evidence, suspect description, and suspect behavior exhibited before, during, and after the crime.

It is the objective of VICAP to provide all law enforcement agencies reporting similar pattern violent crimes with the information necessary to initiate a coordinated multiagency investigation so that they may expeditiously identify and apprehend the offender(s) responsible for the crimes. (Multiagency Investigative Team Manual, 1988).

TRACKERS

The VICAP program has encouraged the development of local, regional, and statewide violent crime information programs. The usefulness of systems like VICAP is highlighted by the way the TracKERS program was developed in Orange County, CA. Late in 1995, Deputy District Attorney Michael Jacobs was assisting Costa Mesa and Tustin police departments in the review of four murders of young sexually assaulted women that had occurred in 1979. Investigators were confident back in 1979 that the same unknown offender had also committed two sexual assaults. The cases are listed as follows:

- 04-01-79, Costa Mesa Police Department, murder of Kimberly Rawlins
- 05-24-79, Orange County Sheriff, rape of Kim Whitecotton
- 07-20-79, Costa Mesa Police Department, rape of Jane Pettengill
- 09-15-79, Costa Mesa Police Department, murder of Marolyn Carleton
- 10-07-79, Tustin Police Department, murder of Debbie Kennedy
- 10-21-79, Costa Mesa Police Department, murder of Debra Senior

Since then, DNA has become a useful tool to the investigator worldwide. The state DNA database at Berkeley, CA, had been building an RFLP database for some time. Mr. Jacobs facilitated the forensic reviews of the cases at the Orange County Sheriff-Coroner's Crime Laboratory.

During the reviews, Jacobs inquired about police resources and databases in order to identify other possible victims or offenders. He determined that investigators had no local hands-on access to a database of sexual assault and homicide information. Additionally, law-enforcement efforts were fragmented among the many different police agencies, which made information almost inaccessible among departments. Worse yet, caseloads, transfers, retirements, and other such issues prevented adequate followup on violent crime investigations.

During Jacobs' inquiry, he discovered that a local police investigator had developed a database based on similar criteria collected by the California's Violent Crime Information Network (VCIN) and the FBI's VICAP databases. That database had been used to track murder investigations for the city of Garden Grove. Arrangements were made to use that database to assist in the Costa Mesa and Tustin police murder investigations. A collection process of homicide and sexual assault information began, focusing on females murdered and sexual assault cases prosecuted in Orange County for the past 30 years. The review included solved and unsolved cases. During that process the following observations were made:

- Orange County's population was approaching 3 million people.
- Orange County was experiencing approximately 100 murders and more than 500 felony sexual assaults annually.
- The law-enforcement community consisted of more than 25 agencies.
- In 1996 Orange County had an estimated 1000 unsolved murders.

By May of 1996, the database had approximately 240 murder cases. A variety of reports had been prepared for the investigators to review. A report of females murdered by blunt force to the head resulted in a list of 33 cases. The report included solved and unsolved cases. Twenty of those cases occurred in homes or apartments. One case had resulted in the conviction of Kevin Green for the murder of his unborn daughter and the assault of his wife. Investigators met to discuss the results aided by database summaries.

Supervising Deputy District Attorney Mel Jensen recognized the similarity of the Kevin Green case and the unsolved murders. He also had been to State Parole Board meetings where Kevin Green had denied having committed the crime when an acknowledgment would have facilitated his parole.

In the meantime, the sheriff's lab had completed analysis of the first Costa Mesa murder. The results were submitted to the state laboratory at Berkeley, and Gerald Parker was identified as the donor of the semen evidence collected from the victim. His DNA had been submitted due to a conviction of kidnap and rape occurring in county territory adjacent to the city of Tustin on February 15, 1980. Parker had kidnapped a juvenile off the street and raped her in his Dodge van.

Gerald Parker was in prison at the time of the "cold hit," but was due to be paroled in a few weeks. Arrangements were made to conduct interviews.

Investigator Thomas Tarpley, Tustin Police Department, took with him the summaries of cases similar to the cases now known to have been committed by Gerald Parker. Skillfully, Investigator Tarpley obtained confessions to the four known cases and, by extracting significant details of other cases, Investigator Tarpley was able to identify two other cases listed in the database summaries: the murder of Chantel Green and Sandra Fry.

During the interviews, Gerald Parker provided details that convinced investigators and the prosecutor that Kevin Green was innocent of the murder for which he had been incarcerated nearly 17 years earlier. Part of that interview even accounted for the misidentification of Kevin as the killer by his wife. The following is an excerpt of the interview conducted on June 14, 1980:

> **Parker:** She's in the bedroom, okay, first when I opened the door, she's in bed and she sits up.
> **Inv. Tarpley:** Okay.
> **Parker:** Almost as if, in recognition, of somebody that she thought that I was, but I wasn't.
> **Inv. Tarpley:** Okay. What was she wearing? Do you remember?
> **Parker:** I don't remember, I think, it could have been a negligee or something of that fashion.
> **Inv. Tarpley:** Okay. And what happened?
> **Parker:** And she laid back down, as if she recognized me, I guess she thought it was her husband or boyfriend, whichever, whichever the case it was.
> **Inv. Tarpley:** Okay.
> **Parker:** And then I just hit, I rushed into the room and hit her over the head with the board.
> **Inv. Tarpley:** Okay, did that knock her out right away?
> **Parker:** Right.
> **Inv. Tarpley:** Okay, so she's knocked out, then what happened?
> **Parker:** Then I raped her.

As a result of the first series of DNA tests identifying Gerald Parker as the killer in four cases and the detailed confession of the Green killing, Jacobs immediately sought Kevin Green's release from prison. The sheriff provided a plane and the district attorney sent two investigators to return Kevin Green immediately to court where he was judged innocent and released. At a press conference that afternoon, Sheriff Brad Gates received DNA confirmation that Parker was the donor in the Green murder.

Subsequently, the Kevin Green acquittal on the basis of a DNA analysis 17 years after he had been wrongly convicted based on evidence provided by his wife became a landmark case in California. The eyewitness identification of Kevin Green's wife, although she still refused to change her testimony, had been completely reversed by the evaluation of DNA evidence showing that not only could her husband not have been the donor but that another person, already in the state criminal database, had committed the crime. The DNA had been the basis for obtaining Parker's confession, which combined with the DNA results, showed just how faulty eyewitness identification could be, especially when made under the stress of an impending attack and the posttraumatic stress after the attack.

Now, imagine applying the specifics of this case to a serial murder case in which there are a number of living witnesses, and victims who survive the attack but who give different descriptions of the attacker and his MO. Imagine the frustration of detectives trying to pull together a composite of the attacker, but who have no database of similar attacks in nearby or contiguous jurisdictions and have to rely only on information from within their own department. The handicaps they must bear in order to investigate the case prove frustrating and may ultimately paralyze their investigation, even though they may have DNA evidence as well as descriptions from witnesses and victims. That was one of the underlying reasons for VICAP and the subsequent databases HITS and TracKERS.

The TracKERS database serves many purposes, but most significantly it is available for investigators do their own searching. Cases are not buried, but can be queried and sifted, enabling investigators to constantly review facts of cases as new information is collected. Of interest in the Kevin Green case is that he had reported a suspicious male by a Dodge van in the area of his apartment. Had TracKRS been available then, possibly investigators could have linked that information to the rape committed a few months later by the man Green saw in the darkness.

TracKRS is available to investigators from their desktop and laptop computers via an Internet connection. The database now has nearly 5000 murders and felony sexual assault cases online. Security is provided by the District Attorney's Office. Since the Parker case, other cases have been solved; the oldest, a 1975 robbery-murder. Sex crime investigations regularly benefit from current data.

Recently, Stephen Morales was sentenced to 101 years for eight rapes. Those cases were linked using TracKRS and the cooperative efforts of local police searching for behavior that identified Morales. The arrest was based upon circumstantial evidence later corroborated by DNA. Noteworthy is the fact that Morales had never been convicted of an offense that would have permitted a submission to the state DNA laboratory. TracKRS is committed to being the advocate for local investigators to ensure them the best tools for the job in a timely manner (Shave, 2001). The TracKERS program is a replica of the HITS program in Washington State.

HITS

With the assistance of the Washington Association of Sheriffs and Police Chiefs, the Washington State Attorney General's Office sought and was awarded a U.S. Department of Justice grant in September 1987 to conduct research and develop a computerized homicide investigation and tracking system (HITS) for Washington State. The HITS program (1) evaluates the critical factors necessary to solve murder investigations; (2) identifies the salient characteristics of homicides; and (3) records information unique to a particular offender, the offender's method of operation, or physical evidence. Any or all of this can be used to determine if a suspect or item of evidence is associated with murder cases in Washington State. After the grant was completed, the Washington State Legislature funded the continuation of the HITS program.

The HITS program is a Pacific Northwest, computerized information system designed to improve the investigation of murder and sexual assault and the apprehension rate of violent offenders. Its primary objective is to assist local law-enforcement agencies in solving murder and sexual assault investigations. The objective is accomplished by collecting murder and rape information from the 274 law-enforcement agencies in Washington State. Most of the information entered into HITS is collected from individual case files with a data collection instrument (HITS form) designed for investigative purposes.

The 1990 session of the Washington State Legislature supported the expansion of HITS to include other serious violent crimes and sexual offenses. The appropriation increased the HITS budget to $941,000 and the total number of personnel to 11. The HITS program structure is being progressively expanded and modified to collect sexual assault information. Five HITS investigators/analysts are each assigned a geographical area of the state to coordinate the submission and analysis of murder and sexual assault information with local law-enforcement agencies.

Currently, there are over 7000 murder cases and 8000 sexual assault investigations, mainly from the states of Washington and Oregon, in the HITS program. These cases represent 100% of the murder cases from 1981 to the present in Washington State. Every law-enforcement agency in the state that investigates murders and sexual assaults participates in the HITS program.

The activities of HITS' complement the FBI's VICAP program. The HITS murder report form contains many of the fields of the VICAP form plus over 80 additional fields. In addition to the VICAP fields, HITS also contains information from many different, yet related, sources. The information from the HITS form constitutes the most vertical file. Another database is Crime Data, which contains information from teletypes, newspapers, and bulletins. Detectives' requests for information are maintained in the Homicide Inquiry Section for record-keeping purposes, and in the event information becomes available in the future to answer a prior request. The Victim List includes basic case information on all murder and sex crime victims. The Crime Line file records the chronological activities of known murderers, particularly emphasizing their movements. The various databases are cross-indexed in HITS and can be searched simultaneously for information that may be relevant to a murder investigation.

The most important feature of the relational-based data management system which operates the HITS is its ad hoc interactive search capability. A homicide investigator can design queries from the 227 fields of the HITS form or from the information contained in other HITS data files. Since the summer of 1988, the HITS program has received about 500 requests for investigative assistance in murder cases per year. Almost one-half of the queries have resulted in some form of assistance, meaning that information was provided that facilitated the investigation.

Finally, the HITS unit of the Washington State Attorney General's Office has demonstrated the critical role of comprehensive, accurate, and accessible information in improving murder and sex crimes investigations. The cooperative effort of federal, state, and local law-enforcement agencies is proving effective in delivering this valuable assistance through HITS. This cooperative effort was highlighted by the arrest of serial killer Scott William Cox.

SCOTT WILLIAM COX

In the latter part of 1990 and early 1991, the Portland, OR, area was the grim setting for the murder of two prostitutes. The first, Reena Ann Brunson, was last seen November 24, 1990, walking the streets in downtown Portland. She was 34 years old and had a prior arrest for prostitution in Seattle. At about 9:15 p.m., she collapsed in front of the Safeway Store on Martin Luther King Drive and Northeast Ainsworth. She died at Emanuel Hospital a short time later. Brunson was severely beaten about the face and died from a single stab wound to the chest. She also had sustained several cuts to her neck, lower chin, and back which appeared to be the result of someone pressing a knife against her, perhaps torturing her. She was found fully dressed and had a pair of police-grade Peerless handcuffs attached to one wrist. The other handcuff loop was closed, and it appeared she was able to slide her hand out, as evidenced by the severe lacerations on her hand.

The second victim, Victoria Rhone, was 32 years old and had a history of prostitution. She was last seen on February 19, 1991, and was found murdered the next day in a railroad cargo carrier in a Portland rail yard. She had been severely beaten. Torn strips from the suspect's T-shirt was found binding the victim's wrists behind her back. Also, a strip from the T-shirt served as a strangulation device and was found around her neck. These two homicides remained unsolved until members of the HITS went to work.

On May 30, 1991, at 12:30 a.m., a female prostitute was sexually assaulted, beaten, and left for dead in downtown Seattle, WA. A witness had observed the victim being thrown out of a tractor cab-over truck in a parking lot under the monorail that leads to the Space Needle. The victim was not a pretty sight; she had been badly beaten and had had a ligature around her neck. She sustained numerous bite marks all over her body. Her assailant forced a Bartles and Jaynes Wine Cooler bottle up her rectum. As a result, the victim required hospitalization for some time.

Seattle detective, Dan Fordice, had contact with HITS investigator Dick Steiner. Fordice related that the victim was uncooperative and did not want to prosecute. Steiner insisted that the case be pursued because the characteristics of this assault were similar to what he had seen other serial killers do to their victims. This assailant was either already a serial killer or was on his way to becoming one. Detective Steiner knew what some of the telltale psychological calling cards were of a serial killer and understood that even if this living victim didn't know it, she had been beaten and tortured at the hands of someone who was already acting out like a serial killer. If he hadn't yet killed, it was only a matter of time before he did.

Witness information revealed that the truck had a logo on the side of Woodland Trucking in Cowlitz County, WA, two counties to the north of Portland, OR. Follow-up investigation with the trucking firm identified a Seth Scott Cutter as the driver in Seattle that day. Detectives interviewed Cutter and were told that he was only trying to help the victim. With the results of DNA analysis weeks or months away and the fact that the victim had fled, Cutter had to be released. Further investigation uncovered that Cutter reportedly had previously assaulted a prostitute on November 26, 1990, at 3:15 a.m.. According to witnesses, he was driving his Mazda pickup with Oregon plates. Cutter gave an address of the Town and Country Motel in Newberg, OR.

Detectives feared the worst with Cutter, so a police informational bulletin was sent to law-enforcement agencies in Washington and Oregon, warning them of Cutter's presence on the street. Detective Ken Summers of the Newberg Police Department received the bulletin and recognized the photograph of Cutter, but he knew the person as Scott William Cox, a 28-year-old local resident of his city. Summers immediately informed detectives with the Portland Police Bureau and a protracted investigation into Scott Cox began.

Cox ultimately confessed to detectives that he had killed Brunson because he was mad at his 53-year-old girlfriend. He said he drove to Portland to take his anger out by severely beating a prostitute. He drank whiskey, used cocaine, and picked Brunson up. He drove her directly to the Safeway Store and parked in the recessed side of the loading dock area. Cox claimed not to want to have sex, so he immediately started beating Brunson with his fists. He handcuffed her but was uncertain if he got both cuffs around her wrists. As Brunson was escaping from his truck, he stabbed her one time. Brunson collapsed near the store entrance and Cox drove back to Newberg. He also confessed to the killing of Rhone and talked of beating several other prostitutes in Oregon and Washington, but would not admit to any other murders (Steiner, 2001).

This information coupled with Cox's mobility made detectives feel that he may have been responsible for many more murders throughout the routes where he had driven his semi-tractor. Detectives from the Portland area, Seattle, and HITS began contacting agencies along the route that Cox traveled. Eventually, 22 agencies identified in the list below contributed information about Cox's travels.

Washington:

- Attorney General's Office HITS Unit
- Grays Harbor County Sheriff
- King County Police
- Lewis County Sheriff
- Pierce County Sheriff
- Snohomish County Sheriff
- Bellevue Police
- Mount Lake Terrace Police
- Seattle Police
- Spokane Police
- Tacoma Police
- Vancouver Police
- Woodland Police

Oregon:

- Oregon State Police HITS
- Oregon State Police Crime Lab
- Yamhill County Sheriff
- Newberg Police
- Portland Police

California:

- Riverside County Sheriff
- San Diego Police
- Oakland Police

Canada:

- Royal Canadian Mounted Police

Detectives from those agencies collected data on Cox from many sources including truck logs, telephone records, social security records, weigh stations for trucks along freeways, state vehicle records, NCIC Offline information, police computer databases, U. S. border crossings, and credit cards. Using these sources, an extensive timeline file was constructed detailing Cox's whereabouts. His timeline file is the largest one in the HITS program, over 4000 entries.

The apprehension of serial killer Scott Cox highlighted the importance of a violent crime information system and how that system encourages and fosters cooperation among law-enforcement agencies. It wasn't the HITS computer system that helped solve the case; it was the detectives communicating with each other about common crimes and, utilizing the technology, recognizing and acknowledging the nature of Cox's criminal career. The vehicle for their communication was vital to arousing enough police interest throughout at least three states so that Scott Cox was stopped from killing any longer. Therefore, right from the outset, the investigative process consisted of the following elements of recognition:

1. Identifying a potential victim of a serial killer even though she lived through the experience
2. Distributing the information to law-enforcement agencies
3. Officers taking that information and solving a series of murders

Because one of the key detectives who had recognized that the crime scene and victim evidence correlated in his mind with what he'd seen serial killers do, he made sure the information was circulated to different agencies. An informational hit with a local agency provided the information that the suspect had been using a false name. When confronted with a police interview, the suspect confessed and, in so doing, opened the door to a wider investigation. As successful as this investigation turned out to be, it could not have begun without the recognition that a nonfatal assault on a prostitute was really the work of a serial killer operating in the Oregon-Washington area. A long, and possibly frustrating and fruitless investigation into prostitute murders was successfully cut short by translating an early recognition of serial killer psychological behavior into a wide informational distribution process.

The utility of homicide information systems monitoring the frequency and types of murders is important for recognition purposes. The conclusion is that a more thorough and comprehensive analysis by an information system may detect the workings of a serial killer much earlier, and, therefore, help prevent future murders by catching the killer.

ACKNOWLEDGMENT

Once recognition is confirmed, an even greater question faces police administrators: Are they willing to tell others that a serial killer is on the loose? The best argument for acknowledging that a serial killer is in operation is that by releasing this information, the investigation can create its own luck. The strategy to inform the public about elements of the murder investigation is that the public may have key information to help in the solution. So disseminating this information will help in the investigation.

For example, in one murder case the killer shot a convenience store clerk. The follow-up investigation revealed that the killer had stolen or eaten beef jerky. Detectives had talked to associates and friends and even the suspect in the third week, but they elected to hold back the beef jerky information. No strong suspicious feelings were discovered, so they moved on. In hindsight, information about the beef jerky should have been publicly released. Later on, this information led to the identity of the offender who was contacted, and many hours of investigation would have been saved.

A second strategy for release of case-essential information is that it is a way to put the heat on the killer. In one such case, the killer was pulling over vehicles driven by females on a freeway. This information was published and led to a female motorist who escaped from the killer, but had never reported the incident until information about the freeway abductions were published in the paper. When the killer either makes a mistake in his own pattern by failing to abduct and kill who he has approached or has a change of heart because the victim doesn't fit his profile and he releases her, information about the killer in the hands of the public can become more than helpful; it can play an essential role in the investigation. As we will see later, living witnesses or victims play a crucial role in the apprehension of serial killers.

Once a series of murders is recognized as the responsibility of a serial killer, resistance to acknowledgment may follow. The most common reason to not release the fact that a serial killer is in operation is that investigative resources are not available. This became blatantly evident when the enhanced Green River Task Force was formed in January 1984. It consisted of 44 personnel from the King County Police, 2 detectives from the Seattle Police, 2 detectives from the Port of Seattle Police, 1 crime analyst from the Washington State Patrol, and 1 consultant—myself—from the Washington State Attorney General's Office. The obvious conclusion here is that the King County Police dedicated major resources for the task force, even though this series was a Seattle regional issue. Why didn't the Seattle Police dedicate more manpower and resources? After all, the Seattle Police Department was over twice the size of the King County Police at the time. Also, there were over 13 missing prostitutes who disappeared off the streets of Seattle while the King County authorities had located 7 murder victims within their jurisdictional boundaries. It was common knowledge among police investigators at the time that those ten missing victims from Seattle were part of the series. It would prove out in the next two years that all ten missing persons from Seattle were eventually linked to the Green River series because their bodies were found in remote areas of King County and within the city limits of Seattle. The question still remains: Did the decision by the Seattle Police Department to resist acknowledgment by providing inadequate resources severely inhibit the performance of the Green River Task Force?

Mixed in with this resistance to acknowledgment of the Seattle Police Department was another strange phenomenon that occurred relating to the recognition issue of the Green River murders. From January through July 1982, there were five prostitute murder victims found on the streets of Seattle before the published start of the Green River series in July of 1982. These victims were found outdoors, strangled, bludgeoned, or stabbed and nude or partially nude. Were they also victims of the Green River Killer? Why weren't these victims part of the same group of Green River killings? The reason was related to the hesitancy to recognize or, worse yet, cooperate fully. Seattle police supervisors refused to admit or consider whether those victims were killed by the Green River Killer.

The strongest argument for resisting acknowledgment is that the suspect will know what we know if we reveal certain facts. Concealing information is a way to avoid linking copycat crimes with the series at hand. After Kenneth Bianchi was arrested for two murders in Bellingham, WA, his girlfriend attempted a kidnapping to mimic the crimes of the Hillside Strangler. She wanted to demonstrate that the Hillside Strangler was still on the loose, and Bianchi was the wrong man. Because she was unfamiliar with the details of the cases, she failed and was apprehended quickly.

Acknowledging that a serial killer is on the loose brings on the good, the bad, and the ugly of an investigation. It is good because the telephone call you may get might help solve the case. It is bad because you may not be ready for the multitude of incoming information. It could get ugly if members of agencies who once resisted the idea that a serial killer was operating are forced to join the investigative effort.

One might think that the police would be as close-mouthed about a serial killer investigation as possible, because they know the killer is listening to every piece of news about the case. Too often just the opposite is true, because the media tracks whatever the task force does, publishes it in morning editions and weekly tabloids, and broadcasts it on the evening news. Most police departments feel obligated to talk because of the media pressure, and this alerts the killer. While the serial killer can lurk in the shadows until he's ready to strike, the members of the task force must do their work under the glare of camera lights and must respond to the media even when they don't want to. High-profile homicide investigations are often so burdened by the media overhead that they make mistakes or even break down. In the case of JonBenet Ramsey, for example, the pressure from the media was so great that police officers never had the opportunity to assess what they had before they had to present it in a public forum and wound up squabbling among themselves.

Acknowledgment warns the public that there is a dangerous situation in the community. Take the case of the Vampire Killer, for example. Richard Trenton Chase was a 27-year-old paranoid schizophrenic who terrorized Sacramento from 1977 to 1978. He began his series with a victim who was murdered with a single shot from a .22 caliber weapon in his front yard. Over time, Chase would cut birds, cats, and dogs and inject and drink their blood. Two weeks later, Teresa Wallen was shot, her midsection cut open, and blood was scooped from her body cavity.

Physical evidence in the form of lead bullet comparisons confirmed recognition that the same killer was at work. Evelyn Griffin was taking bath. She was murdered and blood in the bathtub gave evidence that the killer took a bath in her blood. Her son Daniel, 6 years old, was at her feet. Her new baby was missing from its crib and a .22 caliber hole was found in the crib. There was evidence that the killer was barefoot. There were differences between the Griffin and Wallen cases, but the match of the .22 caliber cartridges gave it away.

Acknowledgment was made public to warn those in the neighborhood that a vicious killer was on the loose. Police conducted an extensive canvass, but nothing developed from that. What did solve that case was that a witness observed a subject leaving the scene of a burglary. The public was reporting everything out of the ordinary until the killer was caught. The witness was able to provide investigators with a detailed description. Based on that description, a former classmate of Richard Chase recognized him as the person in the drawing and notified police. Richard Chase was contacted and the gun he was carrying matched the bullets from the shootings. Richard Trenton Chase eventually died in San Quentin prison of a drug overdose (Biondi, 1987).

Another factor in favor of acknowledgment is that it gives the police a chance to show that they are doing everything possible to solve the cases. It is up to the investigative staff to advertise their successes and problems by getting this information to the public so the public supports the police effort. Some agencies err by wanting to control the press—don't tell them anything, but work the leads the media provides. This is the cart before the horse argument. Sometimes warning the public about the killer is necessary.

The question is what details should the police release? As we will see in our discussion of the DC Beltway Snipers, releasing too much information about who the killer(s)' targets were actually might have encouraged the shooting of a school child. In the case of the Green River investigation, the task force, while they might have watched as the press speculated about various suspects, never released the name of any of their prime suspects in four of the murders until they actually arrested the killer in 2001. Any competent public information officer will tell you that if you set rules early regarding public disclosure, adhere to them as much as you can, and be honest and forthright to the press when you have to deviate, even the most skeptical reporters will cut you some slack. However, if the press smells blood and defensiveness, and they think you're trying to manipulate them, they will be relentless in confronting you with the sources they've developed and will wind up either forcing you to disclose something you don't want to or force you into admitting you're withholding information. Disclosure is a process of balance and honesty driven by trust.

Recognition and its subsequent acknowledgment are the beginning moves in a very complicated psychological game of strategy in which the serial killer investigators are players—whether they want to be or not—pitting themselves and their task force against the psychology of the killer. The sociopathic killer can have certain advantages in this game such as his compulsion to kill, which is almost animalistic in its primal nature. For the killer, who lives in a universe of one until he identifies his next victim and, through his crimes brings her into his universe, his strategies are those of a creature in the wild surviving in his element. He's not a wild-eyed babbling freak running through the streets with a bloody knife. He's a cunning predator who knows how to conceal himself from crime to crime. For police who don't understand the nature of this type of offender—and most police still don't—his elusiveness can be the undoing of any institutionalized attempt to apprehend him.

Absent recognition and acknowledgment, the police almost always defeat themselves because their collective efforts to marshal the resources to track the killer down, while at the same time trying to cut him off at the next pass, are doomed to failure. How can you catch someone you don't even recognize? How can you apprehend a particular type of offender without even acknowledging his presence? On the most elementary of levels, this argument sounds simplistic, but there is a deeper level of purpose at work here.

Recognition and acknowledgment are psychological processes that commit the task force to the job at hand. Without a collective commitment to what has to be done, and an admission that not to succeed would be damaging to the institution, the psychological resources will not be available to the police. The killer will win the psychological game because what drives him is far more vital than simply a set of police strategies put into motion to solve a case. For the killer it's survival. For the police task force on the trail of the killer, survival must be the issue as well if the task force is to have any hope of succeeding.

As we will now see in the Yorkshire Ripper case, strategy itself is the least guarantee of success. The following set of rules and procedures only guarantees that—and not always—the rules and procedures will be followed. Like blind men following a pathway down a maze which actually changes before them, police who only follow rules almost always wind up against a wall. The key commitments of recognition and acknowledgment that put the police squarely in the face of failure have to be made at the outset for them to begin the investigation properly. The more recognition and acknowledgment are delayed, the greater lead the killer will have on the police. At some point in the investigation, whether police want to or not, they will have to recognize what they're chasing; at some point they will have to acknowledge that recognition. It is only at that point that the chase really begins.

REFERENCES

Biondi, R. Presentation on the Investigation of Serial Murders at the Fifth National Conference on Homicide, Unidentified Bodies, and Missing Persons in Nashville, TN, 1987.

David Owen Brooks v. State of Texas, 580 S. W.2d 825, 1979.

Egger, S. A. A working definition of serial murder. *J. Police Sci. Admin.,* **12**:3, 1984.

Egger, S. A. *Serial Murder: An Elusive Phenomenon,* 1990. New York: Praeger.

Evans, R. Interview with Captain Robert Evans, Green River Task Force Commander, March 1989.

Field Supplementary Report # #78–35203, Des Plaines Police Department, 13 December 78, 0330 hours, Officer G. Loconsole.

Godwin, G. M. Profiling and linking crimes, In *Criminal Psychology and Forensic Technology: A Collaborative Approach to Effective Profiling,* Grover Maurice Godwin, ed., 2000. Boca Raton, FL: CRC Press.

Hazelwood, R., and Michaud, S. *The Evil That Men Do,* 1999. New York: St. Martins Press.

Keppel, R. D. Signature murders: A report of several related cases, J. Forensic Sci., **40**(4): 658–662, 1995.

Keppel, R. D. Signature murders: A report of the 1984 Cranbrook, British Columbia cases, *J. Forensic Sci.,* **45**(2): 500–503, 2000a.

Keppel, R. D. Serial Murder: Future Implications for Police Investigations, Authorlink. com, Dallas, TX, 2000b.

Keppel, R. D. *Linking Cases through Modus Operandi and Signature, In Serial Offenders: Current Thought, Recent Findings,* Joseph Schlesinger, ed., 2000c. Boca Raton, FL: CRC Press.

Keppel, R. D., and Birnes, W. J. *The Riverman: Ted Bundy and I Hunt the Green River Killer,* 1995. New York: Pocket Books.

Keppel, R. D., and Birnes, W. J. *Signature Killers,* 1997. New York: Pocket Books.

Keppel, R. D., and Walter, R. A. Profiling killers: A revised classification model for understanding sexual murder. *J. Offender Ther. Comp. Criminol.,* **43**(4): 417–437, 1999.

Keppel, R. D., and Weis, J. P. *Murder: A Multidisciplinary Anthology of Readings,* 1999. Orlando: Harcourt Brace Custom Publishing.

Missing Persons Case Report #78–35203, Des Plaines Police Department, 11 December 1978, 2329 hours, Officer G. Konieczny.

Multiagency Investigative Team Manual, U. S. Department of Justice, National Institute of Justice, March 1988.

Rossmo, D. K. *Geographic Profiling,* 2000. Boca Raton, FL: CRC Press.

People v. Gacy, 103 IU.2d 1, 82 III. Dec.391, 468 N. E.2d 1171, 1984.

Shave, R. Email message from Ron Shave, Orange County District Attorney's Office, TracKERS Unit, January 8, 2001.

Steiner, D. Interview with Dick Steiner, HITS investigator, January 2001.

2

THE ARCHETYPAL SERIAL KILLER TASK FORCE INVESTIGATION: THE YORKSHIRE RIPPER CASE

Peter Sutcliffe: The Yorkshire Ripper

Chronology of the Case

Reference

As a direct result of the mass culture popularization of Ted Bundy, the Atlanta child murders, the Green River Killer, the Hillside Strangler, Zodiac, Nightstalker, and Jeffrey Dahmer over the past 25 years, the popular media has presented us with a snapshot, however inaccurate, of what a serial killer is, transforming him from a sociopathic sexual predator into a larger-than-life horror movie caricature. In reality, nothing could be further from the truth, and police investigators who specialize in serial homicides and violent sexual crimes know this from years of experience. Investigators know that in a stubborn case which seemingly defies resolution, the approach usually taken is to assemble a task-force—whether within the department or multijurisdictionally—and assign tasks to individual units to make sure no clue, tip, lead, or piece of evidence falls through the cracks. This can be a monumental undertaking which defies description.

Accordingly, the best way to explain how a task force is assembled and operates is to look at a specific case in which the task force made many mistakes, but which was reviewed at a higher level to reveal the mistakes and point to recommendations. In so doing, we will see how the task force confronts frustration and disappointment, how it absorbs the futility of a lack of success, and how it perseveres until, one way or another, it either finds the suspect or is formally disbanded. From an examination of what a task force does, we will see how it functions as an institution and what the nature of the underlying institutional psychology is.

Our case study is the Peter Sutcliffe "Yorkshire Ripper" case from the UK in which a truck driver perpetrated a series of bloody murders of prostitutes in the areas around Yorkshire, West Yorkshire, and Leeds. Dubbed the "Ripper" murders by the press because the knife assaults were reminiscent of the infamous Jack the Ripper cases in White Chapel, London, in the late nineteenth century, the Peter Sutcliffe case lingered for six years before the killer was finally arrested and convicted.

The fact that a sexual killer like Peter Sutcliffe could elude the police for six long years while still attacking prostitutes in neighborhoods that were heavily surveilled by uniformed constables almost became a scandal inside the police department. What made matters worse was that Sutcliffe's name had come up in the investigation a number of times, and he had been interviewed repeatedly by inspectors. As a result, a departmental internal evaluation of the entire case was ordered by the police command, and it became one of the only critical reviews of police serial killer task forces ever undertaken.

This chapter examines the Sutcliffe case in detail to show how a serial killer operates and what the task force did to try to apprehend him. Then, we will evaluate the work of the task force to show how the institutional forces that should have led to a successful resolution of the case actually failed as the police allowed themselves to miss the very clues that would have solved the case.

PETER SUTCLIFFE: THE YORKSHIRE RIPPER

Peter William Sutcliffe, born at Shipley, West Yorkshire, on June 2, 1946, was not notably abnormal, although he had gained a reputation for a rather macabre sense of humor while employed as a grave digger at Bingley. During his late teens he developed an unhealthy interest in prostitutes and spent a great deal of time, often in the company of his friend Trevor Birdsall, watching them soliciting on the streets of Leeds and Bradford. Although there is no evidence that he used the services of prostitutes at that stage, it is clear that he was fascinated by them and spent a considerable amount of time acting as a kind of voyeur.

It is apparent that at some point during 1969, Sutcliffe's interest in prostitutes attained a new dimension with a desire on his part to inflict physical injury upon them. Although the police files on two incidents involving Sutcliffe during that year were destroyed some time ago, there is no doubt that on one occasion Sutcliffe attacked a prostitute in Bradford with a cosh consisting of a large stone inside a man's sock.

In 1975, Sutcliffe is known to have embarked on a campaign of murderous attacks on prostitutes and unaccompanied women in the West Yorkshire and Greater Manchester Police areas. This was to gain him the title

The Yorkshire Ripper. It was also to bring into international focus the unprecedented police activity, press, and other news media interest which arose from one of England's most remarkable crime investigations the twentieth century. To the female population in northern cities, especially in West Yorkshire, the successive murders and serious assaults, over a period of five years, obviously prompted great fear and apprehension. This was not to be alleviated until Sutcliffe was arrested in Sheffield on January, 2, 1981.

CHRONOLOGY OF THE CASE

The first of the crimes for which Sutcliffe was convicted was the attempted murder of Anna Rogulskyj in Keighley on the July 5, 1975. Sutcliffe attacked his victim with a hammer in an alleyway in Keighley and left her lying on the ground suffering from severe head injuries and a number of superficial slash wounds to the body. The crime was investigated by Detective Superintendent Perry of West Yorkshire's Western Crime Area, and an incident room was established in the Keighley Division for the purpose of the inquiry. The crime was not linked with any others; nor was it linked with the Ripper series until June 1978 when the West Yorkshire Police issued a "Special Notice" to all police forces about the murders which had, by then, been committed.

On August 15, 1975, just over a month after the Rogulskyj incident, Sutcliffe, after leaving his friend, Trevor Birdsall, in his car, attacked Olive Smelt with a hammer in Boothtown, Halifax, inflicting serious head injuries. Using a knife, he also inflicted two slash wounds to her back after first disarranging her clothing. Although the nature of the crime was very similar to the attempted murder of Anna Rogulskyj, it was not specifically linked with it in police crime circulations, nor was it linked with the Ripper series until June 1978. Detective Superintendent Holland of the Western Crime Area established an incident room at Halifax for the purpose of the inquiry.

No substantial evidence available about either the assailants or about any vehiclethat might have been used was found in either of these two crimes. Nevertheless, for both assaults, the local police established official incident rooms. Because the crimes were sufficiently violent and overtly sexual in nature, they warranted the kind of investigation that would not only result in the apprehension of the assailant but would also put police on alert to keep the assailant from launching into a series of sexual offenses within the police jurisdictions.

The first murder in the series occurred on October 30, 1975, when Sutcliffe killed known prostitute Wilma McCannon the Prince Philip playing fields in Leeds. Once again the victim was hit on the head with a hammer, one of the blows penetrating the full thickness of the skull. On this occasion, however, unlike the tentative slashings of the bodies of Rogulskyj and Smelt, McCann was stabbed once in the neck and 14 times in the chest and abdomen. In what was to become a standard Ripper trademark, McCann's clothing had been disturbed so that before the stab wounds were inflicted the whole of her torso was displayed.

The opinion of the crime pathologist in the postmortem review was that the victim had been struck first with the hammer, probably from behind, while she was in a standing position, and that the subsequent injuries were inflicted as she lay disabled and unconscious on the ground. This, too, was to become part of Sutcliffe's standard method of operation.

This homicide was investigated by Detective Chief Superintendent Hoban of West Yorkshire's Eastern Crime Area. An incident room for the crime was established at the former Leeds City Police Headquarters in Brotherion House and was initially treated as an independent murder and not linked with the attacks on Smelt and Rogulskyj. Police inquiries revealed that a red Hillman Avenger, driven by person of color, probably a West Indian of about 35 years of age with a mustache rounded to the corners of his mouth, had been seen in the area at the time the crime was committed. The driver and vehicle were circulated as wanted for elimination but were not traced. At this point, however, police were investigating three similar attacks across a related geographical area in which the third attack—an assault to the victim's skull with a blunt object and subsequent knife attack—was similar to the two previous attacks, albeit fatal.

On November 23, 1975, less than a month after the murder of Wilma McCann, the body of Joan Harrison was found in Preston. Harrison, a known prostitute and alcoholic, had died as a result of shock and hemorrhage due to multiple injuries mainly caused by violent kicking to her head and body; she had been stomped to death. In this case, unlike the three previous cases in the West Yorkshire area, sexual assault and intercourse had occurred immediately before the victim's death rather than postmortem. The murder was investigated by Detective Chief Superintendent Brooks of the Lancashire Constabulary, whose main line of inquiry was to trace a suspect of the "B" secretor blood group which was indicated by analysis of semen from within her body.

The next Ripper murder occurred in the West Yorkshire area on January 20, 1976, when Emily Jackson, a known prostitute, was killed in a factory yard in Leeds. As in previous cases, Sutcliffe struck down his victim by a violent blow with a hammer after which he disarranged her clothing to expose her torso and inflicted multiple stab wounds to her lower neck, upper chest, and lower abdomen. An additional series of stab wounds was inflicted to her back by a cross-shaped instrument thought to be a Phillips-head screwdriver. As in the McCann case this particular murder was investigated by Detective Chief Superintendent Hoban who established an incident room in the newly opened Miligarth Police Station, not far from the murder scene.

The two murders were linked together in a crime intelligence bulletin issued to all police forces by the West Yorkshire Police on February 19, 1976. Police inquiries in the case established that at about 7 p.m. on the January 20 the victim, Jackson, had been seen to get into a Land Rover near a public house in Leeds where she had gone to solicit for prostitution. The driver of the Land Rover was described as being overweight, about 50 years old, mousy colored ear-length hair, a full beard, and bushy ginger/blonde side-burns. He was also described as having a distinctive scar extending from the knuckles to the wrist of his left hand. This description was included in the Special Notice to all forces.

On May 9, 1976, Sutcliffe attacked Marcella Claxton in the Roundhay area of Leeds. Claxton sustained severe head injuries as a result of hammer blows. This crime, investigated by Detective Chief Inspector Bradley, was regarded as an independent case of serious assault and was not linked with the murders of McCann and Jackson. It was not included in Special Notices about the Ripper crimes issued to other forces and although some senior detectives thought that it might be part of the series, it was not officially linked until Sutcliffe admitted to it following his arrest. Claxton described her attacker as being about 30 years of age with black hair, a beard, and a mustache.

When one looks at the series of murders and sexual assaults in the same or contiguous areas which are confined to a specific area of England and occur within a very short timeline, one should be looking at a way to relate them. Through the very forgiving lens of hindsight, it's also apparent that the offender in all of these crimes began his assaults in the same way: He sought to disable or knock his victim out with blows to the head before removing her clothing, stabbing her, or committing a homicide. With the exception of the homicide, the assaults fit into a very similar pattern that, when dropped into the timeline and the geographical areas, should have been looked at as the work of the same offender. However, the police simply opened up new major crime incident rooms and pursued them as separate cases that, by the end of the series, took different investigators down different paths. Meanwhile the crimes themselves continued.

On February 5, 1977, Irene Richardson, who was believed to be an active prostitute, was killed by Sutcliffe on a playing field in Roundhay, Leeds. The manner of her death immediately linked it with the killings of McCann and Jackson. She had been struck down by three hammer blows after which her body had been exposed and slashed with a knife. The slash injuries to her abdomen were particularly severe. One apparently coincidental similarity between this crime and the murder of Joan Harrison in Preston was the way in which the dead woman's boots had been neatly placed over her thighs.

Detective Chief Superintendent Hobson, who had replaced Chief Super-intendent Hoban in the Eastern Crime Area, investigated the crime and established the incident room at Miligarth Police Station, Leeds. Not everyone was convinced that Richardson's murder was linked with that of Jackson and McCann and a Special Notice to all forces including this case with other similar cases was not issued until May 9, 1977. Police inquiries produced very little evidence, although plaster casts were taken of clear tire impressions found near the scene of the crime and thought to have been made by the assailant's vehicle. The make, size, and distribution of the tires were quickly established, but greater difficulty was experienced in attempting to identify the type of vehicle to which they were fitted.

On April 23, 1977, Sutcliffe killed Patricia Atkinson in the Bradford apartment where she entertained her johns. Although the indoor crime scene constituted a different MO from the previous outdoor attacks in the series, the injuries and general method of operation linked it fairly conclusively with them. Patricia Atkinson was killed by four blows to her head with a hammer after which her body was exposed and stabbed repeatedly with a knife or chisel. Detective Chief Superintendent Domaille of the Western Crime Area led the investigation into the crime and established an incident room at the area headquarters at Bradford.

Very little evidence was forthcoming in this case apart from a footprint on a bed sheet apparently made by a Wellington boot. This print was similar to a print left on the thigh of the earlier victim, Emily Jackson. Because Patricia Atkinson had made a habit of traveling by taxi from place to place rather than walking or driving her own car, an inquiry was mounted to interview all taxi drivers working in the Bradford area. Approximately 1200 cab drivers were seen, but no useful information was obtained. The murder of Patricia Atkinson was linked with other crimes in the series in Special Notices issued on the 9th and 30th of May 1977, and in which, for the first time, reference was made to an attack on Barbara Miller in March, 1975.

This relatively minor attack on a prostitute, of which the police were previously unaware, is not one that Sutcliffe has admitted but was included in the Special Notice because Miller, who came forward in response to publicity about the Atkinson murder, identified her attacker as a 35- to 40-year-old bearded man with a scarred left hand driving a Land Rover. The description was consistent in many respects with that given by a witness in relation to the Emily Jackson murder when a bearded man with a scar on the back of his left hand was regarded as a fairly strong suspect. Perhaps the attacker with the scarred knuckles was not Sutcliffe at all, but another individual. Sutcliffe's criminal record completed in 1965 showed that he had scars on the fingers of his left hand, but the scars could not have been visible to witnesses and did not match the scar described in the Jackson and Miller cases.

On June 26, 1977, Sutcliffe killed Jayne MacDonald, a 16-year-old shop assistant in an empty untended lot in a prostitute area of Leeds near where she lived with her family. Once again the method of operation fit almost exactly the unknown assailant's standard pattern. Jayne MacDonald had been incapacitated by three severe blows to the head and, after exposure of her torso by the removal of her clothing, her body had been repeatedly stabbed through the same chest wound. She had also been stabbed in the back.

This crime was immediately linked with the series in a West Yorkshire circulation issued to all police forces on June 27, 1977, when it was listed together with the murders of McCann, Jackson, Atkinson, and Richardson. Such a serious view was taken of the series at this time that Assistant Chief Constable Oldfield took over personal direction of the inquiry and set up an incident room at Miligarth Police Station where incident rooms dealing with the Jackson and Richardson murders were already operating. A description was obtained of a man seen talking to Jayne MacDonald shortly before the time of her death. The description had much in common with that of the man thought to be responsible for a subsequent attack on Maureen Long almost two weeks later.

On July 10, 1977, Sutcliffe attacked Maureen Long in a vacant lot a short distance from her estranged husband's home. Long, who admitted that she had acted as a prostitute, received serious injuries to her head from hammer blows and stab wounds to her abdomen and back, but fortunately recovered. Because the victim had been drinking at the time and was still under the influence of alcohol, her ability to describe her attacker was severely impaired. She thought she had obtained a lift in a car from a large man of about 35 years of age who had light brown shoulder length hair. She was not able to give a description of the car that was involved, although a night watchman saw a car drive away from the scene and described it as a white Mark II Ford Cortina.

While, with the doubtful exception of the murder of Joan Harrison at Preston, all the established crimes in the series had occurred in West Yorkshire, the next attack occurred in the Greater Manchester Police area on October 1, 1977. The body of the victim, Jean Jordan, a known prostitute, was found on a disused allotment site in Chorlton-cum-Hardy on October 10, nine days after her death. She had been killed by hammer blows to the head after which she had been stabbed in the body. An unusual and curious feature of this case was that there was evidence that the killer had returned to the scene some eight days after the murder, stripped the body, and inflicted further injuries including an attempt to decapitate it.

On October 15, Jordan's handbag was found 189 feet away from the body. It contained a new £5 Bank of England note, which was thought to have been paid to the victim by the murderer. The recovery of this note some two weeks after the death marked a significant new stage in the series inquiry. Detective Chief Superintendent Ridgway of the Greater Manchester Police took charge of the investigation and recognized immediately the possibility of a link with the crimes in West Yorkshire. Weight was added to this initial suspicion when it was discovered that the £5 note recovered from Jordan's handbag was probably from a consignment of £25,000 (i.e., 5000 £5 notes) delivered to the Manningham, Shipley, or Bingley branches of the Midland Bank on September 29, 1977. A team of detectives from Greater Manchester moved to the West Yorkshire area and, accompanied by West Yorkshire officers, undertook extensive inquiries to trace the person to whom the recovered £5 note had been paid. The murder of Jordan had occurred within three days of the bank note's having been delivered to the bank, and attention was concentrated on firms in the Manningham and Shipley areas that had collected new notes from the bank to pay their employees that weekend.

On November 2, 1977, Detective Constable Howard of the Greater Manchester Police together with a Detective Constable of the West Yorkshire Police, following the trail of the £5 note, interviewed Peter William Sutcliffe at his home. It was the first time Sutcliffe's name entered what would become the vast database of tips and clues regarding the identity of the Yorkshire Ripper. Here it would remain, popping up from time to time, as new clues linked him to the crimes. Even though his name would be lost to police until years later and after more murders and assaults, it is instructive that, like a bad penny, it refused to go away no matter how many times Sutcliffe was eliminated as a suspect by the unsuspecting police. When Sutcliffe was finally arrested and confessed, authorities would be amazed at how many times they had interviewed him and took his denials at face value, possibly because the weight of information that might have implicated him early was lost to detectives because of information overload.

Sutcliffe first entered the investigation through routine police work as a followup to the tracing of a piece of evidence found on the victim at the crime scene. Sutcliffe's employers had collected money from the Shipley branch of the Midland Bank to pay their employees. Sutcliffe, who was one of nearly 8000 people listed for interview during the inquiry, denied ever having visited Manchester except during the course of his employment, and said that his last visit had been some 12 months previously when he had delivered goods to an unknown address.

Asked to account for his movements on the evening of October 1 (the date of the Jordan murder), he said that he had been at home all evening and had gone to bed at 11:30 p.m. He was also asked about his movements on the evening of October 9 when the murderer was known to have revisited the scene. He said that he and his wife had been at a house-warming party at their new home. Sonia Sutcliffe supported her husband's account of his movements on both these dates, and, absent any contradictory information, police simply relied on her statements.

After a number of new £5 notes from the Bank of England consignment were identified in the possession of people who could be eliminated from the inquiry, it was possible to eliminate some firms as recipients of the

"Jordan" note and thus limit the scope of the inquiry. T. & W.H. Clark was not one of the firms that could be eliminated, and on November 8, 1977, Sutcliffe was re-interviewed by Detective Constable Leslie Smith of West Yorkshire and Detective Constable Rayne of the Greater Manchester Police. He again satisfied the inquiry officerswho obtained further alibi evidence from his mother in connection with the house-warming party mentioned previously. At this time they were preoccupied with the £5 note aspect and did not examine Sutcliffe's car or its tires, although they did examine some footwear and household tools felt relevant to the Ripper crimes.

On December 14, 1977, the next incident in the series occurred in Leeds, when Marilyn Moore, a convicted prostitute, was assaulted by Sutcliffe in a vacant lot along Scott Hall Street. The inquiry established that Moore was picked up for prostitution purposes by the driver of a car which, by a process of elimination, was subsequently thought to be of the BMC "Farina" type. This was driven by a man who said he was called "Dave" who appeared to know several prostitutes working in Leeds by name. The driver parked his car on spare ground and, having suggested that intercourse should take place in the back of his vehicle, he hit Moore over the head with a hammer as she was getting into the rear seat. She sustained seven or eight lacerations to the head together with a depressed fracture of the skull. She also received injuries to her hands, which she had used to try to protect herself from the hammer blows to her head. Moore was eventually found and taken to Leeds General Infirmary for treatment.

The attack was investigated by Detective Chief Superintendent Hobson from the Eastern Crime area, but it was not linked with the series crimes until May 12, 1978, when it was circulated to other forces in a West Yorkshire Police circulation. Tire tracks found at the scene of the crime were similar to impressions that were found at the scene of the earlier murder of Irene Richardson. Marilyn Moore described her assailant as a white man about 28 years of age, 5'7 or 8" tall, of stocky build with dark wavy hair, a medium-length neatly trimmed beard, and a "Jason King" mustache.

Over 1000 men called Dave or David were identified in the nominal indexes of the series crimes. All were interviewed but none of them could be implicated with the crimes. Unfortunately, although, Moore's description of the car in which she had been picked up was accepted, the police placed less reliance on her description of her assailant. In retrospect, it can be said that her identification of the car was wrong although her description of her attacker matched that of Peter Sutcliffe fairly accurately. Even as the incidents were multiplying, detectives still had difficulties connecting the crimes and keeping track of potential suspects, even those potential suspects who had already been linked to evidence of the crimes.

On January 21, 1978, convicted prostitute Yvonne Pearson, was murdered by Sutcliffe in Bradford. Her body was not discovered until two months later on March 26, when it was found under an overturned settee in a wooded lot often used by prostitutes. In some ways this crime was dissimilar from those in the series so that, in a circulation to police forces on March 29, 1978, it was referred to as an independent case of murder not connected with those circulated earlier. The main reason for excluding the case was that the head injuries appeared to have been caused by a large stone rather than a hammer and that, additionally, death had been due to injuries to the chest area, probably caused by her assailant jumping on her. Although her body was exposed, no stab wounds were inflicted.

One unexplained piece of evidence recovered by police at the crime scene was a copy of the *Daily Mirror* dated February 21, 1978 (exactly one month after she was last seen alive), found under the right side of her body. This newspaper must have been intentionally placed under the body and could not have been in that position accidentally. Had the murderer returned to the crime scene after he had left the body to insert a piece of evidence under the body to confuse the police when the body was eventually discovered?

The crime was investigated by Detective Chief Superintendent Lapish of the Western Crime Area and another incident room was established at Bradford. Little evidence was forthcoming in connection with this crime, largely because of the long time lapse between the murder and the discovery of the body. There was, however, a different conclusion about the case when in May 1978 a West Yorkshire Police circulation linked it with other crimes in the Ripper series.

On January 31, 1978, Helen Rytka, an active prostitute, was murdered by Sutcliffe in Huddersfield in what by then had become the standard Ripper pattern. The body was discovered in a timber yard by a police search on February 3, and the subsequent postmortem examination revealed that she had died from hammer blows to the head together with a number of stab wounds to the body, which had previously been exposed. Another incident room was established at Huddersfield by Assistant Chief Constable Oldfield who ultimately took charge of this particular inquiry and began an independent investigation into the homicide. This ran parallel to the other ongoing incident rooms and lines of investigation into what was clearly a series of similar pattern homicides, even though the police command in Yorkshire had still not established a task force.

The separate police inquiries on their own, however, were fairly productive, and although a number of people were traced and eliminated from the inquiry, details of three motor vehicles were circulated as being wanted for elimination purposes. These were a Morris Oxford saloon, a Ford Cortina Mark I, and a white colored Datsun 160/1 SOB. The Ford Cortina and the Datsun were subsequently eliminated and attention was focused on the Morris Oxford and the BMC "Farina" range of similar cars. Because some of the vehicles in the range did not fit the tire track of the Richardson murder, a new vehicle inquiry referred to as the "Farina Index" was started. After the murder of Rytka the nominal indexes and vehicle indexes from the McCann, Jackson, Richardson, Atkinson, MacDonald and Long cases were centralized at Miligarth Police Station and subsequently amalgamated into an integrated index. This incident room continued to monitor the series inquiry until the arrest of the killer.

Early in March 1978, but before the discovery of Pearson's body, a letter postmarked Sunderland 1.45 PM 8th March 1978 and addressed to Mr. Oldfield was received by the West Yorkshire Police. The letter, written by a person signing himself Jack the Ripper, "claimed that the writer was responsible for the series of crimes. A few days later a similar letter was received by the Chief Editor of the *Daily Mirro*" newspaper in Manchester. This letter was also postmarked Sunderland and was recorded received at 10 a.m. on March 13, 1978. No immediate action was taken following the receipt of these letters, although there was a suspicion that the writer's familiarity with the crimes was more than what could have been gleaned from a study of newspapers and television programs about the Ripper series.

The question of whether the letters were actually written by the killer or by someone who knew the killer and what he was doing was not pursued at first by the police—a serious—mistake because either the separate incidents were pursuing their own paths so independently that a piece of evidence or clue unifying the investigations was overlooked, or the weight of the entire investigation was so great that the police were simply not capable of following up on something as potentially revealing as a letter from a witness.

On April 25, 1978, there was increasing concern within the West Yorkshire force that the administration of the series inquiry was being overwhelmed by the amount of information being recorded and the number of actions required to clear it. As we will see, not only in the Sutcliffe case, but in almost all major task force investigations, this process of becoming overwhelmed by information is the ruptured Achilles tendon of task forces. It's almost always where investigations face potential breakdown. This occurs simply because task forces have no means to manage the enormous flow of information from hundreds, if not thousands, of sources once detectives start researching the separate crimes and developing leads. Once the public gets involved, as we have seen from the Atlanta child murders and the recent DC Beltway sniper shootings, information becomes next to impossible to manage without a consistent system, and navigating through the information becomes a frustrating and often self-defeating process.

In the Yorkshire Ripper case, as a result of this information overload and the lack of progress in clearing the cases, a special inquiry team under Detective Chief Superintendent Domaille was appointed to conduct an internal review of the investigation. The team was asked to establish the lines of inquiry that had been undertaken in connection with each case in the series and to report whether each inquiry had been completed as far as possible and, if not, to give the current status of the investigation. At the time nine murders and four attempted murders were regarded as being connected in the series, but before the team was able to report, a further three murders had occurred. The team, first under the command of Chief Superintendent Domaille and later under Detective Superintendent Slater, was comprised of two detective inspectors, four detective sergeants, and four detective constables. Their report, which was submitted to the Chief Constable in December 1979, was more in the nature of an index of what had and had not been done in the past rather than a suggested blueprint for further action. This lack of blueprint for further action has been, in my experience, an all too typical mindset of case reviewers who simply don't know what to recommend or are too timid to recommend any further action. Reviewers many times will play it safe, focusing on the obvious of what has been done and not done instead of mapping out a suggested course of action. Not only does this limit the value of a case review, it can sometimes leave task force managers and their personnel worse off than they were before. This is what happened in the Yorkshire Ripper Task Force.

On April 26, 1978, Detective Chief Superintendent Domaille contacted the Police Scientific Development Branch and asked for assistance. Members of the branch and the Police Research Services Unit visited the force on May 4, 22, and 25, and as a result agreed to arrange for the results of the vehicle observations in "red light," or prostitution, areas to be processed on the Police National Computer. Observations on vehicles in notable red light areas had by this time commenced in other northern cities within and outside West Yorkshire so that possible leads might be available to investigating officers in the event of a further Ripper crime.

On May 16, 1978, Vera Millward, a convicted prostitute, was murdered by Sutcliffe in Manchester. Her body was discovered in a compound in the Brunswick area of the city the following day; an examination disclosed the traditional pattern of Ripper injuries. Following three severe blows to the head with a hammer, her body had been exposed before being stabbed and slashed with a knife. This crime immediately came under the control of Detective Chief Superintendent Ridgway who was still hunting for the murderer of Jean Jordan, and an incident room was established in Manchester to service the police investigation.

In this case tire tracks and footprints were found at the scene. The make and distribution of the tires on the vehicle which left the tracks were very similar to those found at the scenes of the murder of Irene Richardson and the attempted murder of Marilyn Moore, and the crime was immediately regarded as being part of the Ripper series. As a result of their investigations into the tire tracks at the scene of the Millward murder, the Greater Manchester Police were satisfied that they were not made by a car from the

Farina range. They subsequently discontinued their participation in the Farina inquiry.

The West Yorkshire Police, however, were not as convinced as their Manchester colleagues on this point and continued their inquiry with regard to Farina cars until Sutcliffe's arrest when it became clear that Sutcliffe had never owned a Farina car, and that the tire marks at the scene of the Richardson murder were probably left by his white Corsair, while those at the Moore and Millward scenes were probably from the red Corsair he acquired in September 1977.

By this time, the staff of the Police National Computer and Police Scientific Development Branch had completed their arrangements for the computerization of information from the red light observations. Initially vehicle registration numbers, recorded at a number of fixed observation posts and fed into the computer at Hendon from visual display units in Leeds, Manchester, Sheffield, and Hull, were to be printed out for inquiries if the same vehicle was identified as having been seen in two of the separate areas where observations were in progress. This exercise was begun on the June 19, 1978, and as early as August 13, 1978, Peter William Sutcliffe was interviewed as a result of his red Ford Corsair car having been seen in the Chapeltown area of Leeds and the Manningham area of Bradford.

Detective Constable Peter Smith of the West Yorkshire Police, who knew that Sutcliffe had been seen during the £5 note inquiry, visited him at his home in Garden Lane, Heaton, Bradford. Detective Constable Smith knew that Sutcliffe worked as a truck driver from a Bradford base and assumed that the sightings of his car in Bradford could be explained by journeys to and from work. Sutcliffe denied having visited Leeds or other West Yorkshire towns during evenings in the relevant period. He also emphatically denied using the services of prostitutes. At this point, as my experience with the Bundy and Green River investigations has shown me, with Sutcliffe's name coming up under two separate inquiries should have been enough to make the police suspicious. But the fact was that the police were still so overwhelmed by the evidence and separate inquiries into the case, that a clear hit on a suspect that indicated something beyond randomness was not followed up. Again, this is a common problem in task forces where the volume of information impedes police progress and ultimately adds to the frustration of not being able to get out from under the paperwork.

In September 1978, following a discovery that a number of detectives had not been correctly completing some of the undoubtedly monotonous inquiries allocated to them, an internal audit team of seven officers was appointed to determine the extent of the problem. Team members checked a sample covering about 107 completed inquiries but found no other evidence of such misconduct. Two detectives resigned from the force and 13 were subjected to internal disciplinary action as a result of making false statements during the initial cases. Although the audit showed that the internal mechanisms of the task forces in the investigation were breaking down under stress, it was also self-serving in that it reinforced the police perception that the institutional structure of the investigation was sound. A later audit would find out exactly how unsound the internal structure actually was.

On November 23, 1978, Peter Sutcliffe was observed again by Detective Constable Smith. He obtained details of his Building Society account in connection with the £5 inquiry and also visited the new owners of the red Corsair. He obtained a description of the Corair's tires, which were new, having apparently been fitted after the vehicle had changed hands. Five days later, the reward for information leading to the apprehension of the Yorkshire Ripper was increased to £20,000.

The murders continued with a relentless inexorability. On March 23, 1979, a further letter addressed to Mr. Oldfield was dispatched from Sunderland. The suspicion that the writer might indeed be the perpetrator of the crimes began to grow and was reinforced by two factors. First, the author of the letters went to an unusually high degree of trouble to ensure that no fingerprints were left on either the paper or the envelopes, and second, analysis of the saliva on the third envelope revealed that whoever had licked it was a secretor of blood group B. The last factor was considered to be especially significant, because analysis of semen recovered from the body of Jean Harrison in Preston showed that the person responsible for that crime was also group B secretor and was thus within 6% of the total male population.

This coincidence had two effects. First, it tended to confirm that the Harrison murder was part of the series and second, if Harrison was in the series, the blood grouping pointed to the authenticity of the letters. The two propositions were, however, mutually dependent and, as events were to prove, both wrong. At this stage, police inquiries began in Northeast England to try to trace the author of the letters.

On April 5, 1979, Josephine Whitaker, a Building Society clerk, was murdered by Sutcliffe in Savile Park, Halifax. The murder was in the established Ripper pattern in that the victim was struck down by two hammer blows to the head and was then stabbed 25 times in the abdomen, breasts, thighs, and vagina. Exposure of the body followed the usual Ripper modus operandi (MO). The new element in this case was that whereas most of the earlier victims had been prostitutes or women of loose morals and the attacks had occurred in or near to prostitute areas, Josephine Whitaker was a perfectly respectable young woman who was walking home in a residential area of Halifax not frequented by prostitutes.

Assistant Chief Constable Oldfield set up an incident room in Halifax to deal with this crime while the integrated incident room at Miligarth Police Station continued to operate over the full series of crimes. Such was the demand for manpower to staff the Whitaker inquiry, however, that the complete inquiry team attached to the Miligarth incident room in connection with the series crimes was allocated to the Halifax incident. Clearly, the local police were overwhelmed with the process of the investigation, which expanded every time a new victim was discovered. Subsequently, the processing of all outstanding actions from Miligarth ground to a halt. This is an unfortunate result of the lack of recognition of the realities of a particular case when, in an effort to satisfy the staffing requirements of investigating one crime, personnel and resources are cannibalized from another crime in the same series. Consequently, if the case from which resources are taken had clues that might have led to a suspect, those clues are left untouched while detectives start from scratch on a different crime in the series. If one puts oneself in the shoes of the detectives being shifted back and forth, it should become obvious that the resulting frustration breeds a lack of confidence in the task force leadership and work suffers.

Police inquiries in Halifax and an exceptional public response following the murder of a respectable local girl produced masses of indirect evidence of which the most significant appeared to be the description of a man seen near the scene of the crime in a dark colored Ford Escort. It was later determined that Sutcliffe had access to such a vehicle, the property of his mother-in-law. A Sunbeam Rapier vehicle was also seen in the vicinity but was not traced. The suspect was described as having dirty blonde collar-length hair, an unshaven appearance, and a "Jason King" mustache. Other evidence recorded from the scene showed that the assailant had been wearing size 7 industrial boots with a molded rubber sole.

Based on the (MO), the killing of Josephine Whitaker was linked with the previous series of murders and circulated to other forces by West Yorkshire. On May 1, an entry in the murder log approved the practice of eliminating suspects on the basis of the handwriting from the three Sunderland letters. This was a hasty decision, possibly arrived at because of the information overload, but it resulted in Sutcliffe's early elimination as a suspect based, in part, on his handwriting. No one knew for a fact that the murderer had written the letters, so using the handwriting on the letters as a basis for elimination as a suspect was not a logical conclusion supported by the facts.

Still, Sutcliffe continued to be clever if not downright smart. Like most long-term, street-savvy serial killers, he sensed that witnesses in the area of his murders who would be canvassed by uniformed police as well as detectives would probably report having a seen a Ford, or a Sunbeam, or some other car in the area. By correlating the different sightings of the cars, police would quickly home in on the killer. So Sutcliffe, probably because he was a truck driver, was obviously car sensitive, and on June 4, 1979, he disposed of his Sunbeam Rapier car and acquired a brown Rover 3.5.

On June 18, 1979, another envelope addressed to Mr. Oldfield was posted in Sunderland. It contained an audiocassette tape recorded by a man with an accent, which a voice expert said belonged to a man who had lived within

5 miles of Sunderland for much of his life. On the tape there was a personal message to Mr. Oldfield about his failure to detect the series of crimes. The saliva on the envelope flap was quickly found to indicate a B secretor blood group thus linking it with the third letter and, as a result, with the Harrison murder.

Senior officers in West Yorkshire now appeared to be fully convinced that the author of the letters and the tape recording was indeed the man responsible for the crimes they were investigating, and they decided to attach top priority to this aspect which, they felt, would be bound to lead to the detection of the Ripper crimes. In addition to the major internal police effort, it was decided to seek increasing assistance from members of the public in West Yorkshire and North East England in an attempt to identify the voice on the tape and the handwriting on the letters.

Accordingly, a press conference was arranged for on June 26, 1979, to share with the public information about the killer and the letters police believed he was sending. The impact of it was slightly dulled by the earlier publication of some relevant aspects in the *Yorkshire Evening Post*. Details of the letters and tape were given at the press conference, and police inquiries thereafter concentrated on identifying a suspect who still lived in North East England or a suspect with origins in the North East who had subsequently moved to the West Yorkshire area. From this stage, existing lines of inquiry, some of which had already been suspended because of the demands of the Whitaker investigation, began to attract even lower priority.

Because of the very high number of vehicles listed in the printout by the Police National Computer as having been seen in two separate red light observation areas, this particular line of inquiry also began to suffer from the lack of manpower required to conduct the follow-up action. Of the 21,231 vehicles in the printout, 15,195 were not pursued by further checks. As a result of this overloading, compounded by the effects of the Whitaker inquiry, a decision was then taken to print out only those vehicles that had been observed in at least three separate observation areas, subsequently referred to as "triple area sightings."

On July 29, 1979, Sutcliffe was again interviewed after the registration identification of his black Sunbeam Rapier had been printed out, first as a "double area sighting" and later as a triple area sighting, after having been spotted in the red light areas of Leeds, Bradford, and Manchester. Clearly, he was now on the police radar because of the sightings. As in many investigations, Sutcliffe's name had been entered into the database multiple times, and it seems evident that police knew they had their killer somewhere in their investigative database. However, they didn't know who he was or where they could find his name. Accordingly, the task force kept recycling names as they turned up as new hits without realizing, until it was ultimately too late, that they were already interviewing their killer.

After Sutcliffe's Sunbeam Rapier turned up on the printout, Detective Constables Laptew and Greenwood visited Sutcliffe at his home, not at all aware that Sutcliffe had already been interviewed in connection with the £5 note inquiry and also because of the double sighting of his earlier vehicle. Sutcliffe gave explanations for having been in Leeds and Bradford but denied that he had been to Manchester in his own vehicle. Because of the police decision to keep the red light area observations secret, investigating officers were advised not to challenge those whom they interviewed in respect to any individual sighting but were required to approach the subject obliquely.

Again, despite the interviewer's questions that suggested Sutcliffe's relationships with prostitutes, Sutcliffe emphatically denied making use of prostitutes' services and was, again, loosely alibied by his wife for the dates he was asked to account for his whereabouts. The detectives obtained samples of his handwriting, thinking they might find a match with their letter-writer, and searched his car and garage. Although they found nothing to connect him with the murders, they were, nevertheless, not satisfied with Sutcliffe and reported their disquiet to the Major Incident Room. Unfortunately their report was not linked with previous papers or clues concerning Sutcliffe, and Sutcliffe was eliminated because his handwriting did not match that of the Sunderland letter writer.

On September 2, 1979, Barbara Leach, a 20-year-old student, was murdered by Sutcliffe in the University area of Bradford. A postmortem examination revealed that she had been struck a single blow to the head with a hammer after which she was stabbed in the abdomen and shoulder blade a total of eight times. From examination of the injuries it was possible to say that the weapon used to cause them was, in all likelihood, the one used in the murder of Josephine Whitaker five months previously. Detective Chief Superintendent Gilrain led this inquiry and established his incident room in Bradford.

The Leach homicide was immediately linked with others in the series and Detective Superintendent Holland who, upon hearing of the murder, had immediately returned to West Yorkshire from leave in Scotland. He continued to supervise the overall inquiry from the main incident room at Miligarth. This incident room, due to the shortage of manpower, together with the rapidly increasing response from the general public and the demands of the Northeastern inquiry, was being inundated by a very large backlog of uncompleted actions. The position was exacerbated by the fact that almost no follow-up actions had been processed after the Whitaker murder in April that year.

Police inquiries into the murder of Barbara Leach produced one suspect described as being a white male in his early thirties and of athletic build. He had short dark hair and a thin dark mustache, and was seen to put a "bundle" into what was thought to be a green Hillman Avenger estate car parked near to the murder scene. In addition to this vehicle, a blue Datsun 160/1808 sedan was seen in the area and was sought for elimination purposes.

In the absence of Assistant Chief Constable Oldfield, now on sick leave, his Deputy, Detective Chief Superintendent Hobson, assumed responsibility for all crime matters in the West Yorkshire area but at the same time continued to act as the senior detective in the Eastern Crime area of the force. No arrangements were made for him to assume the rank of Acting Assistant Chief Constable. Although Chief Superintendent Hobson thus had command of the overall Ripper inquiry, day-to-day decisions in connection with the investigation of crimes in the series were taken by Detective Superintendent Holland. Detective Chief Superintendent Gilrain, formerly in charge of CID Administration at force headquarters, was put in command of the Barbara Leach investigation, this being the latest crime in the series.

On September 13, 1979, a Special Notice was issued by the West Yorkshire Metropolitan Police to all forces in the country giving details of 16 murders and attempted murders then linked in the series along with details of the tire tracks from the Richardson, Moore, and Millward incidents. They were also given details of the Sunderland letters and tape. None of the descriptions or photofit impressions provided by surviving victims was included, and a crucial section of the notice said that:

A person can be eliminated from these inquiries if

1. Not born between 1924 and 1959
2. He is an obvious person of color
3. His shoe size is size 9 or above
4. His blood group is other than B
5. His accent is dissimilar to a Northeastern (Geordie) accent.

On September 17, 1979, four days after the Special Notice, things inside the investigation heated up even more when Mr. R.E. Stockdale, a Principal Scientific Officer from the Wetherby Forensic Science Laboratory, was attached to the West Yorkshire Police as a resident scientific officer for the Ripper series of crimes. On September 24, he was joined by Mr. R.A. Outteridge, the Director of the Nottingham Forensic Science Laboratory. The two scientists were provided with accommodation in the Western Area headquarters at Bradford. During a meeting with the Chief Constable, it was agreed that their specific role was one of "liaison and coordination" (of scientific services) and that they should be available to the Ripper inquiry team as consultants on a day-to-day basis. During their period of attachment, the two scientists reviewed the forensic evidence available in connection with all previous Ripper cases and suggested a number of new lines of inquiry in connection with existing and possible future cases to the inquiry officers. The attachment of the two resident scientists who were functioning as forensic consultants ended in January 1980. But the murders still didn't stop.

On October 23, 1979, Sutcliffe was interviewed again, on this occasion by Detective Constables Vickerman and Eland who were investigating the murder of Barbara Leach. This interview resulted from a resurrection of the inquiries made by Detective Constable Smith who had seen Sutcliffe in August and November 1978 in connection with the sighting of the red Corsair vehicle in the prostitute areas of Leeds and Bradford. The officers were told that Sutcliffe's alibi for the Jordan murder was inadequate, and they were asked to check his movements in relation to the murder of Barbara Leach. Unfortunately, they were unaware of the previous interview of Sutcliffe by Detective Constables Laptew and Greenwood and of their reservations about him. When the officers spoke to Sutcliffe, he quickly volunteered the information that he had been interviewed before, but he also said that on the night of Barbara Leach's murder he had been at home working on improvements to the house. This was confirmed by his wife as in previous interviews. A further handwriting sample was obtained and this was subsequently used to eliminate him from the inquiry again.

What seems incredible about the successive interviews the police held with Sutcliffe is that, not only were the police not aware that Sutcliffe's name had come up multiple times in the investigation generating separate interviews, but that only Sutcliffe was aware of the interest the police had in him. Even within the same departments, different detective units were unaware that Sutcliffe's name was coming up time after time. Because there was no system for sharing clue and tip information within the departments or among departments, Sutcliffe was allowed to remain on the street while obviously becoming more concerned that police were closing in him. As we will see from an examination of other cases, this sense that the police are homing in can have a dramatic effect on the killer's pattern of committing homicides. The killer may feel he's invulnerable while at the same time he may deliberately change his MO to throw the police off.

In November 1979, the police command was obviously aware that despite the overwhelming number of personnel assigned to the various task forces across an increasing number of departments, the investigation seemed to be spinning in place, digging itself deeper into a rut. Internal audits were more self-serving than anything else, particularly one performed by Mr. I. Evett and Mr. C. Brown of the Home Office Central Research Establishment, who visited Leeds and Bradford at the instigation of the two resident forensic scientific consultants. They examined the operation of the computerized red light area observations and discussed a number of problems with the senior inquiry officers, but were unable to suggest significant changes in the established system. The police were responding to a sense that something was terribly wrong inside the investigation, but couldn't do anything about it until after they had their killer and were able to retrace their steps.

For our purposes, it's important to realize that by November 1979 the two psychologies we described in the opening chapter were clearly at work. Peter Sutcliffe, the Yorkshire Ripper, had become well aware of the increasing interest the police had in him and, partly because he believed he was invisible to them and, partly because of a hubris that many serial killers develop when they believe they're right in the faces of the police who are incapable of drawing any conclusions about them, so he actually threw back to the detectives knowledge they did not have about previous interviews Sutcliffe had had with investigators. So confident was Sutcliffe, he believed he could throw police off the trail by telling them they had already interviewed and dismissed him as a subject of their inquiry. His gambit actually worked because the police took him at his word that he had already been eliminated and turned away from him.

Meanwhile, as the internal audits of the Yorkshire Investigation indicated, not only were the police overwhelmed and drowning in their own data, the police were also becoming frustrated at their own lack of progress. They did not know, of course, that they had already interviewed the killer four times. They did not know that their investigative process was actually working because it spit out the name of the killer each and every time another series of clues was processed. And they did not know that they were actually surveilling the killer and his vehicles. Furthermore, the paradox was that although they already knew who the Yorkshire Ripper was, they didn't know they knew it. This paradox is typical of many serial killer task force investigations, especially the Ted Task Force, the Green River Task Force, the Arthur Shawcross Task Force, and the Atlanta Child Murders Task Force. In each instance, either the killer himself was right in the faces of the police the entire time, his picture was in their faces, or his name was in their files. The sense that the killer is right there and can't be identified creates a gnawing frustration at the center of the investigation, which only exacerbates the dual sense of defeat and futility that cripples task forces.

On November 21, 1979, Commander Nevill and Detective Superintendent Bolcon of the Metropolitan Police visited West Yorkshire at the invitation of the Chief Constable to examine and report on the overall Ripper investigation. The two Metropolitan officers had discussions with investigating officers from all forces involved and also examined the incident room systems and records then in use. In a report to the Chief Constable on January 8, 1980, Commander Nevill stated:

> The following lines of inquiries were agreed as viable and could be completed in a reasonably short period:

1. Persons born and/or educated in Wearside to be located and interviewed
2. An inquiry throughout England to trace all owners of Avenger estate cars and Datsun 160/180 saloon cars; positive sightings of vehicles of these descriptions were seen near the venue of the Leach murder
3. To trace the history of a £5 note issued at or near Bingley and found in possession of the murdered prostitute at Manchester
4. Inquiries at speech therapists (prompted by the suggestion by a linguistic expert that the author of the letters and tape suffered from a stammer for which he had probably received speech therapy)
5. Inquiries at all banks to attempt to identify handwriting through counter staff.

It will be seen, therefore, that Commander Nevill accepted the letters and tape connection, although in fairness, he introduced a caveat later in his report when he said:

> During the years of the inquiries many persons were eliminated only on the facts known at the time. It may well be prudent to re-evaluate these in the light of all the facts known today. For instance, many have been cleared purely on dialect or handwriting. Whilst it is agreed that the author of the letters and tape is probably the murderer, it is not a complete certainty.

Commander Nevill made recommendations for streamlining the major incident room system with a view toward the accurate monitoring of outstanding and completed actions and to the filtering of information reaching incident officers. He commented on the absence of forensic evidence and the lack of dialogbetween scientists and investigating officers, and he finally warned that other assaults on women in West Yorkshire might well prove to be part of the series of crimes. Yet again there was no evidence of any follow up by the police of Commander Nevill's recommendations.

A month after the official visit, at the end of 1979, the triple area sighting exercise using fixed observation points was stopped and replaced by a less manpower-expensive system of mobile observations. The triple area sighting might have even yielded some results, but because of personnel issues, frustration and the seemingly interminable surveillance, and despondency over the lack of any success had caused the exercise to "decay," according to a West Yorkshire officer, into misuse. This is another obvious example of the ways in which the psychological reactions of individual personnel can affect the ways the institution responds to stress. In this case, because officers had been less than responsive to the demands of the exercise, the exercise itself decayed and had to be terminated, no matter how effective it might have become.

During the autumn of 1979, senior detectives of the Greater Manchester Police decided to re-activate the £5 note inquiry in an attempt to detect the Jordan and Millward murders. With the full cooperation of the Bank of England and the Midland Bank they were able, by experiment, to eliminate several firms as possible recipients of the £5 note. There had, of course, always been the possibility that the £5 note had been paid to a customer cashing a check at a bank but, on the balance of probabilities, it seemed most likely that the note had been included in money drawn for wages by one of only a few firms in the area. The total number of employees to be seen in this resurrected inquiry was a readily manageable 241. Sutcliffe was number 76 on the list, being 44th of 49 employees from the firm of T.&W.H. Dark Ltd.

Before the people shown on the list were seen, their names were searched against the nominal index in the Miligarth incident room to see whether they had been previously involved, other than in connection with the original £5 note inquiry. For some reason, which to this date the police case reviewers have not been able to discover, Sutcliffe's name was marked N/T, meaning no trace, even though he already was in the database and had been interviewed four times previously.

On January 13, 1980, Sutcliffe was visited by Detective Sergeant Boot of West Yorkshire Police and Detective Constable Bell of the Greater Manchester Police who were unaware of the previous double and triple area sighting interviews. Sutcliffe told the officers that when he was not working as a truck driver he spent all his spare time with his wife working in their house and that he did not go out in the evenings without her. His wife confirmed the story, which gave the two homicide investigators, without any disputing evidence or records of the previous interviews with Sutcliffe, no reason to doubt what he was saying.

Sutcliffe then told the officers that he had already been seen in connection with sightings of his motor cars, and that prompted the detectives to check out this information when they returned to their office. The papers relating to the red Corsair sighting were located but those of the black Sunbeam Rapier (which referred to the Manchester sighting) were not, because they were attached to documents that were waiting to be returned to Sutcliffe's employers.

Sutcliffe's car by that time was the Rover saloon in which he was eventually arrested. It was searched, as was his garage. His footwear and the tools he kept in his house were also examined but nothing of interest was found. Unfortunately the search was not thorough enough to discover a pair of Wellington boots in a wardrobe. These boots could have linked Sutcliffe with the murder of Emily Jackson some four years previously. The two detectives knew that Sutcliffe had been eliminated on handwriting but, being suspicious about him, they recommended that another inquiry team should interview him to see whether they, too, might share similar reservations.

Now the interviews with Sutcliffe became more frequent as different teams of detectives, each armed with reservations about the man based on their own case files, began swarming about. Here was a possible suspect whose name had been repeatedly turning up in their files even when those files had not been shared between investigative teams within the same departments. But, when on January 30, 1980, Detective Sergeant McAlisier of Manchester and Detective Constable McCrone of West Yorkshire interviewed Sutcliffe at Kirkstall Forge Engineering works while he was loading his truck, Sutcliffe again satisfied the inquiry officers who were going over past history in connection with sightings of his red Ford Corsair and the £5 note inquiry.

Sutcliffe was interviewed yet again on February 7, 1980, when Detective Constable Jackson of Manchester and Detective Constable Hannison of West Yorkshire visited the Shipley Depot of T. & W.H. Dark Ltd. They, too, were unaware of the sightings of Sutcliffe's black Sunbeam Rapier in Bradford, Leeds, and Manchester and also of the report submitted by Detective Constables Laptew and Greenwood after their interview with him. Detective Constable Jackson decided he was unable to eliminate Sutcliffe but, following a discussion with his senior officers, it was concluded that as he had been alibied by his wife and mother for the nights of October 9 and 10 1977, when Jordan's body had been moved and mutilated, he could be eliminated from the inquiry.

All these interviews, each one of them ending in a seeming dismissal of Sutcliffe as an immediate suspect even though the interviewing officers had reservations about him, only served to alert Sutcliffe that his name was continuously coming up in somebody's records. The searches of his garage and his clothing, the inquiries into the £5 bank note, the inquiries about the different cars he had owned, were all clear tip-offs to him that the police must have had some information connecting him to the crimes, even though it wasn't enough to charge him with homicide. Did he know that he'd left footprints at one crime scene that would have incriminated him had the police only noticed the Wellington boots that were in his closet? Did he know about the tire tracks? At the time, probably not. But he knew that whatever evidence the police were following, it was drawing them ever closer around him.

On June 25, 1980, Sutcliffe was arrested on a DUI. The officers, Constables Doran and Melia, who detected the offense while keeping mobile observations on the Manningham red light area, passed details about him to the Miligarth incident room as a matter of routine. They were informed that Sutcliffe had been eliminated from the inquiry. Here, again, was another lost opportunity to interrogate Sutcliffe or keep him in custody to shake his confidence in his ability to elude the police. As it was, less than two months later, the Yorkshire Ripper struck again.

On August 20, 1980, Marguerite Walls, a 47-year-old civil servant, was murdered by Sutcliffe as she walked home in Leeds. She was struck on the head, as in previous assaults, and knocked down. Then, however, instead of being mutilated she was strangled with a piece of cord. Her body was stripped, sexually assaulted, and hidden under a pile of grass cuttings in the grounds of a large house. When this crime was discovered it was not linked with the Ripper series, because death by strangulation was an entirely new feature in relation to all the previously connected crimes. The police were being exclusive in their categorization of the crime instead of inclusive. Rather than look at the basic pattern of assault, which was to disable a victim with a blow to the head prior to a sexual assault and murder, they looked at the method of murder, strangulation instead of a knife attack. This prevented them from asking whether the Yorkshire Ripper was merely changing his MO to throw them off the track or whether he was actually experimenting with a different type of sexual homicide.

Detective Chief Superintendent Hobson assumed responsibility for the inquiry and set up an incident room at Pudsey Police Station from which he directed police operations. Descriptions were obtained of people who had been in the vicinity at the time of the murder, but none of these was very useful and attention was focused on a number of men living in the area who had previous convictions for serious sexual offenses. Perhaps as a result of this attack, even though the attack was not linked to the "Ripper" murders, surveillance in the red light district was discontinued because the police believed that the killer was now operating outside of his original territory. Also, the victim was not a known prostitute, which also placed her case outside the profile the police had developed for the Ripper prostitute murders.

On September 24, 1980, Uphadya Bandara, a 35-year-old doctor from Singapore, was attacked with a hammer in Leeds after which her assailant tried to strangle her with a piece of cord. For some unknown reason this attack was not completed and the victim was taken to the hospital where she recovered from her injuries. She was unable to offer any precise information about her attacker, except to say that he had a close-cropped beard. Detective Superintendent Newton took charge of the investigation, which was supervised from a major incident room in Pudsey Police Station. Although this crime was not officially linked with the Ripper series, it was linked with the murder of Marguerite Walls in which strangulation had been the cause of death.

Maybe it was the arrest of Peter Sutcliffe that prompted a new rash of assaults or maybe it was the successive interviews. Whatever the reason, Sutcliffe seemed go to into a frenzy of assaults. On November 5, 1980, Teresa Sykes was attacked on a footpath in Huddersfield by Sutcliffe who hit her over the head with a hammer. Fortunately for her, the attack was interrupted by the man with whom she was living who had heard her screams. Although she suffered severe head injuries, she survived the assault.

This crime was investigated by Detective Superintendent Hickley from an incident room at Huddersfield and was not publicly linked with the Ripper series. Many detectives involved in the case had by now reached private conclusions about which were and were not Ripper cases, and there was a strong body of professional opinion that Sykes was in the series. Information gathered about the assailant in this case included the fact that he was alleged to have had a gingery colored beard and mustache.

On November 17, 1980, the final murder in the series was committed when Jacqueline Hill was killed by Sutcliffe near the Arndale Center in Leeds. After being disabled by a number of violent hammer blows to the head, she was dragged onto waste ground and her exposed body was stabbed. Detective Superintendent Findlay took charge of the inquiry and established an incident room at Belle Vue, Leeds. The murder was linked with the Ripper series and circulated to all forces in an edition of *Police Reports* published on November 19. A number of suspects had been sighted in the area and inquiries were also made in tracing a squarish looking car, which had been seen being driven in the wrong direction of Alma Road, a one-way street near the crime scene, at about the time when Jacqueline Hill was killed.

The public response was immediate. The local newspapers, obviously outraged by the impunity of a killer who was able to strike while police had set up surveillance teams all over the area, increased the amount of the award being offered for information leading to the arrest of the killer by £30,000, bringing the total amount to £50,000.

At the same time there was a shake up in the police investigation units tracking the Yorkshire Ripper. In addition the change in the police command, an Advisory Team of four senior officers from other police forces with no previous connection with the Ripper investigation, together with a senior forensic scientist, were asked to review the case and to report their findings to the Chief Constable. The following month their report was submitted and, significantly, included these points:

1. The aim of the inquiry should now be to foster an opinion both within and outside the Police Service that the killer does not necessarily originate from the Northeast of England.
2. We have indicated a number of facts which could point to the wanted man living in/working in the Bradford area.

On November 26, 1980, an anonymous letter was received at the Miligarth incident room, one of many letters received at the time from people trying to insert their opinions and observations into the investigation. This letter, however, suggested that a man called Peter "Sutclifte" was the "Ripper". The claim was supported by a number of minor points about Sutcliffe's employment and character, but particular mention was made of an incident that had occurred within the previous five years of which the author of the letter could not give details because they might lead to him being identified. The author of this letter has since been identified as Trevor Birdsall, a close friend of Peter Sutcliffe.

Birdsall's girlfriend, who had urged him to write the letter, later advised him that its contents were insufficient to enable the police to act and persuaded him to report to the police personally. Birdsall accepted this advice and visited Bradford Police Station late on November 26, 1980. He repeated the suspicions which he had voiced in his letter to Constable Butler. He added that he had been to Halifax with Sutcliffe in August 1975 and suspected that Sutcliffe had assaulted a woman on that occasion. Constable Butler submitted a report on Birdsall's visit to the Miligarth incident room.

By this time the incident room was suffering a progressive collapse both because of the weight of information being put into the system and the number of actions being generated by new and existing information that could not be accommodated by the available officersdealing with them. There is little doubt from the inquiries the reviewers of the Yorkshire Ripper case had made that Constable Butler's report was received in the incident room, but they were unable to trace it despite detailed questioning of the officers concerned.

On January 2, 1981, police surveillance in a key district finally worked when Sutcliffe was observed by the police while he was in the company of a prostitute in the red light area of Sheffield. Police ran the plates on his car to determine the man's identity and discovered that his vehicle did not match the vehicle to which the number plates displayed on it were registered. He was arrested for having stolen plates on his car and detained. At this point, the police started putting together a case against Sutcliffe.

Some 24 hours after his arrest, the arresting officer, having been advised to consider the possibility that Sutcliffe might have connections with the Ripper crimes, returned to the scene of the arrest and recovered a hammer and knife which Sutcliffe had disposed of while allegedly urinating nearby. An additional knife was later recovered from the cistern of a toilet in Hammerton Road Police Station where Sutcliffe had hidden it following his arrest. From that point onward, although on the basis of his record card in the Miligarth incident room, it might still have been possible for him to have been eliminated on accent and handwriting grounds. The finding of the hammer and the two knives prompted members of the West Yorkshire inquiry team to think that Sutcliffe was the man they were looking for.

The police interrogations of Sutcliffe in connection with the Yorkshire Ripper murders began in earnest, especially now that two possible murder weapons had been linked to him. With the name of a potential suspect now right before them, police also began to re-examine Sutcliffe about the bank note, his cars, his association with prostitutes—which association he could no longer deny because he had been picked up in a surveillance in the company of a prostitute—and his name having been given up by Trevor Birdsall. Sutcliffe soon began to admit the crimes with which he was subsequently charged and gave a detailed statement to the interviewing officers. His statements, concerning details that only the Yorkshire Ripper himself would know, were a key part of the incriminating evidence against him and five months after his arrest, on May, 22, 1981, Peter Sutcliffe was convicted at the Central Criminal Court of 13 cases of murder and 7 cases of attempted murder and sentenced to 20 concurrent terms of life imprisonment with a recommendation that he should serve a minimum of 30 years.

Now it was up to the police to determine how a series of sexually violent homicides could have been committed under the very noses of joint police task forces assigned to the cases. How had police managed to mistake all of the clues and apparently obvious evidence that the man they were looking for was in their data files all along? But even more critical for investigators was the need to find out why the task forces themselves had failed. Why, even when the police were assembling the key clues that could have let to a resolution of the case, were the members of the task force so frustrated and despondent that they overlooked vital evidence and let the man slip through their fingers until he was picked up as the result of a license plate check? Was it something about the task force itself that caused it to fail? This was something a subsequent police investigations had to determine.

REFERENCE

Byford, L. (1981). The Yorkshire Ripper Case, private report, December.

3

ANATOMY OF AN
INVESTIGATION

In the wake of the trial of Yorkshire Ripper Peter Sutcliffe, the subject of one of England's longest, most complex, and most expensive investigations in terms of resources and allocation of law-enforcement personnel, there were a number of reviews of the case and subsequent reports made to Parliament about the procedures police followed to apprehend Sutcliffe. The reviews were overwhelmingly critical of the police methods and the way the administration of the case was conducted. But, most importantly, the reviews documented the actual process of management breakdown which allowed the killer, already in the police files from the very beginning of the investigation, to escape detection and go on killing for six years in Yorkshire, Manchester, and Leeds. The case reviews show why police morale on serial killer task forces breaks down in the face of the mounting frustration and hopelessness due to the size of the investigation, even though the clues for the solution to the case and the apprehension of the offender are probably already in the task force records. The paradox of investigations like this, as the management review will show, is that the actual process of police work was successful. However, the information overload was so great, none of the managers of the task force knew they were achieving success, so they let the killer get away for so long.

For the purposes of my examination of the psychology of the case, the reviews also document how the rising levels of frustration and malaise undermined the investigation from the field staff officers to senior managers who lost control of their own data systems. In the recommendations for reform that the case reviewers put forth, they acknowledged the despair that might have even bordered on resentment among officers in the lower echelons, and suggested that senior staff spend more time interacting with junior staff and serving on field teams to keep in touch with the flows of the daily investigative routines. This, the reviewers suggest, was not just a morale booster, although it certainly served the same purpose, it was a way to keep all levels of personnel in communication and keep information from getting lost in the institutional bureaucracy comprising the administrative structure of the investigation task force.

THE MAJOR INCIDENT ROOM

In England, as in the United States, local homicides are usually handled by the local police. Most homicides are usually solved within a very short period of time, because they are crimes in which the perpetrator and victim know each other or may even be related to or intimate with. Most homicides are usually witnessed and a first-time killer will usually leave a trail of clues leading the police straight to him. However, in this case where the homicide was especially heinous with the special circumstances of sexual violence and mutilation, the Metropolitan Police set up "incident rooms" to manage the case.

In a homicide inquiry where 100 officers might be deployed at an early stage, it would clearly be impossible for any senior investigating officer to keep control over such a widespread and diverse operation as part of his own mental process. There is an immediately recognizable requirement, therefore, for an effective administrative support system capable of monitoring the work of the inquiry as a whole. More particularly, it should be capable of pointing the investigating officer to significant elements of the evidence or conclusions drawn from it, of which he might not otherwise be aware. This need is catered to by what is now commonly referred to as a Major Incident Room, a facility, pioneered in the Metropolitan Police area, which until the second World War, was the only police force in the country to have very wide and continuing experience with homicide inquiries.

A Major Incident Room is, according to the officers who reviewed the Yorkshire Ripper case, defined as, "those administrative procedures used to handle all information coming to notice in a major police investigation."

The purpose of the "Room" is to provide the senior investigating officer with an accurate record of all police inquiries made in connection with the crime and the results obtained from them. The records are intended to show the state of the inquiry and how much work in the form of outstanding actions remains to be done at any time. They are also required to enable any police officer making an inquiry to establish whether any person, vehicle, or other factor has previously come to notice in the investigation and to provide investigating officers with a ready means of acquiring all the knowledge the system contains about his inquiry subjects.

A Major Incident Room is also intended to serve a much more positive purpose in that its records are kept to highlight people, vehicles, or other facts which have become subject to inquiry as a result of different lines of investigation. These records are capable of pinpointing suspects to whom the investigating officer can direct special attention. Finally, the room should act as a point of historical reference so that, in a long-running inquiry, officers joining the investigation team can have easy reference to major policy decisions taken at earlier stages of the inquiry.

The Major Incident Rooms are usually staffed by a senior investigating officer, the individual in charge of the inquiry who is responsible for the control of the operation, the direction of the inquiry, and the maintenance of the Incident Room service. Also part of the staff are action allocators, detective investigators in middle management positions whose task is to initiate inquiries under the general direction of the senior investigating officer. They are also responsible for the preparation of action forms or documents serving a similar purpose which are issued to members of outside inquiry teams. These outside inquiry teams are composed of detectives, usually sergeants or constables, who receive action forms and visit and interview subjects of the inquiry. The results of the information compiled by the outside inquiry team members are shown on completed action forms and in statements of evidence, both of which are returned to the Major Incident Room. Completed action sheets are returned to the action allocator who either accepts that the action is complete or issues further actions for additional inquiries to be made. Statements of evidence go to statement readers, a group of middle management detectives whose task it is to read all incoming statements of evidence and to identify the important information contained in them. The other staff members inside the Major Incident Room include telephone operators and indexing clerks who file all information received by the Major Incident Room.

PROTOTYPICAL OPERATION OF A MAJOR INCIDENT ROOM

In an ideal operation, according to the official review of the Yorkshire Ripper Case, the operation of the system is perhaps best explained by the use of a short practical example: Early yesterday morning the body of Valerie Brown, a 20-year-old student nurse, was found on the sports field of a leisure center in an urban area. She had been sexually assaulted and subsequently strangled. (A sexually motivated murder is used as an example because such crimes are usually difficult to investigate.)

In this particular type of case, following or perhaps concurrently with the examination of the scene of the crime and the subsequent removal of the body for examination, several lines of inquiry would immediately be started. A Major Incident Room would be set up and the first actions would usually involve the dead girl's parents, friends, and associates. Her mother, for example, would be interviewed and a statement would be taken from her providing the investigating officer with as broad a picture of the deceased's background as possible. When this statement arrives at the Major Incident Room, a nominal index card would be completed giving details of the girl's mother and cross-referenced with the statement index. The statement would then be read and would almost inevitably produce a number of actions. For instance, if the dead girl had, over the years, several boyfriends who were named in her mother's statement actions would be raised for each one of them to be seen separately to see whether they could give useful information.

Before the actions were issued they would be checked against the nominal index to see whether the subjects had previously been recorded. If not, new nominal index cards would be completed. On the return of the completed actions, the accompanying statements would be read, undoubtedly raising further actions for the inquiry team. The statement reference would be recorded on the nominal index card in each case. At the same time as these elementary background inquiries were being made, separate teams of officers would be conducting house-to-house inquiries which might generate information about vehicles or people seen in the area at the time of the murder. If the information gained was sufficiently positive to allow identification of some person or some vehicle, actions would be raised to have the person seen or vehicle traced and either implicated in or eliminated from the inquiry. Where the available information did not provide an identification, for instance, where there was only a description of a person seen in the area, an action would be raised for the description to be circulated within the Police Service and possibly through the media as being that of a person wanted for elimination. Many other lines of inquiry would be running simultaneously, for instance, inquiries among taxi drivers, at dry cleaners or laundries looking for unusual or unidentified patrons. The results of all these inquiries would be channeled through the Major Incident Room where relevant information would be indexed so that investigating officers might have easy access to it thereafter. Officers completing the nominal index cards would be responsible for bringing to the investigating officer's attention any individual who was recorded for more than one reason.

Accordingly, a person who had been seen near the scene of the crime but had, on interview, been able to satisfy the officers about his presence in the vicinity might also come into the system. He might come in on the separate route because he was a former associate of the dead girl, his description fit that of a person seen with the girl before her death, that he was the owner of a vehicle seen elsewhere in suspicious circumstances, or that he had a previous criminal conviction that was relevant to the inquiry. It goes without saying that in a protracted murder inquiry the number of names in the nominal index, of completed, pending, and unallocated actions, of statements of evidence, of letters from members of the public, and of reports of telephone conversations with members of the public or of visits of members of the public to police stations is very high indeed.

If the murder under investigation could be solved very quickly because it involved a domestic relationship or if there were many witnesses who lead police directly to the suspect, the establishment of a Major Incident Room is obviated. However, if the crime is complex then despite the organization of the incident room, the staff could become quickly overwhelmed with data. In England as in the United States, versions of the Major Incident Room which house *de facto* task forces are far from immune to data overloads and the resulting frustration from investigators and staff that bogs serial killer investigations down. From even a cursory review of serial murder task force investigations, therefore, the task forces most efficient in processing incoming data and keeping investigative staff focused on pursuing leads were the most resistant to the kind of frustration reducing officer morale.

The danger to task force investigations is that even the most efficient structure and data organization system can break down or the officers may decide to shortcut their system and the resulting disintegration of the planning and procedures will have proved futile. This was what happened when one of the best basic systems available to the West Yorkshire Metropolitan Police during the Ripper series began to systematically break down. It is fair to say, however, that, despite the extensive use of Incident Room procedures in previous major crime inquiries, the Metropolitan Police had, until the beginning of the Ripper series, no experience in dealing with a linked series of 13 murders and 7 attempted murders over a 6-year time span. The available experience indicated that a system which worked well in the investigation of a single crime could not be guaranteed to be similarly effective when applied to a long series of similar crimes.

This was much like King County's experience with the Bundy investigation, where members of the homicide task force had never investigated a crime series like Bundy's before and, although they tried to follow the procedures of a major homicide investigation, their experience did not prepare them for what they soon encountered. In King County's Green River Murders case, even though the police had learned from the Bundy investigation, they still never managed to catch up to the amount of information that flooded in. The detailed review of the Yorkshire Ripper case shows exactly how the sheer frustration of coping with too much information overloads even the most efficient organizations to the point where the systems actually defeat themselves.

For example, when the West Yorkshire Major Incident Room system was applied to the Ripper series, the following problems were encountered.

Because the police changed the reference system for suspect vehicles after the sixth murder and because the reference system for murders 1–6 was too complicated, suspect vehicles that came to the attention of the police from murder 7 on could not be incorporated into the main index. As a result, any attempt to cross-check vehicles from the later murders to the first murders in the series required too much time for the filing clerks and was abandoned. Also, subsequent clue and witness-name filing systems broke down because of the number of murders and assaults, and names of potential witnesses literally got lost within the system. As a result, the senior investigating officers did not have records support and knew they were going into the field without valuable backup information from their files. For all they knew, they could well have been interviewing the actual killer a number of times without realizing it—and that's exactly what happened.

Furthermore, the West Yorkshire police departed from their own filing and organization system on at least two occasions during the later murders. As a result, it complicated an already overcomplicated system and prevented the complete integration of all the records from the different murders. Also, the police began new indexes for each person when that person became the subject of a new line of inquiry regardless of whether the police checked to see whether the new people had previously been recorded in their database. If the subsequent search showed that a particular person already had a previous record card, the new card was stapled to it in an attempt to ensure that they would always be referred to together. This was undoubtedly a serious mistake. The existence of duplicate and in some cases triplicate cards (Sutcliffe himself eventually had four cards in the system) led to the possibility of error in that duplicate cards might not be properly stapled together and become detached, so that when the index was being checked only the original card was seen. There was also the possibility that an index clerk facing a tray full of actions to be indexed might omit to refer to the duplicate or triplicate cards and fail to record for the previous papers clerk the important references recorded on them.

How did this affect the investigation? Clearly, from the history of the police contact with Peter Sutcliffe, it can be seen that in many interviews the police conducted none of the officers involved was aware of the previous interview. For instance, when Detective Sergeant Boot and Detective Constable Bell paid the first visit in connection with the resurrected £5 note inquiry, they knew only of the first two interviews in connection with the £5 note. Quite clearly the duplication of main record cards increased the risk of mistakes being made in the searching of indexes.

Did this directly prevent the police from catching Peter Sutcliffe? Probably not, but it indirectly added to the onerous burden of information management, clearly increased the frustration of the investigation officers, and may have contributed to a perception that this case was just about unsolvable. This perception can be one of the factors that prevents the police from seeing through the fog of the case and finding fresh approaches to an analysis.

The final complication affecting the basic functions of the Major Incident Room in the Ripper inquiries was that it had to be expanded to accommodate the records of each new murder in the series. In an effort to control the paper thus generated, each murder was allocated a numerical reference. For instance, the murder of Josephine Whitaker at Halifax in April 1979 became No. 9. All future papers connected with this inquiry were therefore prefixed "9" and filed separately, although the general index cards were filed in the amalgamated index which contained all the murders. This in itself became cumbersome, but the record keeping actually got worse when separate incident rooms were opened for each succeeding murder in the series. These incident rooms also housed records of the crime until their records got folded back into the main index at Miligarth. Thus, records were not only spread out at a number of stations housing incident rooms, but even within the main incident room papers were put into separate files.

This fragmentation of the records of the case probably contributed to the sense of malaise among the investigating officers. They were missing key elements of the case because their own record-keeping system was essentially disconnected and actually prevented the police from doing routine searches on their own data.

This fragmentation of records did not only plague the basic filing system, it also compromised the effectiveness of the area sighting reports and the tracking of vehicle licenses and registrations. There were so many different records in different locations that searches to find relationships among sightings and witness reports were usually unsuccessful. As a result, teams of detectives who went out to interview Sutcliffe usually didn't realize until he told them that he'd already been interviewed about one of vehicles, and that the previous interviewing officers had been satisfied as to his alibi and whereabouts at the time the crime was committed. This allowed Sutcliffe to all but eliminate himself as a suspect and so convince his police interviewers. It also may have contributed to his feelings of invulnerability because he knew police had to have been seeing his name in connection with the cases, but had no idea he was the killer.

Additionally, the police command also complained about the amount of paperwork individual detectives were required to read when searching for information, because routine filing inquiries or other nonessential paperwork had not been filtered out of the case file. As a result, the truly formidable amount of file information, most of it irrelevant to the nature of any individual detective's inquiry at a given time, probably impeded rather than encouraged the investigators' attempts to search for information in the case files.

Another failure of the routine processing of information was the retrieval of critical records on previous convictions of individuals for related crimes. Even though all Major Incident Rooms incorporate systems for obtaining the previous convictions of people who come to notice during the course of the inquiry, the system didn't work in the Yorkshire Ripper case. Normally a system to retrieve previous convictions has two purposes: the first is to identify people who have previously committed similar crimes and are, therefore, capable of being suspects for the crime under investigation; and, second, is that inquiry officers are aware of the previous convictions of people being interviewed, even though such convictions appear to be unrelated to the inquiry in hand.

During investigation of the Ripper crimes, for instance, people with previous convictions for sexual offenses or crimes of violence were considered for interview as potential suspects. Under this heading, Sutcliffe could not have been singled out for particular attention. In spite of that, he had a relevant conviction for "going equipped with a hammer," which would, had inquiry officers known about it, have been of tremendous importance. How did the police managed to miss this key piece of information despite their routine searches through records?

In the final report on the case, it was shown that when Peter William Sutcliffe was searched against the West Yorkshire Criminal Record Office, it was found that in addition to a conviction for the theft of tires and motor vehicle convictions, he had been convicted of being equipped with housebreaking implements. Unfortunately, the West Yorkshire Police record of that conviction omitted the fact that the house-breaking implement involved was a hammer. Thus, a vital piece of information was overlooked in West Yorkshire. However, at the same time, the Central Criminal Record in New Scotland Yard was clearly marked up with the word "hammer" which, had the West Yorkshire Police relied on the national system rather than their own, would in all probability have alerted the officer making the inquiry to the possibility that Sutcliffe could be regarded as a definite suspect for the Ripper crimes.

The post case report on the Yorkshire Ripper also discovered that there was a failure of senior officers in charge of the inquiry to ensure that appropriate staffing levels were available to handle the projected workload from each new line of inquiry, before it was introduced, rather than attempting to eliminate backlogs of work once the new lines of inquiry had been developed. This meant they had to plan for future staff allocations in advance rather than play catch up. Although the standard of staff work on the case had clearly declined before this stage, the turning point in the inquiry, from the point of view of the Incident Room, was the murder of Josephine Whitaker at Halifax in April 1979. The need to handle the outstanding public response to appeals for information in connection with this murder had by that time stripped the Incident Room of its vital outside inquiry teams. Thus actions could not be allocated for both the Whitaker inquiry and the tasks remaining in the Incident Room forming the basis of a backlog, which was never eliminated.

The effect of the Whitaker murder was compounded by the decision to go to the public with information about the letters and tape on June 26, 1979. This caused a flood of information to come into the Incident Room. At that point, all of the uncompleted actions that had been allocated for inquiry and other actions that had not been allocated were stored in a large collection of shirt boxes in the Incident Room. Many of them remained stored for a considerable period thereafter and many of the actions were never carried out.

By December 1980, in addition to this very serious backlog of outstanding actions, there were 36,000 documents in the Major Incident Room waiting to be filed. It is estimated that this would have taken existing staff nine months to complete as long as no new crimes occurred in the meantime. Such a backlog had inevitable consequences for the integrity of the entire investigation as Sutcliffe kept on committing new crimes and generating new lines of inquiry for each assault and murder. The resulting pile up of lines of inquiry thus crushed the investigation under its own weight.

THE BREAKDOWN OF THE CROSS AREA SIGHTING INQUIRY

Prior to the murder of Whitaker on April 4, 1979, Sutcliffe's victims were predominantly, but not entirely, prostitutes. It was reasonably believed, by the investigating officers, that prostitute victims were picked up in red light districts by the murderer who was, in British slang, a "punter" or prostitute's client, who regularly frequented known prostitute areas in a vehicle.

Following the Jordan murder in Manchester, an intelligence operation was mounted in the police areas of West Yorkshire, South Yorkshire, Greater Manchester, and Humberside to gather information about prostitutes and their associates, the areas where they solicited, and the places where they took their customers. Efforts were also made to identify regular punters by recording their vehicle registration numbers. This procedure should have worked very well, but the scale of the problem was far larger than had been imagined. This was met, in West Yorkshire, by the issue of pocket tape recorders with the tape recordings stored against the eventuality of another murder when a list of vehicle registration numbers would be available for checking. Thus the amount of data on audiotape from the area sightings quickly grew to unmanageable levels. Other difficulties encountered included the presence of large numbers of motorists who drove through red light districts en route to other destinations. How to account for the sightings of these vehicles? How to determine who was just passing through and who was a punter?

Consequent to the West Yorkshire Police approaching the Police Scientific Development Branch (PSDB), a study was undertaken by PSDB, the Police Research Services Unit (PRSU), and the Police National Computer Unit (PNCU). Resulting from this study was the decision to store the vehicle surveillance data on the Police National Computer (PNC). The scheme adopted was for the computer to print out a record of any vehicle that was sighted in two different prostitute areas and, from this, the system was called the Cross Area Sighting Inquiry.

It was also possible to retrieve data relating to particular vehicles in particular areas and to search the records by make and description of vehicle. All these facilities, which were available from the computer, became known as the "Punters' Index." This system consisted of police officers recording vehicle registration numbers on to tape with date and time interjected at regular intervals. The tape was transcribed into a handwritten list which was then entered in the computer store via a terminal keyboard. Although the date and approximate time of sightings were transcribed onto the handwritten list, these were not entered into the computer database. However, the time of input via the terminal keyboard was automatically entered. In other words, the street-sighting time was replaced with the terminal input time creating confusion for the investigating detectives who used the computer printout to cross-reference the car sightings. This defeated one of the primary purposes of the entire sighting inquiry. The system created additional confusion because once a vehicle had been input into the computer as having been sighted in two different areas, it was automatically printed out as a cross area sighting. However, subsequent appearances of the same vehicle in the same areas did not result in additional printouts.

Ultimately, the system achieved the objective of producing details of vehicles seen in prostitute areas, albeit not at the times they were seen, but at the times they were entered via the keyboard. However, a lack of detailed understanding of the system and its capabilities, particularly in relation to descriptive searches, was a serious limitation. Because a joint study by PSDB, PNCU, and PRSU had recommended the appointment of a senior police officer with computer experience to the investigation team, it was unfortunate for the investigation that their recommendation was not followed. Had it been followed, perhaps the computer system might have been used to the full extent of its capabilities.

As one can plainly see, the cross area sighting exercise was a mammoth task fraught with substantial problems. The early concept of recording the registrations of all vehicles which passed a given point may well have been effective in the event of another prostitute murder, but it led to the swamping of the information processing system when used as a basis for a continuing series of investigations. This was particularly a problem in the Manningham area of Bradford where the red light district is crossed by a number of main thoroughfares, and the surveillance caught vehicles simply driving by.

Faced with these problems, the West Yorkshire Police changed their system and observation points a number of times while taking into account the tendency of the prostitutes and punters to change their ground in the face of intense police activity. Parallel with this ran changes in methods of recording vehicle numbers including manuscript, tape recordings, radio, and telephone. In December 1979, the emphasis was shifted to only those vehicles containing a single white male with or without a female. Finally in May 1980, static observations were withdrawn and vehicle numbers were only recorded by a small team of task force officers operating mobile patrols.

While the initial strategy of cross-sighting vehicles in red light areas seemed like a good idea at the start, the entire operation also served to overwhelm the incident rooms with paperwork and lots of action items. They involved the allocation of inquiries to detectives, the linking of their inquiries to others being conducted at the same time and the result of all these being collated, in all their aspects, with the main index.

A separate index of motor vehicle registrations existed, which originated from the computer output of, initially, cross area sightings and, subsequently, "triple area sightings." There also existed a vehicle index for the first six Ripper incidents. Thus, although the names of persons coming up for notice through this part of the inquiry were properly carded and inserted into the main index, separate vehicle indexes existed with no automatic method of cross-referencing names with vehicles, unless investigators decided to make the connections by hand. Further complications arose in the course of inquiries related to subsequent murders where nominal indexes were eventually integrated into the main nominal index but where the vehicle indexes were kept separately. Finally, 14 different vehicle indexes were maintained in the Incident Room.

Attempts to deal with the deluge of paper generated by the cross area sighting inquiry led to the increase of staff from a small team of relatively competent personnel to a large anonymous and poorly structured group where motivation and enthusiasm suffered as a result. The system of recording vehicle numbers once and then transcribing them twice resulted in large error rates. These errors, coupled with false registrations and vehicle transfers, resulted in a large index of unidentified vehicles.

For all the complexity of the cross and triple area sightings, the surveillance strategy actually worked, even though the police didn't know it, because Sutcliffe's name popped out of the database. However, it was the information management system itself that failed. Although the system identified Sutcliffe in both the cross and triple area sightings and he was interviewed on both counts, the interviewing officers were inadequately briefed. This was a consequence of poor index searching and failure to locate previous papers despite the fact that the paperwork had been filed in accordance with the information management system's requirements.

Probably as a consequence of the gradual realization that the system could not cope, a high proportion of cross area sightings were filed without the vehicle owners being interviewed. The murder of Whitaker caused the re-deployment of personnel and the cross area sighting inquiry was left with no outside inquiry team. Consequently filing and inquiries were left pending. Eventually all uncompleted cross area sighting inquiries were withdrawn from outside officers and given a rating of importance on a three-point scale with the intention of, possibly, resurrecting the inquiry later.

In spite of the fact that the capabilities of the computerized Punters' Index were not fully understood by operational officers, one particular search on vehicle type was conducted which could have led to Sutcliffe's arrest in March 1979. On March 2, 1979, Anne Marie Rooney, a 22-year-old student at the Horsforth College, was attacked in the college grounds by a man who hit her on the head with a hammer. She survived the attack and described her assailant as a man in his twenties, 5'10", of broad build with dark curly hair and a drooping mustache. More importantly she was convinced that immediately before the attack she had seen the man sitting in a dark-colored Sunbeam Rapier saloon.

Detective Inspector Sidebottom asked for, and obtained, a computer printout of all Sunbeam Rapier and Alpine saloons which had been input on the Punters' Index since its commencement. The printout listed 850 vehicles, including the Rapier NKU 888H owned by Sutcliffe. This vehicle was shown to have been sighted on 46 occasions and while there were a few other vehicles which had been sighted more frequently, only three, including Sutcliffe's, had also been printed out as triple area sightings. Only 21 other vehicles had been printed out as cross area sightings. There were no police inquiries made on the basis of this computer printout which established Sutcliffe as one of three prime suspects for the attack on Rooney, although she was not at that time regarded as a Ripper victim. This clear short-sightedness was entirely due to a lack of appreciation of the information that the printout contained, probably because it was just more information that the police didn't really understand as a direct result of having been inadequately filed.

The need for additional administrative and clerical staff in the Major Incident Room should also have been foreseen, since it was inevitable that the vehicle inquiries would result in a considerable increase in the amount of actioning and indexing that would be required. The failure to anticipate the need for and provide for the manpower necessary to handle this new line of inquiry had serious consequences. For example, although Sutcliffe bought his Sunbeam Rapier in May 1978, and had before the end of the year been printed out as a cross area sightingand before March of the following year been printed out as a triple area sighting, he was not interviewed about these sightings until July 29, 1979. By this time he had disposed of the Rapier and acquired the Rover in which he was ultimately arrested. How much easier would it have been if the officers had been able to talk to Sutcliffe within days or at most weeks of the visit to Manchester on February 22, 1979, which resulted in his being printed out as a triple area sighting?

The most significant failure of all in relation to the cross area sighting inquiry was that of failing to accept the advice given to the force by PSDB and PRSU. This advice included that a senior officer experienced in handling computer information should be appointed to monitor the computer application to ensure that the computer's scope for searching on a wide number of factors was understood. The result of this failure was that the computer was used solely to print out vehicles for cross and triple area sightings and was rarely used for searches on individual types of vehicles.

As a consequence, although the murder of Rytka took place before the computer operation started, the system could have been used subsequently to print out sightings of vehicles in the "Farina" range, bearing in mind that West Yorkshire continued to operate the Farina inquiry until Sutcliffe's arrest. It would appear that the Rooney printout was not used as the basis for an inquiry, because the officers who received it did not know how to interpret the information and were thus unable to grasp that of the 850 vehicles listed, only three had also been printed out as triple area sightings. It is now possible for anyone who understands the codes which were applied to the different red light areas to analyze this printout in terms of "cross and triple area sightings in less than half an hour". No other specialist skill is required and the information is not affected by hindsight. It is also apparent that had a senior officer with computer experience been appointed in West Yorkshire to act as a link between the computer and the force, much more positive use might have been made of the available information; the emergence of Sutcliffe as a prime suspect for the Rooney case, if not for the whole series, would have been inevitable.

THE TIRE MARKS AND VEHICLE
TRACKING INQUIRY

Tire marks found at the scene of three of the crimes were a prominent feature of the investigation, because they were measured at the scenes to gain some indication of the type of vehicle used. Ultimately, the list included 51 vehicle types. This list was then used as a basis for a decision that all vehicles of these types in the West Yorkshire Police area and in the Harrogate area of North Yorkshire should be examined. From a manual search at vehicle licensing offices and a search of computer records by the PNCU, a list of 53,000 vehicles and registered owners was produced. This list was compared with the record of cars eliminated as a result of the night-time check, and the amended list was used as the basis for inquiries at the homes of registered owners. Vehicles recorded in the Leeds Vehicle Licensing Office were examined first, but beyond this, no strategy is apparent in the choice of vehicles for examination. On July 10, 1977, following the attempted murder of Long at Bradford, this line of inquiry was suspended with about 20,000 vehicles remaining to be examined. Sutcliffe's vehicle, a Ford Corsair registration number: KWT 721D, was one of these.

As the course of the investigation proceeded, the tire marks inquiry and other lines of inquiry had so diverged from each other, primarily because of information overload and the logistics of investigative support staff, that connections between leads and tips were not picked up. Therefore, detectives were interviewing Sutcliffe along one line of inquiry without realizing that he was already in the database for another line of inquiry. Specifically, Sutcliffe was interviewed on November 2, 1977, and on November 8, 1977, during the course of the Jordan £5 note inquiry. At this time Sutcliffe was in possession of the red Corsair which may have been running on wheels and tires that would have associated him with the Richardson murder on the February 5, 1977.

It is clear that the interviewing officers did not examine the red Corsair owned by Sutcliffe. Had they done so it is highly likely that the inquiry at that stage would have taken a very different course, since two entirely different lines of inquiry (Richardson tire tracks, Jordan £5 note) would have both led directly to Sutcliffe. This, then, was a vital error in the Ripper inquiry, coming as it did after six murders and four assaults. Seven further murders and three assaults admitted by Sutcliffe were to occur before his arrest on January 2, 1981.

Another major failure of the tire marks line of inquiry was to allow one inquiry to be superseded by another before the first had been concluded. In a small case, this jumping from one pursuit to another might not have become a critical problem, but in the Ripper case, it served to further confuse investigators who had shifted their attention from one series of clues to other sets. This happened several times during the series inquiry.

When, for instance, after 33,000 of the 53,000 vehicles in the original inquiry had been seen, it was discontinued because the demand for detectives to work on the investigation of the assault on Long drew all available manpower, including the officers who had been working on the tracking inquiry. When investigators become confused about the priorities of the case and are summarily shifted from one line of pursuit to another, it can sometimes become difficult to pick up the previous line of inquiry where it was left off. As a result, morale weakens and the case slows.

A further administrative failure affecting the vehicle tracking inquiry was not including the inquiry information in the main index of the individual crimes and subsequently of the series. Had the list of 53,000 owners in the original tire tracking inquiry been included in the index, the name of Peter Sutcliffe would have been in the system before he was first interviewed during the £5 note inquiry. Thus, it would have ensured that the inquiry officers knew before they first saw Sutcliffe that he was the owner of a vehicle that could have left the tire marks at the Richardson scene. The resulting hit between two separate lines of inquiry into the same event would certainly have made Sutcliffe look very good as a suspect. At that point, a deeper search into Sutcliffe's background and records at New Scotland Yard would have revealed his prior convictions involving possession of a hammer, and that would have constituted a third hit. Maybe it would have been enough to allow the police to hold Sutcliffe for further questioning and perhaps even get a confession.

CRIMINAL PATTERN BEHAVIOR

One of the persistent problems in conducting serial task force investigations is the recognition of a pattern of the offender's criminal behavior and an acknowledgment that the pattern may have changed or may be more inclusive than the police investigators first thought. Many task force investigators like to vary restrictive patterns, because it allows them to eliminate cases from consideration that don't fit the pattern. It's less work for the task force both in investigating the new crimes and reducing the overhead of having to go back and re-evaluate previous crimes to see whether the recognized pattern needs further adjustment. Translated into a psychology of institutional behavior, the acknowledgment that the task force's understanding of a pattern of criminal behavior might be flawed can be demoralizing to personnel who've invested themselves in the understanding and recognition of a particular pattern. There is a tendency, therefore, once a particular pattern of behavior is recognized, to make that pattern work no matter what and to throw out the crimes not fitting that pattern. As evidenced in the Yorkshire Ripper case, this can impede the investigation. Valuable leads and clues can be lost by neglecting crimes that were actually committed by the serial offender but were overlooked by the task force because they simply just didn't fit the pattern.

In the Ripper case, the commencement of the series of crimes was not recognized until the murder of Emily Jackson occurred less than three months after the murder of Wilma McCann. Both of these crimes were committed in Leeds, both involved prostitutes, and in both cases the victims had suffered severe head injuries followed by exposure of the body and repeated stabbing. They were thus regarded as having a common author as were the murders of Irene Richardson and Patricia Atkinson. The murders of Richardson and Atkinson occurred in Leeds and Bradford, respectively, after a 12-month interval.

At this stage of the case, the criteria for inclusion of crimes in the series were

1. That the victim should be a prostitute
2. That she should have been hit over the head with a hammer
3. That her clothing should have been disarranged to expose her body
4. That stab and slash wounds should have been inflicted to the body

The unofficial criteria were extended to include Jayne MacDonald who was seen as the first nonprostitute victim, but not immediately to include the assaults on Claxton, Long, and Moore which did not involve stabbing and slashing injuries. Equally, in January, 1978, the murder of Yvonne Pearson was not linked because her head injuries were not consistent with hammer blows—although it is now known that they were inflicted with what is known as a lump hammer—and because the injuries to her body were caused by her being jumped on rather than stabbed.

As the attacks on women increased, it was becoming obvious to the police that either there was a sudden epidemic of crimes against women or a group of sexual offenders had gathered in the areas of Yorkshire and Leeds and had started a collective crime spree. The obvious answer, of course, was that the same offender was operating in the areas in a broader pattern of criminal behavior than had been previously recognized by the task forces. Therefore, shortly after the discovery of Pearson's body on March 26, 1978, the internal review team under Detective Chief Superintendent Domaille was appointed. Included in the very wide terms of reference given to the team was the task, "To examine all reported attacks on women in general and prostitutes in particular and endeavor to find any common link or pattern to formulate any new and profitable line of inquiry." In connection with this task members of the review team sent telex messages to the various divisions of the West Yorkshire Metropolitan Force and to other Northern forces asking for details of relevant offenses which might be considered, in an effort to establish the scope of the series.

The crime files from relevant cases were acquired and read by members of the team who also interviewed victims, witnesses, and investigating officers in some cases. Although evidence of this original research is no longer available, the officers who conducted it recall that a large number of possible offenses was first reduced to 21 and finally to 14, the details of which were included in the Special Notice of June 1978. The crimes included at this stage were those including Rogulsky, Smelt (both linked for the first time), McCann, Harrison (probably linked because of the claim in the first Sunderland letter that had then been received), Jackson, Richardson, Atkinson, MacDonald, Long, Jordan, Moore, Pearson, Rylka, and Millward. Of these 14 crimes, 10 were printed in red on the Special Notice while the remaining 4 were printed in black to signify that they were included with less confidence and should not be used for elimination. These four were Harrison, Long, Moore, and Pearson.

This effort on the part of the review team was a valuable one, but its members applied the criteria so narrowly that a number of similar assaults where good descriptions or photofit pictures of the suspect were available were not included. The review team's criteria were (1) wounds to the head caused by hammer blows and (2) wounds to the body and abdomen (scratch or stab wounds) caused by a knife and/or a star-shaped instrument.

There was also an inference that the attack should have been committed against a prostitute or in a prostitute area. Unfortunately for the investigators, this review exercise was not repeated later in the series. There were subsequent assaults on record in the West Yorkshire area where women had been attacked in several cases with a hammer, by a man whose description included the fact that he had a dark beard and/or mustache. The assaults on Bernadette Cassidy, Gloria Wood, Caroline Brown, and Rosemary Stead were clearly within this category, as was the attack on Marcella Claxton to which Sutcliffe later admitted.

The criteria later established to assess whether or not to include a murder or attack in the Ripper series were

1. Blows to the head with a hammer of diameter 1.2–1.1 inches (±5/7 of an inch)
2. Attack on the body with some other stabbing/mutilating instrument
3. Displacement of the brassiere to give access to breasts
4. Lowering of panties/tights to pubic hair level (in many instances vulva remains covered by crotch of garment precluding penetration)
5. Movement of the body after the initial attack, before the infliction of further injuries, frequently to the trunk
6. The reluctance of the assailant to stab through clothing
7. Assailant's return to the body to inflict further injuries or secrete it

It is now apparent that these very restrictive criteria were in fact used on attacks occurring after the murder of Millward in Manchester so Carol Montgomery, Anne Rooney, Yvonne Mysliwiec, Maureen Holmes, and

Maureen Lee were all excluded from the series. The Rooney case provides a good illustration of unwillingness to include additional cases in the series. It was excluded because the injuries indicated a hammer of a different size from that required by the criteria. In two of these cases the victims were able to provide good descriptions of the assailant including that he had a mandarin or "Jason King" mustache and, in one case, a goatee beard. In the Rooney case the victim said that she had seen her assailant sitting in a Sunbeam Rapier motor car before the attack. Also excluded, because they did not match the criteria, were the murder of Walls and the attack on Bandara. Although both of these cases involved head injuries, they introduced the apparently novel element of strangulation, and perhaps, there was slightly more justification for believing that their attack was by a separate author.

In retrospect, what was clearly established is that had senior detectives of the West Yorkshire Police assembled the photofit impressions from the surviving victims of all hammer assaults or assaults involving serious head injuries on unaccompanied women, they would have been left with an inescapable conclusion that the man involved was dark haired with a beard and mustache. They would also have learned from Olive Smelt, Caroline Brown, and Marilyn Moore, all of whom had spoken to him, that he had a local accent. In other words, had these descriptions been rendered into an artist's impression and circulated, detectives sent to interview Sutcliffe on succeeding occasions would have had a workable character sketch at their disposal further revealing Sutcliffe to have been the suspect in the series of murders and assaults.

Further, when the police compared the descriptions of witnesses and the photo composite with the extended pattern of criminal behavior, it would have been possible for West Yorkshire detectives to have improved their knowledge of thesuspect by collating the evidence and composite pictures provided by women who had survived hammer or head injury attacks in West Yorkshire. The criteria which could usefully have been applied were:

1. That the victims were unaccompanied women but were not always prostitutes
2. That the lead up to the attack was
   - By following on foot (stalking) as seen in Cassidy, Stead, Fox, Leach, Walls, and Hill
   - By walking and talking to the victim, as seen in Wood, Brown, Smelt, and Whitaker
   - By pick up in a car as in Long, Moore, Rytka, and by implication the other prostitute victims
3. The attack itself was always from the rear; in the case of Wood, Brown, Smelt, and Whitaker by dropping behind the victim, and in Long, Moore, and Rytka by persuading the victim to get out of the car

Had these criteria been applied to the list of undetected assaults on women, the overriding conclusion would have been that the suspect:

1. Was a local man
2. Had hair on his face
3. Was not a person of color
4. Was between 20–35 years of age

Accordingly, even as early as November 1977, there is no reason why Sutcliffe should not have been identified as "similar" to the composite of the suspect the police were seeking.

THE POLICE INTERVIEWS INVOLVING SUTCLIFFE

Following Sutcliffe's arrest it was learned that he had been interviewed by police officers on nine separate occasions in connection with the Ripper series of crimes. There was intense speculation about the failure of these interviews to lead to his arrest sooner. Sutcliffe was, in fact, interviewed by the police on 12 occasions between July 5, 1975, the date on which his admitted series of crimes commenced, and the date when he was charged with the 20 crimes for which he was subsequently convicted. The final interview followed Sutcliffe's arrest in Sheffield and led to his admission of the various Ripper crimes.

Sutcliffe had already begun his killing spree when he was first arrested in October 1975, by West Yorkshire police in connection with a theft of tires from the tire-fitting facility where he worked. The stolen property was found in the trunk of his car. This was a simple case of theft and on pleading guilty to it at Dewsbury Magistrates Court on February 9, 1976, Sutcliffe was fined £25. Fifteen days after this interview Sutcliffe murdered Wilma McCann in Leeds, but at the time he was arrested there was no evidence to connect him with the assaults on Rogulsky and Smelt earlier in the year. Although his arrest for stealing tires might not, on the surface, appear to have any significance as far as the series of crimes is concerned, if there was a trigger to his behavior, the arrest might have pulled it and his murder of Wilma McCann was the result.

Sutcliffe was next interviewed in connection with the £5 note found on October 15, 1977, in Jean Jordan's handbag lying 189 feet away from the point where her body had been discovered five days earlier. The bank note had only recently been issued and detectives believed that it might actually be traceable to the individual who had given Jean Jordan a £5 payment for sex. This inquiry led to local businesses in the area who drew their payrolls from the Leeds Clearing Bank which had received the note from Bank of England in September. Sutcliffe was a truck driver for one of the businesses, and he was interviewed by detectives who asked about his alibi, assumed he did not own a car, and eliminated him as a possible suspect. However, they were not as thorough as they might have been because Sutcliffe did, in fact, own a car and his alibi, confirmed by his wife, had a giant hole in it. There was a period of time that night during which Sonia Sutcliffe could not account for the whereabouts of her husband. But this fact didn't come to light until years later even though police did return to the Sutcliffe house on November 8, 1977, to re-interview the couple to make sure the statements in the October interview held up.

But more important than the lack of depth of the second and third Sutcliffe interviews was the lack of seriousness that the interviewing officers gave to the meetings with Sutcliffe. This goes right to the heart of problem of investigator morale. Task force investigators have to believe in the mission of the task force. They have to believe that what they're doing, that the avenues they're pursuing, no matter how narrow, will eventually lead to a solution of the crime. When they don't, they are less than thorough and allow clues and pieces of evidence to slip right by. This is what happened in the early inquiry into Peter Sutcliffe.

During the first few Sutcliffe interviews, especially concerning the mysterious £5 bank note, it seems apparent that the officers didn't believe that what they were doing would lead anywhere. This was the conclusion the senior reviewing officer came to when he was evaluating the performance of the joint Yorkshire Ripper task forces for the Home Secretary. Therefore, perhaps because the interviewing officers did not believe that their conversations with Sutcliffe would lead anywhere, they were less than thorough in their questioning. This is exactly how task forces break down, especially during the early phases of an investigation when the police are not only likely to have the name of the offender somewhere in their files, they're probably already interviewing him but don't know how close they are to the clues that will identify the suspect who's right across from them.

The fourth interview with Peter Sutcliffe, conducted in August 1978, was the result of Sutcliffe's being identified as a result of the cross area sighting inquiry into vehicle owners who made frequent visits to red light areas. Sutcliffe made it to the computerized Punters Index in June and July 1978 when his red Ford Corsair was recorded on seven occasions, six in the prostitute area of Bradford and once in the Chapeltown area of Leeds. What officers didn't know from the printout was that Sutcliffe had also been sighted on nine additional occasions in Bradford in his newly acquired Sunbeam Rapier. A little over a month after his sighting in Leeds on July 7, Sutcliffe was seen at his home by Detective Constable P. Smith of the West Yorkshire Police. He was instructed that the object of his inquiry was to eliminate subjects by accounting for their movements on one or more of the murder dates. A list of the dates was provided and elimination was to be achieved by the examination of diaries, passports, holiday booking forms, records of periods in hospital, or family anniversaries. The interviewers were explicitly instructed not to reveal to the subjects of their interviews that police observations were being carried out in prostitute areas and that they were looking for someone who might have used a ball peen hammer.

At the same time, however, inquiry officers were briefed to find out whether people being interviewed made use of prostitutes. They were further briefed to find out whether they possessed motor vehicles that could have made tire marks found at the scenes of the Richardson, Moore, and Millward crimes. It was emphasized that vehicles in the BMC Farina range were most suspect. But the instructions were that if any vehicle mentioned in the list was encountered during inquiries then full details of the tires fitted to it should be obtained.

Constable Smith was aware of Sutcliffe's two previous interviews during the £5 note inquiry and had copies of the relevant papers with him. He was aware of the loose alibi supplied and it was his intention to obtain a stronger alibi for the most recent murder of Vera Millward in Manchester on May 16–17 1978. When Constable Smith arrived at Sutcliffe's home on Sunday, August 13, Peter Sutcliffe was busy decorating the kitchen. His wife, Sonia Sutcliffe, was present during the interview as well. They explained that they had recently bought the house and spent most of their spare time on alterations and decorating it, they seldom went out, and when they did go out they were always together. Initially they were not able to remember their movements on the May 16 or 17, but Sonia Sutcliffe subsequently said that on the May 16 her husband "would have come home from work and stayed with her all evening."

While his wife was out of the room, Peter Sutcliffe was asked whether he used prostitutes. He denied that he did and was then asked about the use of his car, particularly during the evening hours. The interviewer's strategy here was not to reveal that Sutcliffe's car had already been seen in specific locations during the red light area cross sighting surveillance. Sutcliffe explained to the police interviewer that any sightings of him in Bradford could be accounted for by his commutes between his home and where he worked in the city. He completely denied ever having visited Leeds. Astoundingly, the police interviewer did not pursue this, because the interviewer believed there was a high error rate in the cross area sighting inquiry in Leeds. Again, lack of police faith in the process of the information retrieval caused the interviewer to deny the validity of a piece of evidence and, as a result, gave the killer the benefit of his own doubt. The interviewer not only accepted Sutcliffe's denial and his explanation of the Bradford sightings, he also accepted that Peter and Sonia Sutcliffe were a normal young couple pursuing the path of home improvement.

The police interviewer did not check the tires of Sutcliffe's car, nor did he carry out any search of the house or garage because, he later reported, he had read that Sutcliffe's house had been searched during earlier interviews and that he had been previously eliminated from consideration as a suspect. The officer had no reason to doubt this information even though the previous search was cursory at best, because the inquiry officer at that time took too much for granted.

It should have been apparent to senior officers in the investigation that even though the interviewers were systematically clearing Sutcliffe each time, there was something odd about his name coming up again and again during each inquiry. In fact, no particular suspicion was attached to the fact that Sutcliffe was being interviewed for the cross area sighting inquiry having already been interviewed during the £5 note inquiry. This was because Constable Smith, the Bradford sighting interviewing officer, didn't believe it was unusual for people living in Bradford to become subjects of the two separate inquiries.

The officer evidently agreed with Sutcliffe that because the Bradford red light area sits astride a number of main access routes to the city, many people going about their legitimate business would be recorded there. Unfortunately, Constable Smith did not have the actual times of the Bradford sightings when he interviewed Sutcliffe because these were not available due to the limitations of the printout; only the times of the keyboarded entry appeared in print, not the officer's sighting of the subject vehicle. Had they been checked from the original input documents, it would have revealed that the earliest sighting was at 8 p.m. and the latest 12.50 a.m. This was incompatible with Sutcliffe's assertion that he "rarely went out in the evenings." Failure to challenge Sutcliffe on his denial of having visited Leeds in the evening was also a failure of the process as was the officer's failure to check out the tires on Sutcliffe's car. But most importantly, there was nobody looking at the number of times Sutcliffe's name had been coming up, defying the laws of chance even though Sutcliffe himself tried to explain it away.

Finally, on August 29, 1978, a detective superintendent realized that because Sutcliffe had owned two Ford Corsair motor cars—included in the list of vehicles for the tracking inquiry—the tires of both vehicles should be checked. He also called for details from Sutcliffe's employers and for his personal banking records to be reviewed. This was a countermand of Constable Smith's immediate supervisor who had not noticed anything suspicious in Sutcliffe's statements and simply approved Constable Smith's interview for the file.

But the fifth interview with Sutcliffe, on November 1978, was treated as if it were a matter of simple routine. He had sold his red Corsair, so the officers couldn't examine it. When they tracked it down to the new owner, the tires had been changed so they were no longer the brand of tire in question. The officers did confirm, again, that Sutcliffe had worked for T. & W.H. Dark Ltd., one of the firms involved in the £5 note inquiry. But the interview produced nothing beyond this and after the murder of Josephine Whitaker in April 1979, the notes from Sutcliffe's fifth interview simply disappeared, mislaid for at least another year.

In May 1978, well before his November 1978, interview, Sutcliffe bought a black Sunbeam Rapier motor car which was sighted in the red light areas of the investigation and was entered in sightings logs in the PNC records. Between June 1978, and November 22, 1978, Sutcliffe's Sunbeam Rapier was observed in the prostitute areas of Bradford on 36 occasions and in the Chapeltown area of Leeds twice and was duly printed out as a cross area sighting. By the February 22, 1979, the vehicle had been seen in both Leeds and Bradford on a three more occasions. It was also seen in Manchester and was subsequently printed out as a triple area sighting. This information should have been of the utmost significance had it been related to the earlier cross area sighting of Sutcliffe's Ford Corsair and his earlier involvement in the Manchester £5 note inquiry. However, because of loss of data resulting from the information overload and the inability of the administrative process to take control of its own data, the three Sutcliffe hits were not connected, an omission with the gravest consequences for the future of the inquiry. Because when Sutcliffe was interviewed a sixth time, in July 1979, in connection with a sighting of his car after the Whitaker murder, the interviewing detectives had no idea he'd been interviewed five times before in connection with other car sightings and the £5 note.

The two detectives who visited Sutcliffe in July 1979, were thus starting from the beginning with a man who, to the best of their knowledge, had not been involved at all in the earlier investigations; he had only come to notice because of the triple area sighting of his vehicle. Sutcliffe managed to convince the police that all the sightings of his car were completely innocent because he was commuting back and forth from work. He also denied having been in other areas where his car had been surveilled. However, even after the sighting of his car was verified, no action was taken to confront him with the discrepancy in his story. Even though one of the interviewing police officers felt suspicious about Sutcliffe, his senior officers took no action.

For the first time, however, the interviewing police officers admitted to themselves that they were not satisfied with the outcome of their interview and they discussed a number of points that made them suspicious of Peter Sutcliffe. They were unhappy about Sutcliffe's flimsy alibi, especially his denial of ever having been to Manchester even after they'd confirmed a positive sighting of his vehicle. They noted Sutcliffe's strong resemblance to the composite description provided by one of the victims, a photofit they had previously been told to disregard because the witness was regarded as unreliable. They also noted that Sutcliffe wore a shoe size close to the size of prints found at the scene of the murder of Josephine Whitaker. They also noticed that Sutcliffe had a pronounced gap between his top front teeth, which the murderer of Joan Harrison at Preston was thought to have had. The detectives also thought that for a man who was being interviewed in connection with a series of murders, Sutcliffe's attitude was almost too casual, as if he were confident about the interview because he knew far more than the police did.

Even though the officers considered arresting Sutcliffe on suspicion, they decided against it because they knew of no other information that could be used as a basis for filing charges other than the points already covered during their interview. One of the officers also remembered an instruction that people being interviewed were not to be arrested without the approval of the Assistant Chief Constable after submission of a full report. This instruction was issued in July 1977 headed "Notes for Guidance when Dealing with Potential Suspects". It set out ten points of guidance, the last of which was a directive that a person should not be interviewed as a suspect until the previous nine points had been completely covered and then only subject to the approval of the Assistant Chief Constable. They came to the conclusion that in view of this directive, they should submit a comprehensive report covering all the facts drawn out by the interview including the impression that there was "something not quite right about Sutcliffe." Later in the report they used the phrase "the reporting officers are not fully satisfied with this man." Quite by chance and before their report was submitted, both officers were directed to other inquiries. As a result, they did not take part in debriefings where they could have expressed their doubts about Sutcliffe.

The very nature of the directives to detectives and the rules of engagement and protocols regarding what information could be acted upon during interviews seems to have prevented the detectives who conducted the sixth interview with Sutcliffe from pursuing lines of inquiry into the other sightings of Sutcliffe's car in red light areas. Even though the detectives had intuitive doubts about Sutcliffe's innocence, the administrative structure of the investigation not only inhibited them from acting on their instincts, it also precluded those higher up in the police chain of command from acting on the detectives' recommendation that Sutcliffe be arrested. Perhaps, had the detectives checked the times of the very large number of sightings of Sutcliffe's vehicle in Bradford, it would then have led them to the conclusion that they were incompatible with Sutcliffe's account. The detectives were further inhibited by the requirement to keep the police observations secret and, more importantly, by the difficulty obtaining additional information from the Major Incident Room. They were also inhibited by the "Notes for Guidance." Without this detectives might have arrested Sutcliffe and made him subject to a thorough Major Incident Room search and to a much deeper interview.

This was without doubt the most crucial stage of the whole investigation as there were three strong lines of evidence were available pointing to Sutcliffe at that time:

1. The £5 note inquiry
2. The sightings of Sutcliffe's red Corsair in Bradford and Leeds (with a denial of the latter)
3. The further sightings of his black Sunbeam Rapier in Bradford, Leeds, and Manchester (with a denial of the Manchester sighting)

An efficiently run Incident Room would undoubtedly have connected these three lines of inquiry leading to a more purposeful interview with Sutcliffe; this time as a suspect being asked to account for each of his vehicle sightings individually. His alibis in connection with the £5 note inquiry would also have been put to more stringent testing. But these lines weren't pursued as the investigation ground on, still looking at Sutcliffe each time his name came up, and each time dismissing him as a suspect even though the evidence against him was continuously piling up in the task force's own records.

By the time of the seventh interview on October 23, 1979, the West Yorkshire Police were still not satisfied with Sutcliffe's alibis and wanted to eliminate him once and for all by checking his movements on the more recent murder dates. Still not in control of their own investigation, the police had provided detectives interviewing Sutcliffe with copies of the papers relating to the fourth and fifth interviews. The officers were aware that Sutcliffe had been interviewed twice during 1977 in connection with the £5 note inquiry. They were, however, completely unaware of the vital sixth interview and of the facts surrounding it.

But Detective Constables Vickerman and Eland learned quickly when they went to Sutcliffe's house that the police had been a constant presence there. When they explained to Mrs. Sutcliffe the reason for their visit, this drew the response "Oh, not again." Mrs. Sutcliffe explained this remark by telling the officers that her husband had been seen three times previously. She explained that the police had interviewed the couple a number of times, each time saying they were satisfied at the answers Sutcliffe provided them. Why were they back now?

The detectives told her they wanted to follow up on his alibis They wanted to check his handwriting, they told him, but were completely astonished to find out that Sutcliffe had already provided a handwriting exemplar to the police. While Sutcliffe agreed to provide a full handwriting sample to the police, Sonia Sutcliffe remarked that her husband was not the Ripper. "I think he is," Detective Constable Eland replied, in an attempt to induce a reaction from Sutcliffe and his wife replied. Sutcliffe stopped writing for a moment and looked at Constable Eland, but showed no other reaction. Then he continued writing. If he was nervous, he didn't show it.

Before the end of the interview, the officers dropped another bomb when they told Sutcliffe and his wife that inasmuch they had been unable to supply any satisfactory alibi there was every possibility that they would be interviewed again should further murders occur. Neither officer considered Sutcliffe to be a strong suspect, but they described the couple as "strange" and were unhappy that nothing that was said in the interview could definitively eliminate Sutcliffe from the investigation. The police were, however, convinced at that time that the Sunderland letter writer was the murderer and believed that the handwriting sample they had obtained would either incriminate or eliminate Sutcliffe.

The officers' reliance on the Sunderland writing sample derived from their belief that because the writer seemed to know information about the murders that only the killer could have known, the letter was written by the killer. The police completely eliminated from their consideration the possibility that someone else who knew the killer and his moves could have written the letter. Their assumption that the author and the murderer were one and the same person was wrong. The decision to eliminate people from the inquiry solely on these grounds in the face of other information which aroused suspicion clearly had a detrimental effect on the inquiry. Knowledge that people were being eliminated on accent and handwriting clearly had a psychological effect on officers conducting inquiries and conditioned them to ignore factors which would otherwise have raised sufficient unease in their minds for them to have taken more positive action.

The officers continued to be suspicious of Sutcliffe's alibis even as they were trying to eliminate him as the letter writer and, thereby, as the killer. They noted his unusual behavior in the face of their challenges to his alibis. Although he had been interviewed previously by the police, Sutcliffe had not made a mental note of his whereabouts on the dates of the last two murders in the series. Inquiry officers had found that it was common practice among people who had been interviewed on a number of occasions to have taken positive steps to identify their whereabouts at the time of each new murder.

With the information about the Sunderland letter and Sutcliffe's writing sample buried in an avalanche of information in the Yorkshire Ripper incident rooms, the police, now completely bogged down in the investigation, actively sought ways in which new life could be injected into the inquiry. They returned to the inquiry into the £5 note found at the scene of the still-unsolved Jordan murder, hoping against hope that a fresh look might provide them a new lead or shine a light down a path they previously thought to be a dead end.

Late in 1979, Detective Chief Superintendent Ridgway in Manchester researched ways he could narrow down the number of firms to whom the bank might have given the Jordan £5 note. After conducting a number of practical tests in which substitute money was counted out in an attempt to reproduce events of September 1977, Ridgeway's team reached the conclusion that the £5 note found in Jordan's handbag had been drawn as part of the payroll by one of only eleven firms in the Shipley area which collectively employed a total of 241 people. T & W.H. Clark Ltd. was one of these firms with 49 employees to be seen. They were the employers of Peter William Sutcliffe, the 76th employee on the full list of 241. The Greater Manchester officers had great hopes that the murderer was to be found among the 241 names, either as the actual recipient of the £5 note or as someone who had received it from the original recipient such as a husband from his wife.

In preparation for interviewing the 241 employees, the detectives searched the incident room databases for information on the people they would be seeing. Astoundingly, there was no record of Sutcliffe's involvement with the case or of his previous interviews available to the detectives assembling their notes. The cross-sighting reports were missing as were the tire track reports and the handwriting sample. The detectives did find previous inquiries into the bank note, but, given the other missing interview reports and action items, it was as if, despite the seven previous interviews, the name Peter Sutcliffe had not come up at all in the investigation outside the routine inquiry into the bank note. For an administrative process that focused on the process of information control, this type of grave error, regardless for the reasons, was a critical flaw. Had the full record of Sutcliffe's involvement in the case been discovered in the list of 241 people, there is a strong probability that even at that early in the case he would have been regarded as a high priority suspect.

On January 7, 1980, all the officers taking part in the revived £5 note operation were told specifically that houses, garages, and vehicles were to be fully searched, and that any interview subject who did not completely satisfy the inquiry officer was to be taken to the police station for a more probing interview. Chief Superintendent Ridgway had always had reservations about the use of the letters and tape recording as eliminating factors, and he emphasized that no one was to be eliminated from among the 241 subjects on either handwriting or accent grounds. Elimination was only to be authorized on the acceptance of a verified alibi.

As in previous interviews, Sutcliffe at first seemed surprised that he was being interviewed *again* by the police in connection with an item, the bank note, which he thought by now was a dead issue. He did, however, and much to the astonishment of the detectives, volunteer that he had been questioned before in connection with handwriting samples. This opened the possibility that there might be more information on Sutcliffe in the police files, information they had not seen but might be relevant to their immediate task at hand—the elimination of Sutcliffe as a possible suspect in the case.

The detectives searched Sutcliffe's house and garage, discovered the claw hammer, noted that he drove a Rover, and found that he could not alibi himself for the Leach murder, one of the homicides under investigation in the series. Throughout the interview Sutcliffe behaved normally but at least one of the detectives, Sergeant Boot, found him odd; "a strange runner" he wrote in his note book. Despite the impression Sutcliffe made, Boot could not bring him to mind ten months later in November 1980, when he received Trevor Birdsall's anonymous letter naming Sutcliffe as the Ripper.

Following their interview with Sutcliffe, the two officers visited the murder Incident Room in Leeds where they discovered three nominal cards relating to him: the first in respect of the original £5 note inquiry, the second in connection with the cross area sightings of the red Corsair, and the third, in relation to the triple sightings of the black Sunbeam Rapier. Moreover, Sutcliffe's admission that he had previously been interviewed and had supplied handwriting samples should have given the officers an opportunity to bring this entire confluence of clues and tips to their superiors. Not only could they not eliminate Sutcliffe, they had uncovered a trove of material warranting a much closer inspection of the man. It was at this point where there was a failure in administrative procedure allowing Sutcliffe to remain at liberty when he clearly should have been arrested.

The eighth interview, because it did not eliminate Sutcliffe from consideration as a suspect, set into motion an action report for a ninth interview only a few days later. This time, detectives were examining Sutcliffe's lack of alibis for the Whitaker and the Leach murders as well as his ownership of the Ford Corsairs that could have left the suspect tire tracks at the crime scenes. The detectives were also following up on the cross area sightings reports in Bradford and Leeds. The detectives found Sutcliffe on the loading dock at his job and conducted the interview, all 30 minutes of it, in their police car, because it was the only convenient place where they could have a conversation in privacy.

As the detectives expected, Sutcliffe confirmed his previous ownership of two Ford Corsairs and once again denied the use of prostitutes. He reaffirmed the journeys in Bradford and Leeds which could have resulted in the sightings of his car in the red light areas of those cities. Sutcliffe said that on the night Barbara Leach was murdered he was at home with his wife and that she would verify this information. The police officers conducting the interview indicated that searches of Sutcliffe's house and car were negative, which was actually incorrect because the officer had not visited Sutcliffe's home and contented himself with a search of the cab of Sutcliffe's truck. In explaining this, the interviewing officer later said that because he knew from previous papers that the house and car had been previously searched with negative results he simply included that in his report, appending it to his search of the cab of Sutcliffe's truck.

Less than a month after this interview, the detective supervisors arranged for a tenth interview because they could not establish the dates when Sutcliffe had disposed of his Ford Corsairs. The detective supervisors knew that the Sunbeam Rapier and the Rover 3.5 subsequently owned by

Sutcliffe could not have been responsible for the tracks found at the scene of the murder of Vera Millward. They also knew, as a result of earlier research, that Ford Corsairs were highly suspect vehicles. Inspector Fletcher concluded that if Sutcliffe had disposed of both of his Corsairs before May 16–17 1978, the night of the Millward murder, he might reasonably be eliminated from the inquiry.

As in the previous interviews, Sutcliffe gave the police information contradicting his answers in previous interviews about which car he drove to the critical sighting areas and when he made his trips. He also changed his story about why he was driving through Leeds on the night of one of the murders and about which car he was using. The officers were unaware of his answers in some of the previous interviews and, therefore, accepted his explanations. Sutcliffe also explained that he had disposed of his white Ford Corsair by having it demolished for scrap, but the detectives subsequently found no record of the transaction Sutcliffe claimed had taken place.

The questioning then turned to the murder of Josephine Whitaker, the alibi for which, Sutcliffe said, was that he should either been away on a journey for his employer or at home with his wife. His vehicle log book for that period was checked and showed only that he had traveled 260 miles and finished work between 5.00 and 5.30 p.m. Sonia Sutcliffe subsequently confirmed that her husband had spent the evening at home with her. Accordingly, in his report to Inspector Fletcher, interviewer Detective Constable Jackson said that he had been unable to put Sutcliffe out of the inquiry satisfactorily. He suggested that Sutcliffe should be re-interviewed immediately after any subsequent murder in the series, leaving open the question as to whether Sutcliffe should be considered a suspect or merely a possible suspect that the police should not discount.

After ten interviews with the police, all of which were intended to eliminate possible suspects from consideration, Sutcliffe could still not be removed from the investigation. Moreover, because he had bobbed to the surface in so many lines of inquiry, the mere presence of Sutcliffe's name should have been an alarm to some member of the senior staff on the combined task force that there was a reason Sutcliffe was coming up so often. But the lack of control over the information flow, the refusal to acknowledge facts that kept repeating themselves, and the police's inability to recognize the extent to which the lines of inquiry overlapped prevented them from seeing the obvious—they already had the name of the killer in their records. Now it was only a matter of numbers, counting the times specific names turned up. Had the police been able to do this, Sutcliffe would have stood out like a beacon just as Bundy did in my first serial murder investigation five years earlier.

In the light of the confidence of the police investigators from Greater Manchester that the murderer was to be found within the 241 listed employees who most likely received the £5 bank note recovered from the Jordan crime scene, the interviews of Peter Sutcliffe, whose alibis were so general and so lacking in proper corroboration, should clearly have taken place inside a police station. They should have involved a senior detective who was prepared to take a positive line and ask Sutcliffe for explanations for every one of his motor vehicle sightings including the seven relating to his Rover between May 1, 1979, and November 10, 1979. It may well be that, by that stage, the inquiry had got to the state where even experienced and competent detectives could no longer "see the forest for the trees," because they had lost control of the investigation and had refused to acknowledge it. There was such a pervasive sense of denial through every level of the investigation—from senior management to field investigators—that was more than tolerated, it was embraced. There was confusion about the many different lines of inquiry which by then had been conducted and cross–pollinated one another. There was confusion resulting from the very different information flowing from each of the new crimes in the series. And finally there was massive confusion as a result of West Yorkshire's dependence upon the Sunderland letters and audiotape which, because of a completely false conclusion as to their real nature, became a red herring of mammoth proportions.

On June 25, 1980, at 11:30 p.m., two West Yorkshire Metropolitan Police officers in an unmarked police car on a small surveillance team in the red light area of Manningham, Bradford, saw a Rover 3.5 speeding and maneuvering in an erratic manner along Grosvenor Road. The officers at first thought that the vehicle might be stolen and decided to check it, suddenly winding up in a high-speed chase ending in the driveway of No. 6 Garden Lane, Heaton. The two officers quickly found that Sutcliffe, who had been driving the car, was its owner and lived at No. 6 Garden Lane. They arrested him on a DUI and took him to Bradford Police Station. Before Sutcliffe was released from custody a check was made with the Ripper Major Incident Room as a result of which Constables Doran and Melia were told that Sutcliffe was in the system, but that he had been "eliminated from the inquiry on handwriting." The decision to check Sutcliffe with the Major Incident Room was a matter of routine followed in connection with any arrest in the area, and at no time did the two officers regard Sutcliffe as a Ripper suspect.

The next arrest of Sutcliffe would have to wait for seven months and would only come when Sutcliffe was again spotted in a red light area, this time in Sheffield with stolen plates on his Rover and in the company of a prostitute. When the officers ran his name after his arrest and found out that although he had been eliminated from the investigation his name was still under consideration because of the bank note and the many sightings in the surveillance areas, senior detectives on the task force decided to reinvestigate Sutcliffe as if he were an entirely new suspect. At that point, the original arresting officer in Sheffield returned to the site of the traffic stop and searched the area. He found a knife and a hammer. The chilling possibility that occurred to the police was that perhaps they had intervened and picked up their suspect moments before he was about to strike his next victim. Sutcliffe was re-arrested, this time on suspicion of murder.

With their examination of the Sutcliffe file now complete, the police, who were holding him in custody at Dewsbury, confronted Sutcliffe with questions about his alibis, his possession of the £5 bank note, his ownership of the Ford Corsairs, the Sunbeam, and the Rover, and, finally, the hammer and knife. Sutcliffe soon began confessing to the murders, especially after being confronted with the information that his name was given up by his old friend Trevor Birdsall. With the ultimate success of the manhunt for the Yorkshire Ripper notwithstanding, the police realized that they had confronted Sutcliffe with information about his presence in their investigation eleven times before they put the pieces together clearly enough to see that Sutcliffe had been their suspect all along.

Perhaps, as the official critique of West Yorkshire investigation suggested, given the number of subjects who were interviewed, it's not surprising that some information was misfiled or even lost. But the aim of the task force organization was not only to preserve information, but to store it in a way that it was accessible and retrievable in whatever format was necessary to allow individual investigators to correlate facts from every line of inquiry. In that respect, the task force lost control of its information and, without realizing it, had to rely on the repetitive, almost compulsively obsessive, nature of the serial killer to allow himself to be ensnared in the web of surveillance that had been set up to catch him. In other words, the process of applying overwhelming manpower on the streets to look for a killer worked the way it was supposed to. But in the end that same massive application of manpower to information systems defeated the purpose of the surveillance itself by overloading the police with so much information that the information was either lost or the police couldn't access it in a timely fashion.

The inability to identify Sutcliffe as a suspect on the basis of the numerous interviews represents a systemic failure of police control of the investigation. This failure was so complete that personnel from individual investigators to senior managers were not provided with the information they needed to follow up on leads and manage the list of potential suspects. What is worse, police knew there was a loss of control and that contributed to a general sense of frustration and even hopelessness regarding the progress of the case. Accordingly, Sutcliffe was still able to continue killing and elude the police, even though there were severe credibility problems in his answers to police interviewer questions and inculpatory evidence in his own garage.

There is little doubt that Sutcliffe should have been arrested earlier on the facts related under the heading of "Police interviews involving

Sutcliffe," even though there were thousands of interviews in the Ripper investigations. In many of the individual lines of the inquiry that were pursued the prospects of success were extremely slim. For instance, there was a large list of vehicle owners who were intended to be seen during the first tracking inquiry. It was hoped that one of the vehicles involved might bear the tires which would associate it with the tracks found at the Richardson murder scene. Equally, when the first £5 note inquiry was launched, 8000 people were seen in the hope that one of them could be identified as the recipient of the Jordan £5 note. In the cross area sighting inquiry some of the 20,000 vehicle owners who were printed out were seen in the hope that one of them could be shown to be a suspect for the Ripper crimes, and subsequently all the 1200 triple area sightings owners were seen for the same purpose. Each one of these inquiries only held out a comparatively slim prospect of success taken in isolation and, therefore, it is not too surprising that when Sutcliffe was seen in respect to each of them the results were inconclusive. However, there were so many times that Sutcliffe's came up under all of these inquiries that it was no longer a matter of chance or coincidence. His name came up for a very good reason; the process was working. But nobody knew it except, perhaps, for Sutcliffe himself.

There was undoubtedly another principal reason preventing the operation from being successful. It was simply that the officers directing the inquiry were bogged down with routine paperwork at a level that might have been settled far below their rank. At every level, the filing and paperwork issues were so massive that detectives simply didn't have the time to pursue their own instincts, because they were reined in by the requirements of filing, paperwork, and information storage. As a result, investigator skills were impeded and the investigation was allowed to drift under the control of the paperwork, the management of which became an end in and of itself.

As we will show, once investigations get past the recognition and acknowledgment phases, they can easily stall and break down as a result of lack of control. One of the primary control failures in an investigation is a failure of information management. Since the 1980s, information management in most police investigations, but particularly in serial offender task forces, is an information management system that instills confidence in the process and is usually computer based.

The Ripper police investigation is a good example of where the increased use of computers could have been of invaluable assistance to investigating officers, but it should also be realized that such computer usage would inevitably have led to an increase in the storage of information about innocent people. Examining the criticisms made of the West Yorkshire Police for their apparent lack of use of computer technology in the Ripper case, one must, therefore, consider both the technical and potential aspects of what was or was not done and equally significant, the effect of such considerations when contemplating the ways ahead. In general, the criticisms made imply that had computer technology been used the offender would have been detected at a much earlier stage, greater and more efficient use would have been made of the information available, and, by extension, cost savings would have been achieved. Indeed when one realizes that, today, a meaningful computer workstation for records management and processing across multiple databases can be assembled for about $5000, the rationale for not implementing one is almost nonexistent. As we will see later, these systems not only work, their use may have already begun to change the nature of serial murder cases that actually get to a task force level.

Beyond the installation of computerized data management resources to allow a serial murder investigation to take control of its information processing, there are larger command, control, and resource allocation issues. If successfully implemented, these provide investigators with a sense of purpose and accomplishment, but if not implemented, they create frustration, resistance, and ultimately promote a shared sense of hopelessness with regard to completing the investigation successfully. Because the investigation of a long-term, control-type serial killer frequently requires the slenderest of clues to be pursued by quite large groups of police officers, the management and control of such inquiries often calls for a range of skills sometimes not always well developed in senior police officers. Most homicide investigators in large municipalities either solve homicides within a month or two or the case becomes cold and is usually archived. A serial murder investigation is entirely different because the caseload keeps piling up the more the killer remains at large. Therefore, unless a task force is staffed by and led by experienced serial offender investigators, the entire process can be a frustrating and self-defeating experience. It's necessary, therefore, in order to retain control of the investigation and drive the investigation even when there's little progress to report, that the task force be led by experienced serial killer investigators who can steer the process through difficult periods.

The Yorkshire Ripper task force was a case-in-point not only because the investigators made so many mistakes, but because the lack of experience on the part of senior investigators and managers made for a lack of control that allowed Sutcliffe to remain at large far longer than he should have. The control of investigations into 13 murders and 7 serious assaults during a 6-year period clearly called for unusual leadership qualities and an understanding of such aspects of management as morale, motivation, delegation, communication, training, welfare, and even cost benefit analysis. The senior detectives of West Yorkshire were probably on par with those in other forces. They were, however, not well equipped in management terms to control an inquiry of the size and scale of the Ripper inquiry. In particular, they lacked the flexibility of mind required to identify failures in existing systems and to take rapid corrective action even when they knew the failures were impeding the entire investigation.

There were other command and control problems stemming from the lack of experienced management, probably none more significant than the decision to appoint a different senior investigating officer for each new crime in the series. The intention was to bring new minds to focus on crimes in the series in an attempt to ensure that no possibility was overlooked. But this, in American management terms, was "siloism" at its worst. In practice the proliferation of senior investigating officers added to the complexity of the situation and probably resulted in a tentativeness of officers who didn't want to step on one another's toes or enter into one another's territories. As a result, there were lots of independent investigations for each crime with no single senior manager leading the task force. The independent investigation units were sometimes blind to the work other units were doing and, as can be seen from then number of times Sutcliffe was interviewed, often repeated work or neglected work that had been done. The appointment of a single detective chief superintendent to be in overall charge of the inquiry and to be divorced from any other responsibilities within the force would have done much to have ensured a clear chain of command, sharing of information, and continuity of approach to the different cases.

The second major failure in the management of the inquiry as a whole was that no proper arrangements were made for the delegation of authority to subordinate commanders to deal with different facets of the investigation. This was more common in American serial killer task force investigations than it is now, although among agencies inexperienced in the management serial killer cases delegation of authority issues can still be a problem. Initially a failure in an authority chain usually happens when individual senior investigating officers and the officer in charge of the investigation as a whole have to read a great deal of trivial material that doesn't require their level of skill and understanding. This is what happened in the Yorkshire Ripper case. In that investigation the lack of arrangement for formal delegation of subordinate functions meant that a number of senior officers were overworked while some of their subordinates were underworked and underutilized in terms of authority and responsibility. One can imagine the frustration that results when field officers are underutilized and a bottleneck of work and decision making at the top of the command chain actually prevents the investigation from going forward.

As a byproduct of this, the officers at the top of the management ladder have to work excessively long hours for extended periods of time, draining them of the ability to be creative in the face of negative results from the investigation. In the Yorkshire Ripper investigation, for example, failure to make arrangements for the delegation of subordinate inquiries such as the tracking inquiry, the cross area sighting inquiry and the letters and tape inquiry meant that the initiative of junior officers was often stifled and the progress of the inquiry slowed up because of the need for the senior investigating officer to be kept permanently in touch with developments.

The tracking Inquiry, for instance, was clearly an undertaking that could have been delegated to a competent detective superintendent or detective chief inspector to run in its entirety, only referring to the senior investigating officer when he had positive information to report. Not only was this not done, but arrangements for the control of the inquiry (and others similar to it) did not provide the senior investigating officer with information about its progress in terms of the number of actions completed in comparison with the total number that the inquiry involved. Ideally the senior investigating officer would not have required such detail but should have been given brief progress reports by the officer to whom the inquiry had been delegated, with an estimated completion date and an indication of future manpower requirements. Such action was not taken and the senior investigating officer attempted to control and direct the subordinate inquiries at the same time as he handled the important aspects of more recent crimes. One should not be surprised, therefore, that the inquiries were inconclusive and that they were often abandoned before conclusion and without proper consideration of their potential.

In the Yorkshire Ripper case, as often happens in major serial killer cases in the United States, the motivation of detectives as individuals and in groups can clearly pose problems as the inquiry develops. In the Ripper task force, the disciplinary action taken against a number of detectives who concocted false statements during one of the motor car inquiries rather than continue with the interminable round of interviews of vehicle owners is a clear indication that both motivation and morale had failed to attract the obviously required attention of management. It is unlikely that the detectives who were disciplined were by nature lazy or dishonest, and it would seem that their malpractice was prompted by a lack of confidence in the tasks they were undertaking.

As has been mentioned earlier, the commencement of an inquiry in which 53,000 vehicles were to be examined in the hope that one would bear a combination of tireslinking it to a scene of crime was a daunting prospect. Whether or not the number of vehicles that had to be investigated could have been appreciably reduced by the application of more skillful analysis is one issue. But the fact that the inquiry was attempted without due regard to the motivation and morale problems which were likely to be involved is a further indication of lack of consciousness of management and leadership concepts within the West Yorkshire senior detectives. Protracted vehicle inquiries involving thousands of actions clearly called for the very highest standards of briefing and debriefing and for the adoption of measures calculated to promote and maintain morale within the inquiry teams.

A senior inquiry officer who was not bogged down in the detail of the case might, for instance, have personally joined in the actual conduct of the vehicle and tire inquiries from time to time to demonstrate his willingness to expose himself to the monotony with which the field officers were involved. He would certainly have given frequent encouragement to his teams and emphasized that the successful conclusion of this aspect of the operation was undoubtedly important. This would have boosted the flagging morale of the task force. The failure of a number of potentially profitable lines of inquiry might well have been due to the poor morale and motivation of inquiry teams.

Whereas it is relatively easy to maintain a very high level of morale and commitment for a short-term operation, it is much more difficult to maintain it over a protracted period, especially when there is no evidence that any of the efforts made are proving successful. The available evidence supports the contention that the morale of any group depends upon the extent to which the group identifies its valid and likely to be productive. Also, the group must believe that among them they have the skill, experience, and resources to bring the task to a successful conclusion. These beliefs and preconceptions were clearly not felt in many aspects of the Ripper inquiry as they often are not felt in many American serial killer investigations.

The anatomy of the Yorkshire Ripper case indicates not just that the investigation failed in all three critical areas of recognition, acknowledgment, and control, but how it failed. It is a case study of a failure in procedure leads to a failure of the process resulting in the loss of group morale, decline in the performance of individual team members, and, ultimately, a failure in the collective performance of the group. That Sutcliffe was eventually identified during one of the ongoing task force operations designed to identify potential suspects is a testament to the efficacy of the concept of the operation. However, that Sutcliffe was identified so late during his serial murder career after the area sightings had been in operation for years also underscores the failure of the task force. This was a clear and obvious example of how collective denial in the face of actual success turned that success into failure. Because even senior management wasn't aware of its own success, it couldn't communicate that success to the personnel along the chain. Accordingly, the suspect had been identified, interviewed, and even arrested. Yet, because no one knew or believed the system was working, the suspect was released back into his pool of victims with deadly results.

The Yorkshire Ripper case demonstrates that for a task force to be successful as an institution, it not only must communicate its shared mission to all personnel, even those at the lowest levels of the hierarchical ladder, but that the communication must take place on an almost daily basis to counteract the natural anomie that takes place in any organization not achieving realistic goals on a regular basis. Even when goals are achieved on a regular basis, as the Ripper case shows, unless those goals ultimately and explicitly contribute to the end results of the operation, they may fail to provide the reinforcement for individuals in the group. Individual performance flags, and the group performance suffers as well. Regardless of the serial killer's own state, because the effectiveness of those pursuing him and their collective effort declines, the offender only benefits and keeps on committing his crimes. This is what happened in the Yorkshire Ripper case where Sutcliffe was able to avoid arrest even though he had crossed through the police dragnet and had obviously left a trail that kept turning up in the police files.

REFERENCE

Byford, L. (1981). The Yorkshire Ripper Case, private report, December.

4

THE CONSULTING
DETECTIVE

The Atlanta Child Murders
Profile of the Atlanta Child Killer
How to Catch the Atlanta Child Killer
The First 30 Days
The El Paso Desert Murders
Summary
References

Hopelessness in solving a long-term serial murder case sets in because investigators are constantly faced with the fact that nothing seems to be working. There is an initial tendency to place blame on the task force itself. Managers may think that nothing is working because the task force is too insular, nobody can think outside the box, everybody's protecting his own turf, the "one-minute manager" is taking two minutes, or any other convenient answer. Gradually, under the pressure from senior managers and the relentlessness of the press who believes that it's personnel can solve the case faster than the police—mainly because they are not constrained by such technicalities as the United States Constitution—a sense of desperation creeps into the task force. That's why, at some point, almost every serial murder task force has turned to consultants from various walks of life for answers from the consultant's perspective.

Consultants can come from anywhere, and they usually do. They have included FBI profilers, clinical psychologists, forensic psychiatrists, psychics, people who claim the power of ESP, biorhythm chart readers, forensic theologists, forensic philosophers, and even strange-looking people with dowsing forks conducting their own searches for missing bodies. Anybody can call himself a consultant. Mainly due to the media coverage of high-profile cases and the emphasis on the weekly one-hour shows depicting the television roles of profilers and crime scene experts, there is a perception that these people can help resolve the case, and resolve it fast before the 11:00 news. Unfortunately, they don't solve cases; detectives solve cases.

For the most part, consultants do nothing more than cause a flurry of work for the detective, none of which leads to the productive solution of the case. But there is one type of consultant who can assist in providing information about how to solve these difficult cases, the "consulting detective." The consulting detective is one who has been in the throws of a serial murder case before and knows the pitfalls. In other words, a consulting detective builds on the experiences of the very events the task force is encountering as a result of the investigative process and applies that experience to the actual case. There's no magic, only the ability of someone who's gone down the same road to recognize from previous cases when the road takes a hairpin turn and when to apply the brakes. What follows are how consulting detectives were used to help the investigators in the Atlanta child murders and the El Paso desert murders.

THE ATLANTA CHILD MURDERS

The first time consulting detectives were used in a major serial murder investigation was by members of the Atlanta Task Force investigating a series of murders that occurred between July 1, 1979 and May 1, 1981. Police connected 28 murder cases and 1 missing persons case, most of whom were children, cases that were dubbed by the national press as the "Atlanta Child Murders." Most of the victims were black, school-age children who were kidnapped, assaulted, killed, and dumped within an average radius of 10 miles from their homes. The pattern of assaults and body recovery sites suggested to detectives that a serial murderer using a vehicle was operating in the greater metropolitan Atlanta area. Because most of the victims died from some type of asphyxiation, the cluster of murders was thought to be discrete, that is, a part of one series and related. Because the crime locations were spread over a number of jurisdictions, a multiagency task force involving local, state, and federal officers had been established to investigation a series of murders. The task force had determined that they were looking for a serial killer (Keppel and Birnes, 1995).

Commissioner Lee Brown had assembled a group of highly touted "supercops" as consultants. They were investigators who had previously handled some of the most notorious and high-profile murder cases in the nation. As was expected, their image was overhyped by the media, who represented them as the "seven samurai" aiming to solve the cases for the Atlanta police.

A Supercops II consultation took place on May 21, 1981, of which I was a part. This consultation took place in utmost secrecy. The group of consultants who were called to Atlanta with me had handled basically two different types of cases: those in which investigators had not known that a series of murders had taken place before the offender was caught, and those who were already pursing serial cases but didn't know who the killer was. In the first contingent were Captain Sidney Smith and Detective David Millican, the investigators who had handled the brutal and sexually sadistic murders committed by Dean Coryll and Elmer Wayne Henley, who buried 17 bodies in a boat storage building in Pasadena, TX. With them was Lieutenant Frank Braun, one of the investigators in the notorious John Wayne Gacy Murders. Gacy had buried 27 males underneath the crawl space of his home in Des Plaines near Chicago.

The second group consisted of Inspector Joseph Borelli from the New York Police Department task force that investigated the infamous Son of Sam—David Berkowitz—who kept the city at bay while he executed couples parked in their cars. It also included Lieutenant Ed Henderson and Detective Philip Sartuche of the Los Angeles Police Department who investigated the Hillside Strangler cases in Los Angeles and Bellingham, WA. Also in this latter group was Inspector Jeff Brosch, who investigated the Zebra Killings in San Francisco, that were committed by black religious extremists. Lieutenant Frank Chase and I, from the Ted Bundy investigations, rounded out this group.

A group such as this with as many years of accumulated serial murder investigation experience shared basic assumptions about the cases we pursued. We knew what questions to ask and understood certain axioms about the behavior of a serial murderer. Because of the cases we had solved, we knew how to cut through the administrative protocols between agencies that often got in the way of crime solving. That didn't make any of us very popular; quite the contrary. We knew that we were going to butt heads with the establishment of the Atlanta Police Department, Georgia Bureau of Investigation, and the FBI. We also knew that even if we found the killer, we would be on the wrong side of the political fence. But we weren't there to win friends. We were there to help solve a series of brutal murders.

According to Lee Brown, our consultation had two objectives. The first was to provide a profile of the killer by identifying characteristics of his behavior and the way they related to the signature of his crimes. Then, after profiling the killer, we were asked to develop strategies for catching him. Inasmuch as the FBI had been running around the bushes for years before we were called in, our profile wouldn't fit their profile. Moreover, because they had not caught the guy, our strategies for apprehending him, we thought, might be likely to raise a few official eyebrows.

PROFILE OF THE ATLANTA CHILD KILLER

We believed that at least 23 of the 27 murders on the task force list were connected and committed by the same person. The cases of Jimmy Payne, William Barrett, Larry Rogers, Patrick Baltazar, Lubie Jeter, Terry Poe, Charles Stephens, Eric Middlebrooks, and Alfred Evans were linked to each other. The same fibers and animal hairs were present consistently from one case to another (Keppel, 1989; *Williams v. State*, 1983). Because other young black female and male victims were discovered, probably strangled, in the same rivers or along the same roads in close proximity to the main nine victims, they could not be excluded from the investigation. We did not have any direct evidence that tied their deaths to the nine primary victims, but it was too soon in the process to throw them out on that fact alone. We conceded that with very few or no similar fibers and animal hairs identified, an absolute connection from the other victims to the nine linked victims could not be made. However, there was still a very high probability that 23, if not all 27, murdered children were killed by the same person. Moreover, we reported, we were unable to develop a strong rationale for connecting all 27 murders into one series because of either an incomplete investigation into the murders of the early victims or insufficient data given to us by the Atlanta Task Force. The more information available for analysis, the more effective we would be in attempting to link these crimes. Some assurance that friends and family members were not responsible for some of the murders was necessary before connection to other cases could be made.

The style of killings, with victims missing from areas popular with young blacks and asphyxiation being the most prominent cause of death, didn't fit logically with the most publicized theory that a white racist person or group was eliminating the black children of Atlanta to create fear in the community. These were not terrorist murders in the political sense of the word. The Atlanta child murders were more than likely committed by a black male whose method of operation reflected a personality with a need for hands-on activity with each victim before and after death. This would be a killer who could move about freely, who had relationships in the community, and whose presence in the area on any day he chose would not be considered out of the ordinary. This would be a killer who was trusted by his victims. Thus, we concluded, the killer was part of the community and, like Ted Bundy, was taking victims who had no idea they would ever be in danger.

Probable asphyxiation was the cause of death in a number of cases. A lack of telling marks of death or signs of a struggle were indicative that the killer more than likely got victims into a sleepy stupor by administering drugs or alcohol to them. Then he quietly strangled or suffocated the children. Getting victims to the point of drowsiness took patience and a plan.

That meant the killer spent considerable time with each victim from the point of initial contact until the induction of the state of drowsiness and subsequent murder. To accomplish all of that meant that the killer was deceptively cunning in his approach and was able to get his victims to place their complete trust in him and feel safe.

Some of the boys who had been murdered hung out in the fringe areas of Atlanta, neighborhoods populated principally by the unemployed drug dealers and hustlers. This was the killer's primary trolling ground, and we figured that he had something these young victims wanted. This was how he lured them into his trap. The killer's line of approach was most likely the offer of a short-term job to make quick money. This was the ploy that John Gacy used to entrap his young male victims and that Jeffrey Dahmer would use 15 years later. This is a typical serial killer lure. The job offer might have been for prostitution, posing for photos, or running drugs. To the younger victims the killer might have looked like a role model or big-brother figure, and the victims probably hoped that their association with him would develop into something long term. To the older victims, the killer was nothing more than a very short-lived employment opportunity for the evening, such as a "john" or a drug dealer in the need of an on-the-spot carrier. The killer, we believed, was able to change his approach according to the victim. He might have been able to lure his younger victims with money and his older victims with money and a job offer. Whatever the case, the killer was able to get those male victims from 9 to 28 years old under his complete control.

What added to his ability to attract those young boys was that each one of them was a clone of the murderer's own self image. Even though his choice of victims was purely random, they were a ready pool of handsome boys just like him. He looked, thought, and talked just like his victims, and that is what appealed to them the most. He was someone with common threads. He identified with them so well, the victims were probably never afraid of him, nor was he frightened by them. But his common ground was seductive because he probably presented himself as educated, well-integrated into the community, and always having a good job. If getting someone to trust a complete stranger was the major obstacle a serial predator must overcome with each victim, the Atlanta child murderer easily succeed in all cases. He succeeded primarily because his victims were young and unable to see through his mask of superficiality.

Based on the killer's ability to mingle across a spectrum of elementary school boys, older teenage victims, and adults, you would expect to find the killer comfortable in each of those atmospheres. He could have been or still was a volunteer or employee of a boys' service group, such as the Boy Scouts, YMCA, or other types of boys clubs community groups. He might have been a frequent volunteer, substitute teacher, or vendor around the elementary school scene. He might have frequented boy prostitutes and, at the same time, been part of the gay disco scene. He was not likely to have been an out-of-the-closet homosexual. In fact, he might have been known to hate gays in some circles and be superficially heterosexual with his own family of origin.

On the other side of the killer's mask was evidence of his need for total possession of his victims by engaging in postmortem activities with them. He had a sex drive that embraced necrophilic tendencies and a willingness to spend considerable time with victims after death. Even though direct evidence of sexual assault was not confirmed for most victims, it was expressed through the killer's signature—leaving the nude or partially clad males in a sexually degrading manner. He also partially redressed previously nude victims and disposed of their bodies in obviously posed positions at preselected locations as if he'd rehearsed this before the killing.

The killer's arranging of various victims in contorted or sexually degrading positions or leaving them in open places so they would certainly be discovered was a form of death ritual as well as a message. He revealed that he was treating the police as enemies and demonstrated with his victims' bodies that he not only exercised absolute control over the corpses, but over the police as well. The police were completely unable to catch him even though he was leaving bodies in plain view and in posed positions that said to investigators, "I am a murder victim." The police looked more and more inept to the public as the search intensified, reinforcing the killer's mentality with feelings of extreme superiority even as the hunted fugitive that he knew he was. He wanted the police to feel, psychologically, as he really did, helpless and controlled.

We also knew the killer was very aware of his environment, sensitive to the nature of the police pursuit, and clever enough to modify his patterns the moment he knew people were on to him. His changing of victim dumpsites from mainly land surfaces to rivers, for example, was a response to the publicity his crimes had received. By changing these styles, he revealed awareness of how the media worked and his ability to monitor the progress of the investigation through public sources. How the police were tracking him, primarily with the victim remains examined for similar fibers and hairs, was very important to him. Leaving partially nude or nude bodies in a river diminished the chances for finding that crucial microscopic trace of physical evidence that could be linked back to him. There was no question that the Atlanta child killer was well versed in police procedures. Having police science knowledge was part of his survival technique of acting only when there was least possibility of detection. He didn't want to get caught—ever.

The killer's predilection for postmortem engagement with his victims should have led investigators to those individuals who had been employed at, no matter how briefly, or were applicants for positions at funeral homes or medical examiners' offices. Previously convicted multiple murderers had expressed interest in morbidity by applying for positions in police departments and the death services area. Killers like Ted Bundy and Kenneth Bianchi worked at crisis clinics and applied for positions as a sheriff officer, respectively. Bundy, at one point in our interviews, reflected on his fascination with decomposing bodies.

The distance from where the victims were last seen to the location of their body recovery ranged from a few blocks to over 15 miles. That feature could only mean that the killer had access to reliable means of transportation. Each of the respective multiple murderers whom we had investigated had had several vehicles available to transport their victims to secluded areas. Also, each had driven hundreds of miles pursuing potential victims and checking out prospective dumpsites.

The profile of the killer as a black male in his mid-twenties, with a record of intermittent employment around elementary schools, interest in medical examiner functions, obsession with necrophilia, traffic with boy prostitutes, a role model for young boys, and constantly driving around Atlanta in pursuit of potential victims was a characterization that the task force brass must have wanted to believe. But the pressure was so intense to link the murders to some white racist conspiracy or to the occult that the black lust-killer theory was not emphasized publicly (Keppel and Birnes, 1995).

HOW TO CATCH THE ATLANTA CHILD KILLER

The second task of the consulting detectives was to develop a strategy to catch the killer. It was proposed by the Atlanta Task Force command that supporting the white racist theory through the media would make the killer think that the police were far from his tracks. We didn't think that was a good idea because the killer already knew they had linked cases through fiber identification. Besides that, previous attempts made by law enforcement to play games with a serial killer through the news media had failed miserably. The main reason those strategies were not effective was that the killer was the only person who knew all the facts of the murders. Any attempt to deceive the killer by portraying distorted facts or attempting to lure the killer to a particular location through a remorseful appeal served only to alert the killer to how close the investigators really were to catching him, which was about as close as the planet Pluto is to Earth.

The second strategy suggested by the Atlanta staff was already in place, and they were hoping that this effort would be endorsed by the consultants and would ultimately be productive. Several days prior to our consultation, they had set out to conduct surveillance of bridges crossing the South and Chattahoochee rivers. This rationale was sound because at least six of the last seven victims had been dumped in one of the two rivers, and there was no reason to believe that the next or subsequent murder victim would not be dumped into one of those two rivers. We wholeheartedly endorsed their proactive effort to catch the killer.

The task force planned to watch 11 bridges crossing the two rivers. It was a very labor-intensive proposition, taking at least five officers to watch one bridge, two on each side and one near the water so he could hear the splash of a body hitting the water. The surveillance team had an elaborate notification procedure in place so that when a splash was heard, responding officers would place large nets across the river in an attempt to snag the body that would presumably come floating by. The officer on the top of the bridge would notify the crews on top and the bridge would be barricaded and catch the Atlanta "Riverman" in the act.

On May 22, 1981, the day we left Atlanta, a four-man surveillance team, stationed at the James Jackson Parkway Bridge, reported an encounter with a suspect. A short time later that suspect was identified as Wayne B. Williams, who was later convicted of two of the murders attributed to the Atlanta child killer.

On June 19, 1981, Commissioner Lee Brown wrote the following letter to Sheriff Bernard Winckoski:

> I am writing to express my sincere appreciation to you for having allowed Lieutenant Frank Chase and Detective Robert Keppel to come to Atlanta recently to confer with the Atlanta Metropolitan Special Task Force on Missing and Murdered Children. I believe very strongly in the concept of information sharing among police agencies as one technique which should be utilized in the investigation of complex criminal cases. Your support in our recent information sharing effort and the personal insights of Lieutenant Chase and Detective Keppel have contributed to what has proved to be the most successful meeting we have had to date. (Brown, 1981).

THE FIRST THIRTY DAYS

High-profile and unsolved murder investigations accumulate an abundance of information from various sources as the investigation proceeds. Unlike more routine murder cases, the case files grow exponentially as the investigation remains unsolved. Increased time of investigation yields more and more information that doesn't seem to lead anywhere because of the way clues are prioritized. As the months go on, investigators usually feel the futility of their actions and the psychological stress of pursing a killer they can't find. This feeling doesn't bode well for the average detective. For one thing, many detectives have been groomed to be bean counters, judged by how many cases they clear. Those that have been part of a major unresolved murder investigation know that those beans to count are few and far between. Then when it's over, there's only one bean to show, albeit a big one. But the sizes and numbers of the beans have no relationship to one's performance. The pressure put on by fellow detectives can be obvious by their questions. Have you solved it yet? When is it going to be over?

My research into the conduct of serial murder investigations uncovered a very important discovery for the benefit of those homicide investigations that seem to never end. In some highly publicized cases, detectives have had the name of the killer all along, somewhere in their files in the early days of their investigations, yet their investigative activities did not focus on that name as the killer. Cases like the Hillside Strangler murders in Los Angeles, the Gainsville, FL, coed murders, the Yorkshire Ripper murders, the missing and murdered girls in Seattle, and the Chi Omega murders in Florida committed by Ted Bundy all had the name of the actual killer somewhere in the files in the early stages of the investigation. This eye-popping realization has strong implications toward the solutions of these types of cases.

In the Ted Bundy cases, Janice Ott and Denise Naslund disappeared from Lake Sammamish State Park, 15 miles east of Seattle, on July 14, 1974. Before the first of August 1974, information poured in, overwhelming detectives with many leads to follow up. However, one of those leads, buried with hundreds of 3×5 cards, proved to be the first information related to Theodore Bundy. The card had the license number of Bundy's VW Beatle. The card did not identify the caller or give information about where the VW was seen. Over 13 months later, we would realize that during the first 30 days of those missing persons investigations we had Bundy's name snitched off to us at least twice. The other tip came in from a university professor who thought Ted Bundy matched the composite drawing of the suspect seen at the park on that warm summer day.

Remarkably, we were not alone at having the name of the killer in the first 30 days located somewhere in the file in investigations that took months to identify. Another high-profile killer with his name in the file was the Hillside Strangler, Kenneth Bianchi, in Los Angeles. Many long conversations I had with Detective Sergeant Frank Salerno of the Los Angeles Sheriff's Department discussed "what if". Salerno related one reason why they might have at least identified by name the possible killer much sooner than receiving the crucial telephone call from Bellingham, WA, authorities. Salerno sensed that they probably had the killer's name but were unsure how to prioritize the correct information among thousands of names of possible suspects. The fact was that Kenneth Bianchi's name was in their files very early in the investigation because he was an applicant for the Los Angeles Sheriff's Office. Checking on former applicants was a tactic developed by Salerno and his fellow detectives. They felt the Hillside Strangler was a police applicant. His name was there along with many others, but they were unable to prioritize Bianchi for further follow up. Too many other leads were being worked.

In 1987, I received a federal grant to study solvability factors in murder cases. Because of the experience encountered in previous serial murder cases, I tracked when the police had the name of the killer in their files during the investigation of murder cases. A most astounding fact came to

TABLE 1   When any Information about the Offender is Known (N = 943)

When	Number	Percent
Before the Murder Investigation Occurs	206	21.85
As the Murder Investigation Begins	86	9.12
Within the First Hour	210	22.27
Within 24 Hours	221	23.44
Within 72 Hours	87	9.23
Within the First 30 Days	85	9.01
Cumulative Percent Up To 30 Days		94.92
Within the First 6 Months	23	2.44
After 6 Months	25	2.65

light: The police had the name of the suspect some place in their case file 95% of the time within the first 30 days of the investigation (see Table 1 above). This didn't mean that the investigators had focused on the killer, just that the killer's name was listed someplace in the file. It would not be long before I could test this theory on an unsolved serial murder investigation in El Paso, TX.

THE EL PASO DESERT MURDERS

So much about our knowledge about how to investigate murders is passed on by the only medium available, homicide seminars. In November 1988, I was a guest lecturer at the National Law Enforcement Institute's Seminar on Homicide Investigation held in Dallas, TX. My block of instruction lasted 3 hours and was on serial murder investigation. After I finished, Lieutenant Paul Saucedo of the El Paso Police Department approached me. With the usual gathering of investigators around me commenting about their cases at the close of my presentation, Paul waited diligently. He asked if I would be available to consult with his staff on what they had called the El Paso Desert Murders, a serial murder investigation with six prostitute victims and one prostitute who had escaped from that same killer. In 1989, I traveled to El Paso and was set up in a hotel with five archive boxes full of case materials. The consulting arrangement was simple. They would take any recommendations I could provide and pursue the leads until charges were filed.

I reached into the first box and pulled out a supplemental murder report on Ivy Williams. On March 14, 1988, the skeletonized remains of Ivy Susanna Williams were located in a shallow grave in the desert area 300 yards west of the 11000 block of Dyer in El Paso, TX. The remains were clothed and tentative identification was made through items found in the victim's wallet. The burial site was just southwest of and off the same dirt road and in the same three-quarter mile stretch of desert where murder victims Maria Casio, Karen Baker, Dawn Smith, Desiree Wheatley, and Angie Frausto were found buried during the previous year. The investigation revealed that no missing persons report was ever filed for Williams. All the desert area murder victims were between the ages of 14 and 28.

Information developed within the first 30 days revealed that the girl-friend of David L. Wood stated that he was introduced to Williams sometime in 1987. A fellow topless dancer also observed Wood pick Williams up from work on two occasions.

After reading the supplemental report, I pulled out a report titled "Suspects Developed in the Desert Death Investigations." The first suspect listed in the five-page document was David Leonard Wood. It read:

> He became a suspect in the desert death investigations during the investigation into the disappearance of Cheryl Vasquez Dismukes. He was last seen talking with Cheryl shortly before her disappearance. An active missing persons investigation involving Karen Baker led investigators to David Wood through descriptions given by witnesses that matched his vehicle (Nissan pickup truck and red Harley-Davidson motorcycle) and his physical description. David Wood was positively identified by witnesses in a physical line up as the person seen with Karen Baker on the night of her disappearance. When the bodies of Desiree Wheatley, Dawn Smith, and Ivy Williams were found, investigations into their deaths ultimately led back to David Wood. He was acquainted with the victims and in some cases was seen with the victims prior to their disappearances. In the cases where he was last seen with the victim, the bodies of the victims were found with the same clothing they were reported wearing at the time of their disappearance. Fiber evidence collected from the truck belonging to David Wood was sent to the lab for comparison with fiber evidence found at the grave sites of the victims. The DPS lab found no dissimilarities between the fibers collected in the truck and the fiber found in the grave of Desiree Wheatley. Although the investigation has failed to realize a source of the fibers, it is suspected to be a blanket disposed of by David Wood when he reported his motorcycle stolen, two days after the murder of Maria Casio.

At this point, I realized that not only did the police have the name of the killer within the first 30 days of each murder investigation, they investigated him. But their case against him was flimsy. The next report I read was the sexual assault complaint of Judith Brown, a crime for which Wood was in prison. The main evidence against Wood was Brown's identification of him. Her account of contact with Wood is quite telling for crime assessment purposes:

> I had left my apartment and walked over to the Circle K store on Dyer and Kemp streets. This was about 7 or 7:30 p.m. I came out of the store and as I started to walk by the street a small beige pickup truck stopped next to me. The truck had a brown strip across the bottom of it. There was a guy in the driver's seat and he asked me if I needed a ride somewhere. I then told the guy that I was going out toward Sunrise. The guy told me that he would give me a

ride so I got into the truck. This guy I describe him as being a white male, 25 to 30 years of age, 5'7" tall, slim build with a slouch, blondish shoulder length hair with a slight wave, wearing a black T-shirt with a Harley-Davidson emblem, blue jeans, dark colored baseball cap, walked with a limp, had a tattoo on one of his forearms. I don't remember the kind of tattoo. After I got in the truck, we headed down Dyer toward Titanic, and when we reached Titanic I told him to make a right turn, but he just kept going and he told me that he had to stop with a friend and that he would bring me back. We went past Titanic and to McCombs where we turned right. We went into some apartments on McCombs. I don't remember if they are the Trans Mountain Apartments or the Mt. Franklin Apartments. He drove on to the back of the apartments and then to the left and parked in the parking lot. The building where he got out of the truck and went in was to the northeast side of the complex. He told me to stay there and about five minutes or so he came back out, and this was when I noticed that he had a piece of plastic that looked like a rope. The plastic was in his right front pocket.

He got in the truck and as we were leaving the apartments, we made a right turn onto McCombs going toward Chapparal. This guy then told me that he had to make another stop because he had buried some coke (cocaine) out in the desert. I then told him that I didn't want to go out in the desert with him. He then told me that it would not take but a second and that it was by the side of the road. He then lit up a joint and made a right turn on to a dirt road. We drove on to Dyer and crossed over Dyer Street. We continued about a mile or so when we came upon a gate and stopped. He got off and tried to open the gate but he was unable. He even kicked the gate. He then turned around and walked back to the truck and made a U-turn. He even said, "This is the wrong fucking place." He started back down the same dirt road the same way we had come in. We crossed over Dyer and continued on where there was a dirt road. He made a left turn onto this dirt road and we continued on.

All during this time he became very watchful and kept looking around. He was very nervous and acted very paranoid. I then told him to just take me back. I then told him that I knew that he was up to something so I again told him to take me back to my apartment or let me out. He then told me, "No, I'm going to rape you." I then told him that I knew that he was up to no good so for him to please take me back. He just kept smiling and laughing. I then looked at him and told him that he would pay for this one (meaning that he would be caught). He continued down the dirt road and suddenly stopped and got off. He came back almost immediately and got in the truck and drove on down the dirt road. We came to another dirt road and made a left turn and continued on. We came to an area where there was a bush to the side of the road. He circled around the bush and stopped. He then reversed the truck into some bushes that were across the dirt road and parked the truck facing north. He got off and he asked me to get out. I didn't want to get out and he went around the passenger side and opened the door and pulled me out. I grabbed the back part of the bed of the truck and told him, "Come on, just take me back." He then grabbed me and pulled me to the front of the truck and told me to face north. I asked why and he told me "I don't want you to see where I buried this coke at." I saw him go to the bed and saw him looking for something. I then saw him get a shovel from the bed of the truck and started walking out (south) from the truck.

All during this time, I kept looking back to see what he was doing and he would yell at me to turn around. I saw him go behind some bushes and digging. He came back about 15 minutes later and threw the shovel in the back of the truck. I did notice that he was sweating. He then walked over to me and grabbed me by the shoulders and told me, "I told you not to turn around." He also told me, "You would not live to walk." He then grabbed me again and faced me north, and he walked to the back of the truck. He had some trash in the truck and I saw him taking out the trash and taking it behind the bushes where he had been digging. There was also a dark colored blanket that looked like he had something large and long wrapped in it. I saw him pick up the blanket in both arms and carried it behind the bushes. It looked like it was heavy because he had to get into the bed of the truck to take out the bundle.

After he took the bundle to the bushes, he came back and walked over to me and threw me to the ground. He then tried to tear off my blouse. He said, "Did you hear anything?" And I told him, "Yes, I hear some voices." He first told me to shut up and then he asked me if I heard some voices and this was when I told him that I did. He then told me "let's go," and he grabbed me and picked me up and threw me into the truck. He drove out the same way and out to the hard dirt road. He made a left turn on the hard road and continued across McCombs. He drove on and passed some water wells. He came up to a water tank and made a right turn and continued on. He came up to a fence where there is a dead end.

At the other side of the dead end is another steel water tank. At the water steel tank he made a left turn onto a dirt road and again another left turn. On this dirt road he drove a little ways and turned around and came back out the same way to the steel tank. From the steel tank he went out a little ways and turned left onto another dirt road. He continued on this dirt road until he came to a clearing and drove right up to the clearing. He then told me to get out. I got out and walked about ten feet. He then told me to get my fucking clothes off now. I stood there for a minute and he walked up to me and tore my sweatshirt off. After my sweatshirt was off I then decided to comply with his demands because I felt that he would hurt me or even kill me if I didn't do what he told me. I then got my pants off and my shoes off. After I had taken all of my clothing off he told me to lay down. He then grabbed me and forcefully laid me down. I was face up and he tried to have sex with me. During this time I was trying to fight him off. He then told me that he liked to fuck women when they were tied up. He then tied my hands in front of me and he also tied my legs onto some bushes that were that were near by. He then began to have sex with me and I continued to fight him. During this time, he kept asking me if I was 13 years old or 15 or 16 years old. He also told me that he liked young girls. He saw that I was still fighting him so he undid my hands and feet and turned me over on my face. He tied my hands behind me and again tied my legs to some bushes. He also put a bandana around my mouth. I was telling him that it was too tight and he was saying, "How tight is it baby?" He then started to have intercourse with me while I was facing down. His penis penetrated my vagina and after about five or ten minutes he jumped up and while he was pulling up his pants he said that he heard someone. I told him that I did not hear anything. He untied one of my legs and took the bandana out of my mouth and picked up all my clothing and got into the truck and left me there. Before he jumped into his truck he told me, "Just remember, you are free and walking free." I picked up a piece of cardboard and headed on out the dirt road and onto McCombs. The first truck that saw me, he picked me up and gave me a ride home (sworn statement of Judith Brown, 1987).

For purposes of crime assessment, there were three main recommendations that were given to El Paso police detectives. First of all, Judith Brown

was a living victim. I was concerned that the police had not used the information from Brown to aid their investigation into the desert murders.
Experience has shown that living victims from a series of crimes of one
killer provide crucial information regarding common scheme and plan, and,
certainly, this was another one. The first recommendation was to have
Brown point out the location she was taken in the desert by David
Wood. It appeared from Brown's account that Wood had every intention
of killing and burying her near where the other victims were discovered.
After the police were escorted by Brown to the area she was initially
taken, amazingly, it turned out that she was taken to the same place where
one of the other victims was found buried. This information would add
greatly to the probable cause against David Wood for the murders of six
women.

Secondly, Brown spent a great deal of time in Wood's pickup truck, and
he also had a great deal of contact with her clothing, allowing for the transfer of hairs and fibers from Woods' environment to his victims. The next
recommendation was for police investigators to search out all known
vehicles and places where Wood resided during the time of the murders.
The goal was to obtain standards or samples of all fibers from Wood's environment. Additionally, I noticed from the reports that detectives had not
compared evidence taken from one burial site to the next and had not
requested that fibers and hairs be compared to samples from David
Wood and his environment. Therefore, there was much more evidence that
could be connected to David Wood from each of the burial sites, and, it
eventually was.

Finally, David Wood did an excessive amount of talking to Judith Brown,
much in the fashion of a power assertive rapist or rape murderer would.
There was no reason to believe that Wood would not have confessed or
bragged to fellow inmates about what he had done and why he was in
prison. So the last major recommendation was for detectives to interview
cellmates of David Wood to determine if Wood had confessed to them.
Wood did not disappoint detectives. He bragged to one of his cellmates and
that evidence was used against him.

SUMMARY

Even though some types of consultants have been useful in understanding some aspects of serial murder investigations, the most valuable is the
consulting detective. But there is one caution about those who speculate
about cases that comes from the insightful Sherlock Holmes and should be
the credo of all experts from any walk of life: "It is a capital mistake to
theorize before you have all the evidence. It biases the judgment" (Doyle,
1887).

REFERENCES

Brown, L. Letter addressed to Sheriff Bernard Winckoski, 1981.

Doyle, Sir Arthur Conan, *A Study in Scarlett*, 1981. New York: Penguin Books.

Keppel, R. D. Serial Murder: Future Implications for Police Investigations, Authorlink. com, 1989.

Keppel, R. D., and Birnes, W. J. *The Riverman: Ted Bundy and I Hunt the Green River Killer*, 1995. New York: Pocket Books. Sworn statement of Judith Brown Case No. 04–371057, El Paso Police Department, 1987.

Williams v. State, 251 Ga. 749, 312 S. E. 2d 40, 1983.

5

THE PAUL BERNARDO CASE

In the similar cases I'm looking at examples of task force breakdown, the second one is the Paul Bernardo case, which dragged on for about five years even though the Canadian authorities had the name of the killer in their files. They also had the killer's DNA, and there were living witnesses who had been raped by Bernardo who had given descriptions of the suspect to the police. The breakdown of the task force system in the Bernardo case, like the breakdown of the task force system in the Yorkshire Ripper case, was so extensive, that it prompted an official review of the investigation to find out what went wrong and what could be done about it (Campbell and Archie, 1996).

The best and clearest description of the problem is set forth in the introduction to the 1996 Bernardo case report itself which says:

> Between May 1987 and December 1992, Paul Bernardo raped or sexually assaulted at least 18 women in Scarborough, Peel, and St. Catharine's and killed three women in St. Catharine's and Burlington.
>
> Paul Bernardo is a unique type of criminal, a determined, organized, mobile, sadistic serial rapist and killer who demonstrates the ability of such predators to strike in any Ontario community. The tragic history of this case, and similar

cases from other countries, shows that these predators pose a unique challenge to the systemic investigative capacity of local law-enforcement agencies throughout North America and Europe. The Bernardo case proves that Ontario is no exception.

The Bernardo case, like every similar investigation had its share of human error. But this is not a story of human error or lack of dedication or investigative skill. It is a story of systemic failure.

It is easy, knowing now that Bernardo was the rapist and the killer, to ask why he was not identified earlier for what he was. But the same question and the same problems have arisen in so many other similar tragedies in other countries.

Virtually every interjurisdictional serial killer case, including Sutcliffe (The Yorkshire Ripper) and Black (the cross-border child killer) in England, Ted Bundy and the Green River Killer in the United States, and Clifford Olsen in Canada, demonstrate the same problems and raise the same questions. And always the answer turns out to be the same—systemic failure. Always the problems turn out to be the same, the mistakes the same, and the systemic failures the same.

The answer to the problem, the report explains, is not simply better motivation of the troops in the field or more accountability on the part of those handling the information. When there is a systemic failure in an investigation that so impedes the ability of the police to find the offender that they are at a loss to explain why, they impart to the offender unique powers of invisibility or camouflage and they blame their own skills as a reason for their failure. In short, when systems fail, the collective psychological reaction on the part of task force members is that the killer grows in his ability to elude detection and the police are diminished in their abilities to find him. The report quotes one Metro investigator, in 1992, as saying: "The boy is better than we might give him credit for, or he's fallen through the cracks." Either way, the killer has defeated the police who are on his trail.

But, as the Bernardo report suggests, the Metro officer was correct. Bernardo had indeed fallen through the cracks, but the cracks were of the task force's own making because of "the inability of the different law-enforcement agencies to pool their information and cooperate effectively." This is also what happened in Atlanta during the Atlanta child murders, and I had seen it with my own eyes.

THE SCARBOROUGH RAPES

According to the official history of the case set forth in the 1996 Bernardo case report, between May 4, 1987, and May 26, 1990, "a violent sadistic predator sexually assaulted 14 young women in Scarborough and 1 in Missigauga. The victims were in their teens or early twenties and were returning home at night, often between a bus stop and their home." The predator was violent and quick. His modus operandi (MO) included:

stalking, then attacking from behind, dragging the victim into a driveway or bushes, punching and beating, raping anally and vaginally, taking trophies such as jewelry or an article from the victim's purse, sometimes personal identification. Some of the rapes were accompanied by death threats, oral intercourse, tightening a ligature or electrical cord around the victim's neck, digital penetration, biting, threat of further violence, gagging, cutting clothes and underwear with a knife, smashing the victim's head on the ground, forcing the victim to say she loved the attacker, forcing the victim to utter words of self-deprecation, threatening to return later to the victim's house and rape and kill her, and cutting the victim with a knife.

Most of these are displays of what I call "signature behavior" and portend that the offender is already on an arc or continuum of violence in which he experiments with behaviors that drive his sexual desire or rage. He changes his MO as it becomes necessary, either to throw the police off the track or to find new ways to satisfy himself. Signature analysis is a vital way to determine where the offender's crimes are going, as we'll see below, and to predict what the offender might be capable of. In this instance, the Scarborough rapist, a good signature analysis of what the unknown rapist was doing to his victims might have led investigators to link up the later murders with the earlier rapes on the basis of the perpetrator's signature behavior (Keppel and Birnes, 1997).

However, Police Superintendent Joe Wolfe, who later became head of the task force, did understand from the second rape onward that a link was apparent in all the rapes, and that the police were dealing with a serial rapist. Unfortunately for the police, because there was no case management system in place, their investigations resulted in an overflow of about one thousand possible suspects, some of whom may have actually committed sexual offenses not in this series. But tracking their stories and following up on evidence was often an exercise in redundancy and tied up more police resources than possibly were required.

Bernardo's name first emerged as a suspect after the fifth Scarborough rape, having been tipped off by a family friend of a police sergeant at Toronto Island. The informant said that she was having troubles with Bernardo, who'd borrowed money from her and was giving her trouble about repayment. The friend thought the sergeant could help her.

The sergeant interviewed Bernardo and realized that from his behavior, he could well be a candidate for investigation in the Scarborough rape cases. In his report, the police sergeant described Bernardo as "manipulative and aggressive." During his relationship with the informant, "his behavior progressed from gesturing to slap her in a joking manner to threatening to do so, to giving her light taps, which became harder and harder." Then the threats and violence became menacing. "On at least one occasion in November," the report continues. "when they were in his car, he wanted her to have sex with him. He pulled out the knife and wanted to have an orgasm while he held it to her throat. She states she did not have sex with him in this way."

That same month, the informant went out with Bernardo again, and this time, in an incident similar to the statement made by a prostitute in the Green River case that tipped off police to the suspect, the informant described in detail an evening where she feared for her life at the hands of Paul Bernardo.

> In late November," the witness statement continues, "the two were out for the evening and on the way home, he drove to an isolated factory area. He had been smacking her and yelling at her. They had an argument, and Ms. [F] wanted to leave the car, but he wouldn't let her. He worked himself into a frenzy and was looking for the knife, but didn't find it. At one point, he started saying: "Why do I do this, why?" She got out of the car and hid from him. He spent some time looking for her, making promises and threats. She wandered until she found the home of a friend. This was the last time she saw the man. (Prior to the final escape, she had gotten away once. He had caught her, punched her, kicked her, and rolled her in the mud bringing her back to the car).

The sergeant's report, according to the Bernardo case report, showed that Bernardo had lived in Scarborough and was "a violent, knife-wielding, sexual sadist with a pattern of frenzied sexual assaults." It seemed important to the sergeant and just as obvious that the man should be investigated as a suspect in the Scarborough rapes. The sergeant submitted the three-page report on January 22, 1988. However, there was no record of any contact between the Scarborough investigation and the police sergeant. In fact, from the time the sergeant submitted his report until Bernardo was identified as the Scarborough rapist five years later, there was no attempt to get in touch with the sergeant or with his informant. The informant, like Carol Da Ronch in the Bundy investigation and like Rebecca Guarde-Day and Dawn White in the Green River investigations, was a living witness of an assailant. The investigation of this witness might have short-circuited his criminal career.

Bernardo was tipped off at least two more times over a period of the next couple of years. One informant was so persistent she eventually showed up at the Sexual Assault Squad office for an interview and told detectives that Bernardo not only fit the composite description that had appeared in the papers, but displayed violent sexual tendencies, carried a knife in his car, talked about picking up girls and raping them, and had actually confessed to getting a young girl to pass out, whereupon he took her up to his room and raped her. The informant also said that Bernardo was relocating to St. Catharine's. It should have been a trigger because it linked two sets of crime series.

Ultimately, in 1990, the two detectives who had interviewed this informant found the sergeant's report on Bernardo in the files. Although neither the sergeant nor the family friend who had contacted him were interviewed, the two detectives did make an appointment to interview Paul Bernardo and recovered hair, saliva, and blood samples from him. Their instincts were correct, and they classified him as a possible viable suspect who was not in the highest category of suspects to be investigated.

One can argue why there was no urgency to the Bernardo contact. Perhaps, as the case report suggests, the fact that the rapes had stopped in May 1990, and Bernardo had not been contacted until seven months later, seemed to have taken the pressure off. The task force was winding down its work, was no longer a unit dedicated to the Scarborough rapist, and was going back to what the report called "business as usual."

In my own experience, we've seen that even though an offender ceases operations in one area, he often does not stop the serial sexual predatory behavior that necessitated the task force in the first place. In fact, when one looks at the Bernardo continuum of violence, it's easy to see that in a new area with new victims and a police precinct not already inured to the crimes taking place, he could start another series in the expectation that he would not be caught. In Florida, there was a similar pattern of crimes involving Bobby Joe Long who had committed a series of rapes in North Tampa as "The Classified Ad Rapist," and then went on to commit a series of sexual homicides in another Florida community. Such would be the case with Paul Bernardo. As far as the task force was concerned, when he stopped committing rapes and sexual assaults in Scarborough and started committing sexual crimes in St. Catharine's—stalking, raping, and killing—it was as if he'd moved to another country to begin a new career. That was how separated in time and place the different investigations were.

Because there was no centralized database repository for violent sexual offenses, the commonalities defining Bernardo's crimes or the cessation of sex crimes in one community and the start up in another community had no significance because they did not alert any of the responsible police agencies. It was almost with a sense of relief, the Bernardo Investigation Review notes, that the authorities in Scarborough became aware that there were no new reports of rapes in this series, which allowed them to move the case to a back burner. For the authorities in St. Catharine's, the cases had just begun.

THE MURDER OF TAMMY HOMOLKA

The St. Catharine's murders began after the murder of Tammy Homolka, the intended victim of a joint rape by her elder sister, Karla, and Karla's lover Paul Bernardo. The police noted that Tammy, a virgin, was supposed to be a "Christmas present" from Karla to Paul, to satisfy what he claimed was his lust for virgins and to reinvigorate their relationship. From what the police ascertained years later after they interviewed Karla, the last thing on

Karla Homolka's mind was the murder of her own sister. However, as a result of the sedative and anesthetic administered to the victim to render her unconscious, Tammy, who had eaten just prior to being anesthetized, vomited the contents of her stomach, aspirated the vomit, and choked to death.

The police who investigated had no way of knowing at first that Tammy was a victim of a premeditated rape, the evidence of which was on video-tape and hidden by Bernardo and Karla Homolka. They had no way of knowing that while Tammy was sedated with drinks heavily laced with Halcion, her own elder sister covered her face with a cloth soaked with Halothane and then took turns performing sex acts on her body with her boyfriend Paul Bernardo. Tammy was so completely anesthetized that she didn't even stir during the sexual activity until she began to retch from vomitus and then choked as she reflexively gasped for air. Her breathing stopped and nothing Bernardo or her older sister could do, not artificial respiration or any chest compressions, could start it again. They dressed her naked body and moved it to the bedroom, dumped the remaining Halothane down the toilet and hid the bottle, removed the video tape from the camera and hid it as well, and called 911 to report that the young Tammy Homolka had vomited in her sleep and stopped breathing. It was the early morning of Christmas Eve, 1990.

Over the course of the ensuing months, as the skein of abduction rape/murders began in St. Catharine's, the police had no way of knowing that the Tammy Homolka death they'd investigated and ruled as "natural causes" was at all suspicious. They were unaware of the existence of the videotape, which would have inculpated Bernardo and Karla Homolka. They had not found the bottle of Halothane and couldn't explain the reasons behind the strange burn mark on Homolka's face. But because Tammy's death was listed as natural causes rather than "unexplained," the police had no reason to suspect Bernardo, even after his name had turned up in connection with the Scarborough rapes.

THE ST. CATHARINE'S SEXUAL ASSAULT SERIES

About four months after he killed Tammy Homolka, Paul Bernardo raped a 14-year-old girl walking south from her home in Port Dalhousie to rowing practice on Henley Island. Bernardo stalked her at first, following her about 20 feet. Once she noticed she was being followed, she quickened her pace. But her stalker was too fast, and before she was able to walk away, he grabbed her from behind, put his hands over her nose and mouth, told her to not to make a sound, and dragged her across the street, through a ditch, and into a thicket of woods where he sexually assaulted her for over half an hour. This was a violent attack, which the victim described in such complete detail that a later investigator who read it in a report said that he had no doubt the culprit was the Scarborough rapist.

The Henley Island attack was the first after the murder of Tammy Homolka and began a series of stalkings, rapes, and two murders. Particularly gruesome was the murder of Leslie Mahaffy who was abducted from outside her home at knifepoint in June 1991, by Bernardo who brought her back to his place where, while Karla was still asleep, raped her. Then when Karla awoke, Bernardo ordered her to make love to Leslie while he videotaped the entire sequence. Paul killed his victim shortly thereafter, cut her into parts which he embedded in concrete, and then dumped them in Lake Gibson where they were discovered by a man and his wife canoeing on the lake on June 29, 1991.

Paul's subsequent murder of Kristen French, which took place almost a year later in April 1992, began with her abduction by Paul and Karla at knifepoint when she was walking home. The witnesses to this abduction told police that the car, a Chevy Camaro, had been in the Grace Church parking lot shortly before the abduction and was driven by a woman who, apparently, had stopped Kristen to ask for directions. What police later learned was that Paul got out of the car and forced Kristen inside. The couple took her to their home on Bayview Drive where they sexually assaulted her and then Bernardo strangled her to death.

Bernardo drove Kristen French's body 2 km from the lake where he had dumped Leslie, but across a jurisdictional line so that the crime report would go through a different police agency. Later, during a confession, Karla Homolka explained to the police,

> And Paul wanted her to be dumped in Burlington because he said that he wanted to confuse the cops, like then they wouldn't know if the guy was from Burlington or from St. Catharine's. So he picked the spot. Later on, he also said that he wanted that spot because, "it was so close to where Leslie was buried and close to her house.

Bernardo was aware, therefore, the police surmised, that jurisdictional boundaries would somehow impede the police investigation because police don't cross boundaries when investigating homicides. This, the Canadian police inspectors said, was an "eerie echo" from the Ted Bundy case where in the official commentary it read: "Jurisdictional boundaries and the inability of law enforcement agencies to communicate with each other allows transient killers to avoid identification and capture." (Campbell, 1996).

That was the situation in 1975 when I was managing the Ted Task Force in King County and was also the situation to a large degree in Atlanta in 1978 during the Atlanta child murders investigation. To a similar extent, it was also the situation as late as the 1990s in Bellevue, WA, during the George Russell murders. However, over the course of the Bundy investigation we set up a task force of Northwest police agencies and later in Atlanta the De Kalb County Sheriff, the Georgia Bureau of Investigation, the FBI, and the Atlanta Police managed to work together despite any jurisdictional disputes. American police agencies tend to communicate more with each other rather than less.

Of particular note were the comments made by the sheriff of Orange County, CA, after a four-day ad hoc task force comprised of local and state agencies and the FBI searched for the missing 5-year-old Samantha Runnion. When the Riverside Sheriff's Department found the young child's body in a desolate rural area of the national forest, they called Orange County homicide investigators to the crime scene and allowed them to work the crime, something, Orange County Sheriff Carano said, was not the usual practice among law-enforcement agencies who sometimes jealously guard the integrity of their crime scenes.

By 1992 it had become an understanding among police agencies both in the United States and in Canada that serial sexual offenders don't necessarily confine themselves to a single jurisdiction and will sometimes cross jurisdictional lines specifically to throw off police who are on their trail. So, Bernardo's attempt to confuse the local police fell flat. When a Halton homicide detective made the discovery of Kristen French's body, he called his counterpart in the Niagra Region, and the two investigators, standing at the body site, immediately agreed that the French case should be turned over to the Green Ribbon Task Force investigating the string of rapes, murders, and stalkings in the adjoining regions.

THE INVESTIGATION OF PAUL BERNARDO: TIME AND WEIGHT OF EVIDENCE

Many times during the course of a serial homicide task force investigation, the statement of a witness or a tip that might have started years earlier finally works its way to the right person bringing together different strands of evidence leading to the naming of a suspect. It happened just that way in the Green River case when one of the living victims finally told investigators what happened to her when the suspect tried to strangle her ten years before he was finally arrested. And it happened just that way in the Scarborough rapist investigation before police realized that Bernardo was responsible for the murders in St. Catharine's.

For the over two years that Bernardo was raping women in Scarborough, his MO remained consistent. He would sneak up on a victim from behind as she got off a bus, fondle the victims sexually, and talk to them the entire time. He wanted them to talk back to him as well, as evidence of their submission. The attacks occurred within a narrow radius of a specific neighborhood, and the police had a composite description from the victims, which looked almost exactly like Paul Bernardo. But the picture was not distributed, so witnesses or friends of Bernardo never knew that the police had his likeness until years later.

Even after one of Paul Bernardo's old girlfriends had complained to the police repeatedly about how he had physically and sexually abused her, the police did not seem to pick up on it. However, in 1990, three years after the majority of the Scarborough rapes had occurred, the police decided to make their composite sketch of the unknown offender public. Suddenly the police were showered with tips, many of them from Paul's old acquaintances who recognized him immediately from the police photo. Still, the police did not follow up.

Detective Steve Irwin, however, convinced that the rapist would be readily identifiable if he could only start interviewing suspects, pulled together all of the physical evidence the police had collected and put it under one forensic specialist, Kim Johnston. It was determined that all of the blood-type factors put the suspect in a group of 12.8% of the population. At the same time, Irwin was now seeing Bernardo's name turn up among the tips and leads from people who said they recognized his photo. So Irwin interviewed Bernardo, and although he did not suspect him right away, nevertheless collected blood, saliva, and hair samples and turned them over to Kim Johnston. Johnston's analysis showed that from among the 230 other suspects she had analyzed, Bernardo's blood factors were among the 5 people who fit the biological profile of the attacker based on blood evidence. Even though Bernardo was asked to resubmit samples for additional testing, the rapes had stopped and the case no longer had the urgency it had two years earlier.

Bernardo's name arose in the St. Catharine's investigation as a result of a tip they'd received after the Kristen French murder. The police were looking for owners of Camaros because a witness had told them that she'd seen the victim talking to someone in a Camaro right before she disappeared. But when the police interviewed Bernardo, they noticed that he owned a different type of car and were impressed by the way he lived. He didn't, on the surface, look like a murder suspect, particularly in the investigation of the dismemberment of Leslie Mahaffy. Paul admitted to them that he had been interviewed by the police in Scarborough about the series of rapes there because he looked like the composite. Perhaps he thought the police would find that out anyway so it was a good idea to come clean. In that respect his behavior was much like Sutcliffe's who told police during subsequent interviews that he, too, had been interviewed earlier by police in Yorkshire in connection with the Ripper murders.

Green Ribbon Task Force detectives contacted Detective Steve Irwin to follow up on Bernardo, who told them that the final testing on Bernardo's blood samples had not been completed. Bernardo had not been eliminated from the investigation, but the nature of the conversation was that he wasn't really considered one of the top suspects on the list, at least not yet. Nor did Detective Irwin send the Green Ribbon detectives any of the interview notes regarding the assault complaint of Bernardo's girlfriend. It would be almost a year later, in 1993, when the final testing was completed and Bernardo's name came up as the prime suspect in the Scarborough rapes.

By the time that happened, however, Bernardo's wife, Karla Homolka, had had enough. For years, she had endured abuse from Paul and been forced to submit to humiliating sexual activities. She had been his accomplice in killing her younger sister and had lured Kristen French to her death. But finally Karla's parents convinced their daughter to leave Paul and live with her other sister whose husband was a Toronto police officer. By the time Paul had become the prime suspect in the Scarborough rapes and was now being looked at in the St. Catharine's murders, the police were also interested in Karla Homolka.

In exchange for a light sentence and doing her time at a psychiatric ward, Karla pled guilty to being Paul's accomplice in homicides and, in turn, was a witness against him. Of course the videotapes Paul made of his murders and the scrupulous journal he kept of his crimes were devastating evidence against him in court, but prosecutors also knew that they would not have made their case against him had it not been for his wife's testimony.

THE BERNARDO INVESTIGATION REVIEW

In June 1996, 3 years after the Bernardo case was solved, Mr. Justice Archie Campbell transmitted his report on the case investigation to Canada's Solicitor General. In his report Justice Campbell (1996) evaluated the procedures used by the Toronto and Ontario police in solving the Scarborough rapes and St. Catharine's murders. The review covered not only the specific police procedures used by the different jurisdictions to investigate the crimes, but the way the police marshaled the data to follow up on the investigations and keep the process moving forward. Of particular note to Justice Campbell was the drop off in urgency to solve the rapes after the rapes themselves stopped. The suspect had moved to the St. Catharine's area and was committing crimes in a different jurisdiction, crimes that the original Scarborough rapes investigators did not necessarily know about. As a result, even though Bernardo's blood work and forensics were at the police lab and Bernardo was among the top five suspects, the final tests on his biological samples wouldn't take place for almost a year.

It seemed to Justice Campbell that police seemed to be working at cross-purposes at times. The investigation was marked by rivalry among different departments, an inability to recognize links between cases (linkage blindness), and an inability to coordinate information sharing and even management decisions among different agencies. At the top of Justice Campbell's list of criticisms and recommendations was that the departments lacked and needed to implement a major case management system for the investigation of serial predators. Not only would such a system help ease the frustration of a seemingly unsolvable serial sexual offender stalking women in the community, it would promote cooperation across jurisdictions and among agencies, provide specialized training for senior management and senior investigators as well as establish liaison protocols for officers dealing across jurisdictional lines, coordinate forensic analyses among the different jurisdictions, and unify management. Most importantly for both the police and the victims' perspectives, a major case management system allows police agencies an early recognition of linked offenses.

Justice Campbell's review and recommendations addressed what American police departments across the country and the FBI realized in the time after the Ted Bundy investigation. They realized that sociopathic control-type serial sexual predators—Bundy-type predators—are different kinds of offenders who, though not likely to be found legally insane by a court or even of a diminished capacity, are nevertheless driven by a psychology that can easily defeat short-term law-enforcement efforts to apprehend them. These killers are pathologically narcissistic, at the extreme end of the scale, and see their victims only as extensions of their own sexual gratification requirements. As such, they are in it for the long haul, deriving follow-up sexual pleasure from all aspects of the control over the victim, including from the police investigation itself. They are self-sustaining, and, as we have seen, can remain out on the street for years or even decades. That's why the short-term, bottom-line solutions of a serial killer task force are unrealistically naïve when stacked up against the type of predator they're trying to stop.

Worse, the longer the investigating agency or agencies take to recognize the nature of the Bundy-type predator and establish the kind of case management system necessary to amalgamate and integrate all of the data such a series of cases will likely generate, the longer the predator will be able to extend his series. Ultimately, as the Bernardo case shows and as we will see later, key clues and tips will float to the surface of such an investigation, catch the eye of one or more investigators, and result in someone taking the initiative to assemble the evidence that will lead to a prime suspect. However, if the agency itself has established a case management system, that event—the amalgamation of critical data to identify a prime suspect—will happen sooner rather than later, sometimes right after the first two linked events.

As the Bernardo case, the Green River case, and the George Russell case in 1990 revealed (Keppel and Birnes, 1995), police can spend so much time chasing the "flavor-of-the-month" suspect because of command pressure or media pressure that evidence linking the real suspect to the crimes can lie just under the surface in an otherwise fallow field for months or even years. The inescapable logic of Justice Campbell's review is best expressed in a quote attributed to former U.S. Secretary of State James Baker: "Proper preparation prevents poor performance."

In this instance, a methodology of codifying, logging, storing, and retrieving case information data, particularly as it relates to potential suspects and leads, is not only the most efficient and productive way to manage a complex investigation, it also generates a sense of confidence among officers at all levels that data garnered from the field won't be lost. As field investigators from the Yorkshire Ripper investigation complained, because they had a loss of confidence and a sense of frustration over the totality of the information that was irretrievable from the files, they became less than thorough on their own follow-throughs and as a result, valuable information was never checked and information was never brought back from the field.

In addition to an across-the-board case management system for all of the agencies involved in the Bernardo case, Justice Campbell also recommended a much speedier turnaround time for DNA testing and other biological forensics. The fact that it took almost a year for a potential suspect who had made it to the top five suspects in the Scarborough rapes to have been confirmed as the rapist when the lab had the confirming information all the time is less than acceptable. In Archie Campbell's own words, had the laboratory been quicker to identify the DNA retrieved from Paul Bernardo and execute search warrants on his home, the lives of two murder victims might have been saved and a series of sexual assaults in St. Catharine's might have been cut short if not completely prevented.

The Bernardo case review was also unhappy with the length of time it took one of Bernardo's victims to have her complaints taken seriously by the police. From my own experience, victims' complaints should be taken seriously because they are actually the reports of living victims. In the Ted Bundy case, it was Carol Da Ronch's complaint against Bundy in Utah that pushed the investigation into his activities to the point where he was taken out of circulation by the attempted kidnapping charges filed against him. Bundy had already been brought to the attention of Utah authorities after the traffic stop and the discovery of burglary implements in his car. When Utah law enforcement searched Bundy's car, despite his having thoroughly steamcleaned and vacuumed the interior, they still managed to find a strand of hair from Melissa Smith that eventually led to murder charges against him. In Green River, the complaints and information retrieved from Dawn White and Rebecca Garde-Day encouraged police to keep their suspect under scrutiny, even though the evidence against him was only circumstantial until the DNA hit.

Mr. Justice Campbell recommended a continuing contact between the investigator and the victim. He also recommended recognition that if police don't understand that the investigation itself and their attitudes toward sexual assault victims can result in what criminologists call "revictimization," victims will be reluctant witnesses, if they are witnesses at all. Part of this ongoing contact with victims also helps them remember details they might have overlooked in the wake of the immediate trauma of the assault. It's important as well to remember that living victims become witnesses in court and that after the offender is arrested—which ultimately will happen—the testimony of witnesses is vital to help the prosecution.

Finally, the case review suggests that the very presence of a case management system almost automatically redefines the concept of coordinated law-enforcement agency operations when a serial predator strikes. The predator doesn't even have to cross jurisdictional lines to commit crimes for a serial predator alert system to go into operation, because the very nature of such a coordinated operation is to confine a predator within the borders of surveillance.

Just such an alert system operates in California. Called the "Amber Alert," the system triggers law-enforcement agencies across the state whenever it's suspected that a child abduction has taken place and the suspect may be fleeing with his victim. It was recently triggered by the abductions of Tamera Brooks and Jaqueline Marris from a "lover's lane" area of rural Los Angeles County by career criminal Roy Ratliff who was later shot and killed by Kern County Sheriff's deputies who were returning fire. The alert system flashed the suspect's vehicle description and license plate numbers on electric signs across California freeways and alerted law-enforcement agencies across the state. The suspect's white Bronco was spotted by a Kern County animal control officer in a dry river bed.

This spot was where the two teenage victims told police and news correspondents they believed Ratliff would kill them. While Ratliff nodded off to sleep, Jacqueline Marris reached for a Bowie knife near the gear shift while Tamera Brooks picked up a liquor bottle from the back seat. Jacqueline stabbed Ratliff in the throat while Tamera smashed him across the face with the whiskey bottle. Stunned, he made his way outside of the car and threatened the girls until they let him back in. But the police had been notified and were on their way. The alert system had worked. As police helicopters and fixed-wing aircraft made it to the spot in minutes, Ratliff pointed his gun at the girls and prepared to shoot. That's when sheriff's deputies on foot confronted him, apprehended him, and, after he pointed the gun at police, shot and killed him.

The alert system itself forced different agencies across jurisdictional lines to work together to catch up with a fleeing suspect before he had a chance to kill his two teenage victims. In a similar way, Archie Campbell's suggestion is that a permanent case-management system would ultimately forge the same kinds of relationships between departments across jurisdictional lines. Such a system, he wrote:

> transcends any localized mindset, discourages tunnel vision, recognizes that the capture of a serial predator involves a provincial public interest wider than the interest of any single community or police force, and encourages unified investigations with clearly defined leader and accountability." In place early enough to "recognize links between crimes," the system allows agencies to "pool information and converge the separate investigations onto the same target.

In other words, Justice Campbell suggests, the mere existence of such a system provides a backstop for the different agencies and protects them from their own worst defensive tendencies when it comes to sharing case information across jurisdictional lines.

Although the Bernardo case was frustrating to detectives and took longer to resolve than it should have, it nevertheless resulted in the kind of comprehensive case review that, through evaluating the shortcomings of the police procedures, resulted in an understanding of the key areas of serial predator task force success. It established the principles of early recognition that the patterns of the offender pointed to a serial predator, it suggested that once the agencies acknowledged that possibility they should also acknowledge the necessity of cross-jurisdictional coordination and cooperation, and it pointed out the obvious necessity of a joint hierarchical command structure that would centralize investigative functions without duplicative procedures that would result in lost data. In so doing, such a command structure and major case management system would alleviate the frustration of working in the dark and the desperation of police officers who can never seem to make headway against a killer who always remains just a few steps ahead.

Bernardo, for example, was so confident that the police would be unable to find him, or be able to incriminate him even if they did, that his psychological need to hang on to the video evidence that would ultimately inculpate him in the crimes was allowed to control his preternatural fear of discovery and self protection. Bernardo's extreme and pathological narcissism trumped his self-preservation and his fear of discovery. The videos that fed his sexual gratification were more important than his fear that they would eventually become evidence against him. Thus, his narcissism and need for self-gratification was ultimately his undoing.

For the police, even though they may not appreciate the narcissistic drives of the killer, the psychology driving their investigation needs to feed on the confidence the police have in the way the case is being managed from the top down. This will allow them to dig in and follow logical directions that will lead them to the suspect instead of reacting to the desperation of senior managers who have to show progress even at the cost of the investigation itself. Justice Archie Campbell's review explains those procedures.

REFERENCES

Campbell, A. (1995). The Bernardo Report.

Keppel, R., and Birnes, W. (1995). *The Riverman: Ted Bundy and I Hunt for the Green River Killer*, New York, Pocket Books.

Keppel, R., and Birnes, W. (1997). *Signiture Killers*, New York, Pocket Books.

6

PROFILING THE
SERIAL KILLER: THE
EFFICACY OF PROFILING

Homicidal Pattern
Suspect Profile
Case Examples
Summary and Discussion
References

This chapter is about profiling: the magic, the myth, and the reality and how profiling relates to the core of the serial killer task-force investigation. Profiling can be central to a task force's ability to understand the nature of the offender they're looking for. Unfortunately, profiling can usually be a disaster leading investigators down wrong trails and prolonging the investigation. Meanwhile the killer, either knowing for sure or by instinct that the police have incorrectly profiled him, throws monkey wrenches into the task force investigation by changing his modus operandi (MO) for no other reason than to trick the police. He becomes the fox doubling back on the hounds because he knows where the hounds are.

Profiling can be central because in a serial killer task force investigation, especially one that's very quickly overwhelmed by information and that's very public and heavily covered by the press the public can place too much emphasis on it. For example, as in the DC sniper case, the frustration built up very rapidly as killings kept taking place before the very eyes of the police and none of the traditional methods—heavy surveillance, immediate crime scene response, intense canvassing of neighborhoods to find witnesses—seemed to yield the results to find the killer. As the frustration level builds among the rank and file detectives on whose backs the investigation rests and those at the top of the chain of command report to their civilian bosses that "today was just another day" have to go back to their offices with new deadlines and demands for a speedy resolution, the task force itself feels it. And when the media is out to show that it can solve the case before the task force can, because everybody's a Sherlock Holmes at heart, confidence erodes in the task force mission itself.

Then someone announces that the official profile has arrived and suddenly personnel believe in the power of the profile. Somehow someone's pulling together a bunch of facts to come up with a prediction about the killer that will solve the unsolvable case. It's all part of the mystique of the profiler, as if he is Pharaoh's prophet. But when the profile doesn't help and the killer keeps on killing and victims turn up who don't fit the victim profile or who were killed according to a different MO, those in command managing the investigation also begin to lose confidence in their own instincts. Their honest, street-trained instincts have been hijacked by the profile. At that point, confidence can collapse completely until the offender himself decides to change the rules of the game. This is how the perceived magic of the profile can actually destroy the gains made in an investigation and why profiling is central to the study of the psychology of serial task force murder investigations.

THE MYTH AND REALITY OF PROFILING

In almost every task force investigation of an unknown sexual serial predator, at some point, the police will decide to profile the killer to figure out just who they're after and what his proclivities are. However, when the motivation for a murder is unknown and the identity of the killer has not been established, it is hard to explain the critical questions of who, what, when, where, why, and how. Without such information, there's nothing the police can do to catch the killer. Accordingly, the public is left with the uneasy feeling that a killer's on the loose and another murder is possibly forthcoming. In an extreme case, like the DC Beltway sniper shootings, the public was near panic that the police, despite all the profiling that was turning up on television from so-called experts, were unable to stop the shootings.

But profiling, at least the way it's done on television, doesn't solve any crimes and can even make matters worse when the killer hears a profile that's off the mark. Hearing this he keeps on killing and maybe even raises the stakes for the police. And the public, having been told that the police now have a profile, calms itself with the false assurance that an arrest is just around the corner. But the only thing around the corner is the next murder. And the police keep refining the profile.

This lack of knowledge has created a forensic investigative dilemma since the beginning of police inquiries. When this dilemma is the primary stumbling block to the work of a serial killer task force, as we have seen in the Yorkshire Ripper and Paul Bernardo investigations and possibly with the combined DC Beltway sniper task force, even though there is recognition and acknowledgment of the presence of a serial killer, the task force still can suffer from a pervasive sense of collective defeat, because key questions about the case have not been answered. Therefore, even before a series is established, if the psychological calling cards the killer leaves at the crime scene can be evaluated, it's critical to investigators to work up an understanding of the psychological patterns of the offender's crime.

Past efforts to address unsolved murders by developing theories of investigations have not been empirically studied (Keppel and Weis, 1994). Researchers and investigative practitioners with limited experience at investigating violent crimes have attempted to analyze murder and the people who commit it by constructing self-styled categories of killers that were hypothetical inferences developed from some individual case studies of convicted murderers. In their Crime Classification Manual, John Douglas, A. W. Burgess, A. C. Burgess, and Robert Ressler (1992) discussed a wide range of information focused on concept identification. The killers were categorized into groups in which one expected outcome became the single and significant identifier. For example, a lust killing is described as a sexually oriented killing. Similarly, a murder arising from a business dispute was called a power or greed killing.

Unfortunately, although their typologies of murderers have descriptive value, they have consistently failed to provide investigators with the elements necessary for crime scene assessment. For example, greed may have been the original motivation for killing an elderly woman and classified as such. This type of characteristic does not explain the motivation if the woman was also severely beaten, stabbed, and placed into a sexually degrading and posed position. Although general indicators may apply to a broad variety of circumstances and possible categories, the static descriptors of these types of classification systems only address the obvious; they do not address the hidden and inferred behavior of the killer. In addition, other authorities, such as Holmes and Holmes (1996), cited typologies of serial murderers that were labeled "visionary, mission, hedonistic, and power/control." These categories have a wide range of function, are of limited service to investigative work, and are unsupported by empirical study (Keppel and Walter, 1999).

Very few police investigators use the typologies in the Crime Classification Manual (Douglas et al., 1992) or those developed by Holmes and Holmes (1996) to generalize about a population of murderers. In fact, the major homicide tracking systems such as the FBI's Violent Criminal Apprehension Program (VICAP); the Homicide Investigation Tracking System (HITS) in Washington, Oregon, and Idaho; and the Royal Canadian Mounted Police's (RCMP) Violent Crime Linkage Analysis System (VICLAS), which are centralized databases for homicide information, do not use either typology to classify murderers (HITS form, 1995; Johnson, 1994; VICAP Form, 1991), because the characteristics of killers and crime scenes by the Crime Classification Manual and Holmes and Holmes are not rich in detail. Therefore, their utility in aiding investigators to apprehend killers is limited (Keppel and Walter, 1999).

Homicide investigators have noted generally that crime classification systems have provided little assistance in solving a particular murder (Copson, 1995; Copson, Badcock, Boon, and Britton, 1997; Geberth and Turco, 1997; Keppel, 1995; Keppel and Birnes, 1995; Morneau and Rockwell, 1980). This is the problem in basing profiles on criminal classifications. It simply doesn't help catch the offender. That is, despite a general description of incidents of murder, the information from homicide classification systems currently mentioned in the literature does not address the key issues relating to the offender's identity. Also, this information does not affect his apprehension. Accordingly, when the logical flow is broken or incomplete between theories and reality, the direction and function of the classification concepts become defused, limited, and sometimes meaningless. Therefore, despite best intentions, the end result may be that the homicide investigator is left with some abstract notions, a dead body, an unknown offender, and a general public on edge and waiting for the next body to be discovered (Keppel and Walter, 1999).

When all traditional methods of investigation appear to fail, and the investigation is bogged down by a multitude of suspects, invariably someone suggests that a profile be requested. Past serial murder investigations that have used experts to profile the unknown offender have had two types of experiences with its use; both are bad. The first involves a diversionary effort on the part of the task force commander or chief of police to get the press off his back for the day, and the second is the claim that the profile will help investigators winnow down a long list of suspects into a smaller number of suspects that should be investigated.

Regarding the use of the profile as a diversion, in the height of media frenzy in a serial murder case, the task force commander can temporarily divert the media from its purpose by claiming that a profile has been requested. The media believes in the magic of profiling even if most field-level investigators don't. But this act alone, announcing that a profile is on the way, gives a transparent delay for the commander's having to deal with the press that day. And because the profile will take weeks to obtain, the media interest in profiling is put off by just saying that it will take a while. This gives the commander a momentary respite from the day's media release obligations. However, when the profile is completed, the media resumes its pressures on the executive, sometimes with greater intensity, for more information.

In some cases, the profile has even been released to the media in an attempt to give the public information that will theoretically lead to a suspect being tipped off. This concept, while noble in its intentions, has never worked in a serial murder investigation. Releasing a profile assumes that the application of its characteristics will be correctly applied by the public at large. Under these conditions, the investigation is no better off than before the profile was released, because the public inundates the task force with useless information. In fact, most investigations are worse off because the reaction of the public at large is to flood the hotlines and tip lines, sometimes sending detectives off on wild goose chases for phantom suspects and draining valuable personnel from the real task at hand—to follow up real clues. If all that is released are behavioral characteristics and no description of a person or vehicle, many people will embellish those characteristics and mold them into their version of who the killer must be. Then you even have more phantom suspects to run down, none of whom really exist because they've been created in the image of the people who've tipped them off.

CASE EXAMPLE

The headline of the December 25, 2002, news release of The New Orleans Channel.com read "Another Victim Linked to Serial Killer." It went on to say:

Investigators confirm that a 23-year-old Lafayette woman was murdered by the same man responsible for the deaths of three women in Baton Rouge. The nude body of Tenesia Colomb, 23, of Lafayette, was found by a hunter in a wooded area in Scott. Colomb's car had been found November 21, the day she disappeared in Grand Coteau. An autopsy revealed that Colomb was bludgeoned to death. Detectives with the Lafayette Sheriff's Office were meeting Monday evening with the serial killer task force in Baton Rouge to discuss the link, which was confirmed Monday morning. Investigators would only say that Colomb was a Marine and that she lived alone. She is the fourth victim to be tied to the serial killer. The other victims are Gina Green, who was found strangled in her home September 24, 2001; Charlotte Murray Pace, who was found stabbed to death May 31; and Pam Kinamore, who was abducted from her home July 12. Kinamore's throat was slit and her body was found about 30 miles from Baton Rouge.

In November 2002, the police task force investigating the first three murders released a serial killer profile developed by the FBI. It read:

It is important to note that no one or two traits or characteristics should be considered in isolation or given more weight than the others. Any one of these traits, or several, can be seen in people who have never committed a crime. Instead, these behavioral traits and characteristics should be considered in their totality.

Based on the age range of the victims and their physical appearances, the age of this male offender is estimated to be somewhere between 25 and 35 years of age. However, no suspect should be eliminated on the basis of his chronological age.

This offender is physically strong and capable of lifting a weight of at least 155–175 pounds. Crime scene information indicates a shoe size of approximately 10 to 11.

His socioeconomic situation is likely average or even below average for the Baton Rouge area. In other words, his finances would be tight. His employment is likely to be in a job that requires physical strength, and does not involve significant or regular interaction with the public. He does have a certain amount of mobility either from his employment, lifestyle, or both.

These homicides occurred on two Fridays and a Sunday. It is possible that on those days this offender was not accountable to anyone, unlike the rest of the week where he was accountable due to his employment or for some other reason.

This offender appears to have developed limited information about the three victims—before the homicides. Because he put himself in a position to see them, observe them, or even casually run into them prior to the assaults, he would have obtained information about where they lived, and something about their patterns of behavior. However, it is important to point out that following these women could have involved merely "spot" checks which would not have raised the women's level of suspicion or awareness. This offender may also have perceived more of a "relationship" with these women than what was there. He may have even "bragged" to others, co-workers, other male friends, about having different relationships with certain very attractive, well-off women, without identifying these women specifically.

This offender wants to be seen as someone who is attractive and appealing to women. However, his level of sophistication in interacting with women, especially women who are above him in the social strata, is low. Any contact he has had with women he has found attractive would be described by these women as "awkward." He might demonstrate an overt interest in certain women, complimenting them, etc., in an effort to get closer to them. However, he may misperceive the intentions of some women who are "nice" to him because they don't want to hurt his feelings. His misperceptions might cause him to think there could be more to their "friendship" than what the woman perceives.

It is likely that this offender spends a significant amount of time watching women and following those in whom he is interested. Whether he is at work, at a bar, on his days off, alone or with others, he watches women. At times, this behavior could be excessive and something he engages in to the exclusion of other daily activities. Watching women and following them would be exciting for him. When questioned about it, he would defend this behavior and attempt to normalize it by telling others "I just like women."

This offender does not just follow women from a distance. It is likely he will attempt to interact with them. He has interacted with other women in the Baton Rouge area that he has not killed. However, his low-key style would not have caused suspicion. What may draw attention to him is when his watching and following women becomes obviously inappropriate. He may be so intent on watching them, he can become almost oblivious when he "crosses the line," and they finally notice him or even confront him about it.

Persons who know this offender would likely be aware of this behavior and probably have made comments to him about it. He would deny his behavior is inappropriate.

Women who have been or will be questioned by investigators may not even think to mention this individual because he seems so harmless. The women he follows, watches, or interacts with may not even be aware of him because he "blends in" with the community and his physical appearance is normal. He may come across to some women as a "nice guy" who might have tried to get a little too close too soon, but otherwise is a nonthreatening person. He may go out of his way to be helpful to women in an effort to get closer to them. This veneer of harmlessness is his shield of protection from suspicion.

This is a person who will not handle rejection—real or imagined—well, particularly by women, and he will become angry, sullen, and determined to retaliate.

There are behavioral aspects of each of the three assaults which are considered very high risk for the offender. This includes home intrusions at times when people are around or could return home and find him. This high-risk behavior exposes this offender to being identified or even apprehended. However, he does it anyway because it is probably enjoyable for him and adds to his sense of thrill and excitement. People who know this offender will recognize his propensity to engage in behavior, which is high risk, to live on the edge—even in normal, everyday activities.

This is an "impulsive" individual. When determined to do something, he disregards the consequences of his acts. However, his impulsivity should not be confused with lack of planning. This impulsivity has likely brought him to the attention of law enforcement in the past, even if for seemingly minor offenses, including trespassing, breaking and entering, and peeping. His decision to attack each of the three women when he did may have been spontaneous or impulsive. However, because he had knowledge of these women's schedules and lifestyles, it would have lessened the "recklessness" of having made a spontaneous decision.

The BAU (Behavioral Analysis Unit) believes that this offender lost control during the assault of Charlotte Murray Pace. Losing control would have angered him. He does not like losing control, and he would have been noticeably angry and agitated for some time after the Pace homicide. People around him would have seen this agitation and will recall any disparaging remarks he might have made about Ms. Pace when her homicide was discussed—either by others or in the media. They would have thought his remarks were inappropriate and insensitive.

He would have appeared very interested in media reports following the homicide.

If the offender was accountable for his time on the day Pace was murdered, and he had to return to his normal schedule, his distraction would have been very noticeable to others around him. However, if at all possible, he would not have returned to his normal schedule, and his absence from that schedule would have been noted by others.

People who know this offender, know that he hates losing control—even in everyday situations. But when he does, he becomes every agitated and upset, and blames others for what happens.

This offender is determined and mission oriented. Even under stress he is able to complete his assaults on his victims, which was his intention when he entered their residences. This ability to be cool under pressure is also a trait that those who know him have seen in the past. At times, when others are upset, and unable to function, he will appear unaffected and detached.

This is a determined individual who likely became upset at certain times in the last 12 months since the death of Gina Green on Sunday, September 23, 2001. People who know him or were around him specifically during key critical times will be aware of this anger and would have seen this agitation.

People should pay particular note of these times, which are outlined below:

1. Following the death of Charlotte Murray Pace on Friday, May 31, 2002, this offender would have likely behaved in a very angry and agitated manner for a period of time. News reports and other mention of Ms. Pace and what happened to her would have precipitated his making particularly disparaging remarks about her, even blaming her for what happened.

2. On July 10, when it was made public that the Green and Pace homicides were connected through DNA, this offender would have again felt agitated and angry and seemed preoccupied. He might have asked those around him seemingly casual questions about the reliability of DNA analysis and how DNA is obtained. He would also have made disparaging comments about law enforcement; for example, they were unable to solve these murders because whoever is responsible is too smart to get caught.

3. This offender did not want, nor did he expect for Pam Kinamore's body to be found. On Tuesday, July 16, 2002, when it was announced that her body was found near the Whiskey Bay Exit off of Interstate 10, he would have been noticeably upset—agitated, angry, and preoccupied. Those around him may recall his having made comments that there was no way the Kinamore murder was connected to the other two.

This offender may have even returned to the Whiskey Bay area—to the scene where he left Kinamore's body—because he was so perplexed about her having been found. This return to that area may have appeared to have been for "legitimate" reasons, for example, he was "curious" about what the area looked like.

This offender has followed this investigation in the media. His attention to the media reports would be inconsistent with his prior behavior about current events in Baton Rouge, in which he displayed little interest. On Friday July 12, 2002, two days after the announcement the Pace and Green murders were connected by DNA, Pam Kinamore is taken out of her home. It is likely this change in his MO is a direct result of his having learned about the Pace–Green connection through the media.

If involved in a relationship with a woman, or living with a female, (mother, sisters, etc.), he can become unpredictably moody, volatile, and abusive. These women would know this side of him and be afraid of him. They would also likely describe him at times as being cold and without empathy.

This offender may have given "gifts" to women in his life, even at times when there was no apparent reason. These gifts could have been wrapped as though they were new and may have seemed strange to the receiver, because they did not reflect their personal "taste" or it was something they neither wanted nor needed.

This offender will be very interested in the release of the "profile" information today. Although on the outside he may try to appear very disinterested, he will in fact feel very anxious that some of his own traits as identified by the FBI might make him suspicious to others.

Since the Kinamore homicide this offender has felt less anxious and concerned about being arrested. His level of confidence has increased over time and things have returned to "normal" for him. However, the release today of some of the offender's traits and characteristics will raise his anxiety level and also produce some paranoia. The offender now knows that he has made mistakes before, during, and after the commission of these crimes, but he cannot go back in time and fix them. These mistakes make him vulnerable.

In addition to the mistakes he has made, this offender will likely be very concerned about people around him who might suspect him. He will be concerned that once they read this profile they will recall specifically his agitation and anger at the critical times identified above. He will wonder about comments he might have made in the past concerning these homicides and the victims, and to whom he made these comments. This paranoia will continue for awhile, particularly because he doesn't know what the entire "profile" says about him, and he doesn't know what will happen next in the investigation as a result of the release of this information. If he is still in the Baton Rouge area he may be tempted to leave at this time, at least temporarily. However, he is concerned about how his absence would look to others.

This was the profile that came out of the BAU. The BAU is a component of the FBI's National Center for the Analysis of Violent Crime (NCAVC) which is located at the FBI Academy, Quantico, VA. This specialized unit, featured in Jonathan Demme's 1993 Oscar-winning movie *The Silence of the Lambs*, is frequently referred to as the "profiling" unit, and those who work there are referred to as "profilers," who, ostensibly working from the crime scene and other information they've gleaned, develop what amounts to a psychological portrait of the suspect.

Criminal profiling is a process now known as "criminal investigative analysis." Profilers, or criminal investigative analysts, are highly trained and experienced FBI agents who study every behavioral and forensic aspect and detail of an unsolved violent crime scene in which a certain amount of psychopathology has been left at the scene. Psychopathology is an offender's behavioral and psychological indicators that are left at a violent crime scene as a result of his physical, sexual, and in some cases, verbal interaction with his victim(s). A profile, or criminal investigative analysis, is an investigative tool, and its value is measured in terms of how much assistance it provides to the investigator.

The purpose of criminal investigative analysis is to assess the offender's interaction with the victims from a behavioral perspective. In this case in New Orleans, in order to offer an opinion about the offender, the BAU factored into this assessment the offender's "victim selection process" and the victimology of each of the victims, including each of the victims' risk levels, the risk level for the offender, the degree or control exercised over the victims, the nature of the attack, the location of the Gina Green and Charlotte Murray Pace homicides, the Pam Kinamore home from where she was taken, the location where Kinamore's body was found, the types of injuries suffered by each of the victims, and the overall nature of the activity that occurred with each victim.

This analysis is based on a thorough review of submitted investigative materials, in-depth discussions with each of the three detectives assigned to these homicides, and on-site visits to each of the victim's homes, as well as the location where Kinamore's body was found. The investigative materials used in this analysis included: investigative reports, autopsy reports, crime scene photographs, aerial photographs of the areas, and victimology data.

A Criminal investigative analyst must have access to the most sensitive investigative materials in order to develop a sound assessment of the crimes and the offender. This access to sensitive law-enforcement information case materials is not afforded to non-law enforcement persons. Any comments or remarks that these persons make regarding a "profile" of the offender is based, in large part, on media reporting of the events, and therefore should not be considered a reliable analysis of either the crimes, the offender, or the profile.

Baton Rouge law enforcement and the FBI recognize that it is not typical to publicly release any portion of a profile in a serial homicide investigation. However, it is the opinion of the FBI's BAU that there are persons in the Baton Rouge area who know this offender and may even suspect he is responsible for the deaths of Gina Green, Charlotte Murray Pace, and Pam Kinamore. Identifying what the BAU believes are some of the offender's key personality and behavioral traits—gleaned from the three crime scenes—may give the person who knows him, whether that person is a co-worker, family member, or friend, the confidence to contact law enforcement. The information contained in this release does not constitute the complete offender profile, which is reserved strictly for law-enforcement personnel (The NewOrlenasChannel.com, 2002).

The careful observer has just read the FBI cookbook version of the demographic and behavioral characteristics of the serial killer operating in Baton Rouge between September 2001 and August 2002. The release of a profile like this causes great difficulties for the continuity and the process of investigating. First of all, where is the evidence stating that releasing a profile has ever done any good in the past in serial murder investigations? Other investigations, not necessarily through a task force public relations officer, but through leaks or court documents, have had characteristics of the unknown offender mentioned in a profile released to the public. In the Green River murders, for example, the profile was used as justification for details in a search warrant affidavit. Because of a civil suit brought by the family of Wendy Coffield against the State, the media was able to get their hands on the details of the profile through the civil process. The presence of this knowledge in the hands of the public diluted an already massive amount of information and didn't further the investigation. It only created an influx of calls from the public, none of which ultimately lead to an arrest of the suspect.

Secondly, where, in this profile report, is the research that says that the profile characteristics identified here are in fact correct? How were these characteristics chosen as opposed to something else? Are we at the mercy of the criminal analysts who picked and chose what they thought were the most salient characteristics without providing any substantiation for their choices? Also, where is the evidence that any of the characteristics that the FBI profilers have developed in the past actually matched the real offender? I am quite familiar with the FBI behavioral scientists' methodology and, quite frankly, they engage in speculation, much like the talking heads that appeared on television in the DC sniper case.

Thirdly and more specifically, the three times noted above to which the public should pay special attention is nothing more than poppycock. This information may be more counterproductive to the entire investigative process because the focus of the public was initially prescribed by previous police news releases. This profile release does not inform the public about what they were supposed to interpret from this based on what they were told in the past. In fact, there is no mention anywhere in this profile about the other important things for which the police wanted the public to be on the lookout.

Now that a fourth victim in New Orleans has been discovered and linked to the other three, what is the public supposed to do with the previously released profile? Has the profile now changed based on new information from a fourth crime scene? Having served on many serial murder task forces, I am quite certain that the police investigators are now sorry they ever released that profile due to the amount of unusable information that came in.

The second use of a criminal personality profile to the task force investigation is to prioritize possible suspects from an already voluminous number of suspects to be ruled out by detectives. But I have never seen a profile that was totally correct, especially when it came to the age and race of the killer. The FBI missed in these two categories in the Arthur Shawcross (age) and George Russell (race) murders before those killers were known by name.

The profilers in the Genesee River murders in New York said that Shawcross was much younger than he actually was and then accounted for it by saying that the fact that Shawcross spent over 20 years in prison was the reason for their mistake. They simply subtracted the 20 years and said that the age matched. They didn't bother to try to explain away the fact that their profile sent local and New York State Police on a wild goose chase for a man in his twenties while Arthur Shawcross, 40 plus and gray-haired, sat down to his morning coffee with local Rochester police at a Dunkin' Donuts near the red light areas where he was killing to ask them about the progress in the case.

The George Russell case in Bellevue is another example of a profile that sent police in the wrong direction. Here, the profilers had their heads stuck all the way back in the 1960s when they said that the man who killed three white women had to be white. The standard doctrine, though incorrect, was that a black serial killer wouldn't kill white women. In fact, George Russell was a young black man who was raised on Mercer Island, WA, in a largely white community and grew up with white friends. He dated white women, lived with a group of white teenagers, and the first person he murdered, Mary Ann Pohlreich, was a waitress he was trying to date. The profilers simply continue to get it wrong, and yet the police and media rely on them as if they are predictions from the oracle at Delphi.

Ted Bundy had definitive thoughts about using profiles. He claimed that behavioral scientists lend absolutely nothing toward telling us how to catch serial killers. Some of the profiles Bundy had seen were wrong. He said, "If they are wrong, then you are taken down the wrong path." Bundy felt that trying to figure out "what's in a guy's head" tends to lead you down the wrong road anyway. Bundy pled for the police to focus on the certainties of the investigation, because the "guy"—Bundy's term for a serial killer—is right front of you, not sticking out like a sore thumb. There are dates, places, and times that have more factual merit to the investigative process than the behavioral characteristics identified by FBI, psychological, and psychiatric profilers. When law-enforcement officers ask me for a profile, I ask them: "Do you want a profile or do you want to know how to solve the case?" Invariably, they choose the latter.

But just the term profiling has come to represent such an overhyped cure-all in the media that in the recent DC Beltway sniper slayings reporters repeatedly demanded when a profile was going to be completed. By that point, even if the police had not initially contemplated a profile, the pressure was so great that they had to acquire a profile just to prove they were conducting a state-of-the-art investigation. But even this wasn't good enough because the intense media coverage in the sniper cases required that the media executives themselves resort to consulting their own profile experts.

This resulted in the talking-head society speculating about what the killer(s) were like. And they did it right on television where the killers could hear them and enjoy not only the speculation but the predictions about what they would do next. The major problem with that type of discussion is that those so-called and self-declared experts violated every precept about the process of profiling. Profiles should be based on the expert examining the entire case files, that is, all the police reports, crime laboratory reports, autopsy reports, photographs, video- and audiotapes, crime scene drawing, maps of the crime scenes, and even the impressions of the investigators themselves. And profiles, as shall be seen from those that follow, should be able to place the offender on what I've called a "continuum of violence" (Keppel and Birnes, 1997) to determine what the killer's signature is and where his psychological forces might be driving him.

A crime assessment is different from a straight psychological profile. Here, the profile operates from what the analyst believes is the killer's own projection of reality. The analyst tries to place the killer at the scene and along a point within his serial murder skein. The underlying logic for this methodology is that because a serial killer represents the ultimate form of pathological narcissism—he exists as a psychological singularity in a universe of one—the serial killer views the victim, the crime, and the crime scene through the prism of his own desired reality. The victim, the crime scenes, and the tools or weapons the killer uses are all extensions of himself, physical manifestations of his wants. Because the killer is satisfying his own needs, he cannot help but leave his calling card at the crime scene.

THE CRIME ASSESSMENT

The examination of police investigative materials should be more properly referred to as a crime assessment. Crime assessment is a systematic evaluation of the probative evidence (circumstantial, physical, and direct) found at the crime scene. The absence and/or presence of this evidence are the hallmarks for the foundation that results in investigative outcomes. Several outcomes are possible from crime assessment (Keppel and Walter, 1999): (1) determining the physical, behavioral, and demographic characteristics of the unknown offender (profiling); (2) developing post-offense behavior of the offender and strategies for apprehension; (3) developing interviewing strategies once the offender is apprehended; (4) determining the signature of the offender; and (5) determining where evidence may be located.

These, Richard Walter (2003) has said, when posed with respect to the evidence collected at crime scenes, are the "right questions" to ask in the discipline of investigative methodology. In a broader sense, however, the entire science of profiling brings together the disciplines of criminology and psychology, which have their own methodologies, but each discipline has a unique set of characteristics that differentiates and identifies one from the other. Here, it is noted that criminology is identified as the study of crime and criminals in a social setting. That is, the issues of interest are toward crime patterns, interview strategies, methods of operation, police work, and probabilities for crime subtypes. The language of criminology is that of deviancy. Alternatively, psychology is the study of the mind and behavior. Again, psychology is focused upon the behavior and cognitive processes of an individual and/or specific group. Accordingly, the applied methods are directed toward diagnosis and treatment of the individual. The language of psychology is that of disorders, psychopathology, paraphilias, and an extended array of restricted diagnostic and/or treatment descriptions that are acknowledged within the field of study. Now, once the distinctions and similarities of criminology and psychology are understood, it becomes possible to discuss in context the related concepts of crime assessment and profiling.

Crime assessment is the systematic evaluation of the crime scene for the presence and/or absence of probative evidence, be it circumstantial, direct, or physical in nature. For example, the presence of evidence would be identified as a gunshot wound, knife, ropes, and the posing of a body. As for the absence of evidence, this would be the missing clothing of the victim, wallet, and/or body parts. Once the probative evidence has been collected, it is evaluated and reconciled with criminological known patterns of homicide, suicide, sexual misadventures, etc. At this point, dependent upon the uniqueness and specificity of the information, an assessment of what is among the evidence pieces and known patterns allows for the determination of crime types, motivational structures, and sophistication of the crime/acts. Subsequently, the accumulated information can result in probability factors for investigative clues related to who, what, where, when, why, and how. Here, armed with dimensional information and understanding, the investigator often can formulate an informed investigative strategy. Finally, noting that the process of crime assessment asks relevant questions within the criminological continuum, the methodology is reflective in nature and it is subject to verification and review. Accordingly, subject to validation, the courts have admitted such evidence into the testimony.

A crime assessment, in the criminological continuum, is a systematic process of recognized patterns within the crime itself that offers evidence of motivations and inferred probabilities within the crime type. Again, this is a reflective process by which one can examine the information in an attempt to further refine the inherent motivational dynamic, homicidal pattern and suspect profile. Here, a traditional psychological profile can contribute a silhouette overlay that can possibly add knowledge about the offender's age, race, work, education, hobbies, and other proclivities. Again, the profiler is viewing the unknown suspect from inside the psychological continuum for individualized identity factors relevant to the known crime factors that can be ascertained from what is learned about the victim and pulled from the crime scene.

Notably, there are times when the crime scene profile may not be as helpful as it can be toward solving the crime or, at least, as will be shown later on, in directing the police along a path of dos and don'ts in their investigation. In these instances, if and when a crime assessment protocol does not clarify the case investigative needs, a psychological profile can be created to augment the crime assessment investigative leads. Under these circumstances, the profile can be quite valuable to the investigator for understanding the behaviors, dynamics, and motivations most likely to occur in that type of offender. Again, if done correctly, although the inherent nature of the profile is projective and speculative to the unknown offender, it can provide valuable insights and refinement of investigative clues. With that said, it should not be forgotten that, despite the investigative value of a profile, by its composition, the profile does not provide verifiable measures. Subsequently, the profile does not meet the standards of the courts.

Still, it is unfortunate that many profilers—both the professionals who work for law-enforcement agencies and the self-proclaimed work-for-hire profilers who pop up on the evening cable news—do not have the experience and or know how to do a proper crime assessment in preparation for a profile. Hence, they create a profile from a shopping list garnered from lecture materials and books that may, or may not, apply. As a consequence, the inexperienced and/or untrained criminal profiler can do much more harm than good by sending investigators down a wrong trail to chase clues that wind up as dead ends. Even those investigators, who are savvy enough to avoid these profiles like the plague, still have to react to their bosses who will react to media pressure. And in a media-driven universe, police may sometimes have to satisfy the appetite of the 6:00 p.m. hungry bear rather than work the ion trail of clues they do have to lead to the offender.

In the cases of Washington's "anger-retaliatory" Shoreline killer and Minnesota's Joe Ture, a true "power assertive" killer, one can see how this plays out. In the case of the power assertive DC Beltway sniper, we can see how even efforts done in the best of faith and professionalism go completely askew because the media-driven profile of the killer failed to come up with precisely the key that should have told the police chiefs and the White House Press Secretary to **never** disclose their thoughts about the case to the media.

HOW CRIME ASSESSMENT WORKS

Given the dynamic and synergetic components of two or more murders committed over time by the same person, a systematic look at a viable murder continuum offers the opportunity to explore elements left at the crime scene by the killer. Here, the investigator can assign meaning to (1) the presence or absence of evidence, (2) methods of operation, (3) signature, (4) the comfort zone of the killer (the place where the killer feels at ease), and (5) an inferred motive for the murder. In addition, there may be indicators for emotional intensity, rationale for the murder, and a constellation of additional factors associated with the known and specific type of killer responsible for a certain murder. If used properly, a dynamic classification system can be applied to the murder. The system can then provide information that could be further analyzed to determine methods of approach in the investigative process of the murder. It also may provide reasons for inaccuracies, additional crime scene analysis, and behavioral indicators of the killer.

The intent of criminal profiling, crime scene assessment, or psychological profiling, as it is sometimes called, is to identify the key crime scene and behavioral factors related to the killer, thereby enabling the homicide investigator to more effectively analyze murder scenes, interview killers, prioritize leads, and apprehend killers (Warren, Hazelwood, and Dietz, 1996). The methodology employed by experts varies with the type of expert doing the analysis. The forensic psychologist and psychiatrist base their opinions on the experiences gained from their individual clinical practice. So their interpretations must be taken in context from the type of clinical practice they had been involved with (Keppel and Walter, 1999). (Although a psychologist or psychiatrist may come in from a clinical perspective, it does not mean that he independently can ask the right questions as an expert in crime assessment. Again, the focus is asking the right question from the right discipline.)

Based on our experience in analyzing and investigating many murder and rape-murder cases and interviewing numerous rape-murderers, psychologist Richard Walter and I identified four categories of offenders who were known to commit multiple murders over time.

What follows is detailed information about power-reassurance, power-assertive, anger-retaliatory, and anger-excitation killers. The crime assessment offender profile categories are divided into three different sections: dynamics, homicidal pattern, and suspect profile along with material from actual cases.

POWER-ASSERTIVE RAPE MURDERER

DYNAMICS

The power-assertive rape-murder is a series of acts in which the rape is planned, whereas the murder is an unplanned response of increasing aggression to ensure control of the victim. The acts within the rape-assault are characterized by forceful aggression and intimidation. Specific to the expression of virility, mastery, and dominance, a direct and overpowering assault is necessary and often results in multiple antemortem rapes of the victim.

For the homicide itself, the central issue becomes one of maintaining control over a vulnerable victim by an exaggerated machismo overreaction. To quickly overcome a victim's resistance, the killer may say, "You don't want to get hurt. Just give up." Characteristically, the killer demonstrates mastery by taking charge or command by the use of an assertive image and dominating violence. For the individual killer or his followers, the finality of the killing ensures the success of the killer's power and control through the elimination of the threat posed by the victim and the secrecy of the performed acts. Because of the satisfaction that the rape-murder gives the killer, he analyzes, plans, and seeks methods to improve his aggressive and masculine image in his everyday life and in times of murder.

HOMICIDAL PATTERN

The homicidal pattern in the power-assertive murder is characterized by the sating of power needs through sexual assault and murder. Once the perpetrator has decided to commit either the initial or a repeat rape-murder, the methods for victim selection and acting out will be determined by previous experience, the stress of internal pressures, and opportunity. Accordingly, in selecting the victim, the perpetrator may choose one by opportunity and surprise. Often, the victim is a stranger who is available by surprise on the street or through breaking and entering into a home. If the rape-assault occurs in a home and the husband is present, he may be required to watch the assault or participate.

When the victim has been assaulted on her own territory, the body is left undisturbed. Alternately, when the victim has been abducted from an outside location, the killing and disposal sites vary. That is, when the killing was perpetrated elsewhere, the body was generally dumped.

If the perpetrator has co-conspirators, there is often evidence of multiple sexual assaults. That evidence in or around the victim's body can be found in the recovery of ejaculate that is later analyzed and determined to come from several persons.

Consistent with his need to overpower and portray an image of the military warrior, detectives will find that clothing is torn off the victim. In addition, the killer will brandish weapons of symbolic importance to him. Generally, his preferred weapon is part of his normal image. The weapon may be a knife or rope or something else that is easily concealed. He views weapons as an extension of his own power and therefore will bring them to the crime scene and take them with him after the murder.

The victim, male or female, may show evidence of bruises from beating and pummeling at the death scene. When the perpetrator senses a challenge to his control and masculine image—or a revelation of his internal weaknesses—he may become even more violent. Here, extreme forms of violence will occur short of what he, in his own mind, considers to be deviant, perverse, and atypical of his self-image. Although violence inflicted on the victim may have been severe, there is generally no mutilation of the body; that would be perverse in his mind. With this in mind, investigators must be cautious when interviewing the power-assertive killer. If the perpetrator senses that he may be seen as a pervert, he may instantly turn off during the interview process and refuse any further contact with authorities.

After the killing has occurred, the perpetrator does not maintain contact with the victim. On departing from the crime scene, he often will leave an organized crime scene, as defined by the FBI behavioral scientists and Geberth (1996), in an effort to cover up and protect his identity. Because the crime scene reflects his image of being in the clear from suspicion, he can emotionally exculpate himself from any responsibility for the murder and repeat it within a short time span. Although he remains intellectually precocious and alert, his desire for power will demand credit for the killing. That is, the murder does not count unless someone knows or suspects him of the killing. Therefore, due to his need for glory and recognition, he may betray his secret to a bar patron, fellow worker, admirer, cellmates, and sometimes the police.

SUSPECT PROFILE

In the power-assertive type of killer, the offender is usually in his early twenties and somewhat emotionally primitive. He is primarily preoccupied with projecting a macho image and orients his life accordingly. Despite a wide range of physical characteristics and types, the power-assertive offender is sensitive to his characteristics of masculinity. Therefore, he often is a body builder and portrays a muscular image and/or displays tattoos for a show of machismo and power. In addition to displaying a confident body posture, the offender cruises in his well-attended car, carries weapons, and shows an arrogant and condescending attitude to others. Although a heavy use of alcohol and drugs may be used to bolster the offender's courage and power, he does not abuse these substances to the point of blacking out.

Although the offender may associate with people, he is not seen as a team player. Socially, he may not be a hermit but at times because of his level of frustration with social contacts, he lives on the edge of being a loner. Although he may have an active interest in sports, they are generally limited to individual contact events such as wrestling, judo, and karate. For the most part, he seeks to gain power and displays a winner-take-all attitude. Although he may have a history of multiple marriages and relationships, he does not view them as successful.

In demonstrating his potential for power, he has a history of perpetrating crimes such as burglary, theft, and robbery. Unless the criminal history has resulted in a mental health referral, he may have had no contact with mental health workers.

Educationally, he is typically a school dropout. Based on the limits of the masculine image, his sexual preferences will not accommodate the variety of materials contained in hard-core pornographic literature. He is especially conflicted over unconventional sexual interest and may display a strong homophobic attitude. For the most part, if he reads magazines, they will likely be Playboy and Penthouse types of literature.

Although he may have served in the Marines or the Navy, his service record is generally poor, and he may have terminated his service prematurely. He is generally viewed as antisocial.

CASE EXAMPLE

The case of Joe Ture, currently in prison for the 1980 murder of Diane Edwards, a 19-year-old waitress in rural Minnesota, is an example of a power-assertive killer who focuses his attention on a certain type of victim. In this instance, Ture focused on waitresses and raped dozens of waitresses before his conviction for the Edwards murder. The Edwards murder might not ever have taken place had Ture been arrested when, as one of the suspects in the brutal murder of a St. Cloud family two years earlier, the police realized that the list of women's names, phone numbers, and license plates in the stolen car Ture was driving was actually a list of potential or actual victims. What police didn't realize was that the person they stopped was a child killer who'd almost wiped out an entire family days earlier.

In 1978, an unknown killer broke into the St. Cloud residence of Alice Huling, shot her, and then went methodically to her children's rooms and shot each one of them except for 13-year-old Billy Huling when he missed at point blank range. Then the killer fled. That killer, the police now believe, was Joe Ture.

The list Ture had in possession was more than just a little black book. As one of the detectives told a reporter for the CBS show *48 Hours*, "He'd have a description of what she wore, looks like; he had over a hundred, close to two hundred waitresses, where they worked, what they wore, what they drove." Ture was stalking waitresses.

Three weeks after Ture killed Diane Edwards, he raped another victim but didn't kill her. He dropped her off in an alley. Then in June 1979, he beat 18-year-old Marlys Wohlenhaus to death, a case that was never solved until police came across a confession that Ture made to his cellmate while in prison. In his confession, he told his cellmate that he came upon Marlys Wohlenhaus when she was home alone, he asked her to have sex with him, and when she refused, he hacked her to death with a hatchet.

Ultimately, after the Ture story was aired on *48 Hours* other witnesses came forward to say that they had been attacked by Ture. In fact, dozens of women, most of them waitresses, had complained to police that Ture had assaulted them, but had gotten no response from the police. Now, however, with Ture's confession and his implication in the Huling family murders, a truer picture of this convicted killer is beginning to emerge.

It is likely that he forced sex with the victims, a profile of a certain class of victim with which Ture had some power base. Ture believed they were or should be subservient to him. Therefore, the attack was an assertion of his power. However, when they refused, Ture attacked them and, in fact, committed at least six murders, three of them members of his victim class. Yet, for Ture, it was more important that he spell out the details of at least the Marlys Wohlenhaus murder, because that was the validation for his assertion of power. Even though he later recanted the confession, calling it a lie perpetrated by his cellmate, the fact that the confession contains facts about the homicide that only the killer would know made Ture the prime suspect in that murder.

The DC Beltway sniper is likely another case example of a power-assertive killer, possibly of a nonsexual type, which will be explored in greater detail in subsequent chapters. There, it will be seen, had the police been able to categorize the offender to understand where he was on the arc of violence, they might have altered their tactics in such a way that may have prevented the later homicides in that series.

POWER-REASSURANCE RAPE MURDERER

DYNAMICS

In the power-reassurance rape-homicide, a planned, single rape attack is followed by an unplanned overkill of the victim. Motivated by an idealized seduction and conquest fantasy, the killer focuses on acting out a fantasy and seeks verbal reassurance of his sexual adequacy. When the victim does not yield to the killer's planned seduction scenario, a sense of failure and panic thrust him into a murder/assault. In the murder/assault, he gains control and lessens the threat to his sexual adequacy in the situation in which the victim was not compliant. After killing his unrequited lover—even though the lover was only a relationship in his own mind—the offender may act out his sexual fantasies through exploratory postmortem mutilation.

The power-reassurance type tries to express his sexual competence through seduction. When that fails, the subsequent killing permits him to reintroduce the fantasy system for further sexual exploration that he was not allowed to do prior to the killing. The quest for sexual competency and personal adequacy dominates any fantasy drawings he may do.

HOMICIDAL PATTERN

In planning the rape, the power-reassurance type selects and watches a female victim. He may choose a casual acquaintance, neighbor, or stranger. No matter which type of victim, he applies his fantasies to that victim. In the power-reassurance rape-homicide, the murder occurs after the attempted rape—a sexual groping—has failed and the perpetrator feels a need for emotional catharsis and victim control. Although the offender has no intent to harm or degrade the victim at first, the failure of the rape-assault and the rejection from the victim panics him into a homicide overkill. Believing that he can act out sexual fantasy as reality, he prepares a selected scenario designed to seduce the victim into validating his sexual competence. When the victim does not follow his plan, he feels threatened and attacks the victim.

Often, the selected victim is 10 or 15 years older or younger than the perpetrator. If he perceives a victim as "damaged goods," he may also target a victim within his own age range.

The power-reassurance type uses threats and intimidation to gain initial control and sometimes enters the crime scene with a weapon. But, usually the first time he attacks, a weapon is not preselected and brought to the scene. The second time, he may bring a gun and display it as a force of his own bravado. The third time, the weapon may be a knife.

After the initial attack on the victim, the offender tries to act out the preprogrammed fantasy. In this respect, he has been called the "polite and gentleman rapist" due to the verbal dialog that he tries to carry on with the victim. During the assault, he may ask the victim to remove her clothing and be quite polite with other such requests. While assuring her that he is not going to hurt her, he seeks reassurances of his sexual competency from her. Typically, he may ask, "Is this nice; do you like this; is this pleasing to you; am I better than . . . ?"

When the killer finds his sexual competence threatened through ridicule, challenge, and counterattack, he loses control of the situation and kills the victim through pummeling and manual strangulation. Because he fears the revelation of his failure at sex, he initiates the homicidal attack to control the victim and protect his self-image.

Because the incomplete sexual assault does not validate his sexual competency, after the killing he will often explore the mysteries and curiosities of sex on the postmortem body. Consequently, there is sometimes mutilation of the body coupled with evidence of sexual exploitation. Given the case of uncompleted sexual assault, often there is not any firm evidence of sperm left at the crime scene. Nevertheless, the postmortem activities and sexual experimentation can, and often do, satisfy him. From his point of view, the killing was a success. Therefore, when the need arises, it can be acted out repeatedly until his needs are satisfied.

As a result, the behavior of the power-reassurance murderer may be episodic in nature with one or more killings within a cluster of similar offenses. Notably, when the offender views the murder as successful, he may attempt to extend the relationship with that victim by collecting small souvenirs and newspaper clippings to enhance his imagined relationship. Finally, the reader should be aware that nighttime is the friend of fantasy development. Therefore, the offender acts out in the nighttime hours because that's when he feels most comfortable.

SUSPECT PROFILE

In considering the age of the power-reassurance murderer, the general acting out age is in the mid-twenties range, but this is not restricted to or absolute to the age factors. Although most cases fall within the above parameters, there are key cases where the serial killer has been in his mid forties or early fifties. Therefore, the age can be variable and conditional on circumstances such as the incarceration of the offender for other crimes during his mid-20s. Although intellectually equal to other types of offenders, the murderers rely excessively on fantasies that allow opposing ideas to come in close proximity. This often makes the offender appear dull and somewhat emotionally scattered. He prefers to satisfy his needs through certain fantasies rather than risk rejection. As a consequence, he is often plagued by an inadequate sex life and uses sexual fantasies and relationships to overcome the dysfunction and pain of reality.

In developing his extensive repertoire of rape fantasies, he borrows notions from erotic pornography and a long history of substitutions for sexual activity such as window peeping, fondling of clothing, and obsessive daydreaming. Developmentally, the onset of absorbing fantasies may have started in the early juvenile years. Because his fantasies have taken him into a private world, he is generally viewed as socially isolated with no male or female friends. He is viewed as a loner and a weirdo. Generally, he is an unmarried person without a history of normal sexual activities.

Educationally, he may be identified as an underachiever who suffers from a learning disability but who still squeaks through the system. His military service will not be marked with unusual problems. He will simply be viewed as a nonachieving passive soldier who takes orders.

Because he does not have any interest in athletic activities, he will often compensate for his lack of machismo through compulsive behaviors. Mentally, he may have had a professional referral because he does not live up to what he is capable of achieving.

Due to the dominating influences of fantasy activities, his life tends to leave him an immature person who views life as a spectator not a participant. In other words, he lacks the interest and/or confidence to participate. He does not value criticism from team members, or if he could avoid the team, he would. Again, because his activities are dominated by compressed and edited illusions and the fact that he does not have control, he often bypasses the social intermediate steps in developing normal social-sexual interactions.

Given the excessive energies directed toward his own self-stimulation or self-designed world, the offender may live at home and try to subsist on little income. If income is not available, he may perform menial labor to support basic needs. Accordingly, he often lives, works, and plays in a neighborhood familiar to him. A common form of transport would be walking.

However, if the subject does have a car, it would likely be an older model in need of repair and care.

The subject's criminal record may reflect his interest in fetish activities, unlawful entry, and larcenies. Basically, the killer is fantasy driven and once the satisfaction is over, he leaves the disorganized crime scene (Geberth, 1996) laden with very valuable evidence.

CASE EXAMPLE

John Wayne Glover came to be known as "The Granny Killer" in New South Wales, Australia, because his victims were older women from their sixties to their nineties. In a police investigation scenario that almost followed the Yorkshire Ripper case as if it were a template, the police task force tracking the Granny Killer, led by Michael Hagan, worked night and day to find a suspect who almost defied reality. Thirty-five of the most experienced investigators the police department could assemble were assigned to catch a suspect they'd profiled as either being in his mid-twenties or even an older teenager from outside the local area who systematically isolated older women, bludgeoned them with a hammer or blunt instrument, sexually groped them, then, if they weren't already dead from the blows to their skulls, strangled them with their underpants. The trademark of underpants tied tightly around the victims' necks as a ligature became the calling card of the Granny Killer.

By 1989, Hagan's investigation had bogged down much like the Green River investigation had stalled around 1985. The creativity of the task force had been drained and Hagan himself had become stressed, along with those around him, because they could not get any results from the investigation. Meanwhile the killings continued even as the police looked for someone who matched the profile, young, possibly a teenager, and someone who didn't live in the area where the killings were taking place.

But their suspect, as almost all serial killer suspects are, had no outward appearance as a serial killer and, in fact, blended right in among the group he was preying on. Just like Ted Bundy belonged to the community in which he was killing because he lived among students, was a student, and worked at a rape crisis center, this suspect was a local resident. He didn't stand out because he was a pie salesman visiting the very nursing homes where his victims lived. And, not at all a young man, he was already in his late fifties, outwardly friendly, completely nonthreatening, and apparently very trustworthy. Glover was married, had two daughters and, like John Wayne Gacy in Chicago, he did charity work. He even belonged to senior citizens' groups, socializing with members of the victim profile. Glover fit into the classic serial predator profile of living and working within his group of victims, but because he looked and acted completely normal on the surface, no one, especially not the police, could see through his camouflage.

Typical of a power-reassurance killer, Glover attacked his victims as if he were committing a sexual assault and then bludgeoned them beyond the application of force necessary to kill them. It is as if this overkill seizes the killer who can't stop until his violence completely reassures him of his own potency. And usually the killer is impotent.

Also typical of most serial killers is a record of previous crimes, sometimes theft or breaking and entering, not just as a source of obtaining loot, but as an assertion of power. Typical, too, is a prior record of assaults similar to the assaults that lead to the skein of murders. This was Glover's pattern as well. He had perpetrated sexual assaults against women 25 years earlier. He was arrested, convicted, and released on probation, only to be arrested later on another charge but released from prison after serving only a few weeks. Upon his release, Glover seemed to straighten out, although he only found equilibrium in his life which would keep him functional until some event—internal or external—started the motor resulting in the skein of granny killings.

That event, or series of events, began when Glover's mother showed up in Australia in 1982. After Glover and his wife moved into her parents' home, where Glover quickly fell under what he would later describe as the tyrannical domination of his mother-in-law, he believed things could not get any worse. But things did get worse when his own mother moved to Australia from England and moved into the household with Glover, his wife, and his wife's parents. Shortly thereafter, however, Glover moved his mother out, and a few years later she died of breast cancer. Glover himself was diagnosed with breast cancer shortly after his mother died, had a mastectomy, and later developed a prostate hyperplasia, which rendered him impotent. By January 1989, less than a year after his mother's death, his own cancer, and subsequent impotence, the first of the granny attacks began. Although this biographical information is relative to the story in chief, the turmoil only enhanced his demand for external power-reassurance from killing. For a complete synopsis of this case and greater biographical detail, one should read Paul Tripp's *The Granny Killer* on the Internet at the True Crime Files website.

Glover did not kill his first victim. He attacked her with his fists and stole her handbag. The police didn't file this as a sexual crime, only a street theft, and let it go at that. Two months later, Glover attacked his second victim, a victim of opportunity that he saw walking along the street, with a hammer that he carried in his car, bludgeoned her to death, and stole the money from her purse. Police had no way to connect this homicide with the earlier robbery. They finally made a connection between this attack with the murder of another elderly victim a little over two months later, because she was in the same profile as the previous attacks. In this attack, however, Glover not only bludgeoned his victim, but strangled her with her underpants, an act that would become his calling card.

During the ensuing months, Glover began attacking elderly residents of nursing and retirement homes along his sales route as a pie salesman. But these sexual assaults were gropings in which Glover entered the victims' rooms and either put his hand down the front of their nightgowns or up their nightgowns and then left. And also because these incidents were so far from the locations where the two murders had occurred, police didn't connect them to the homicides until much later in the case.

Glover attacked and robbed another elderly victim in August 1989, and the molestations at nursing homes continued. However, in October 1989, after Glover attacked an Alzheimer's victim he had met and walked home and then left for dead after bashing her head into a wall, the victim survived. She told police that her assailant was a young man, and that, the first real clue from a living witness that the police believed they could rely on, sent them off on a chase to find a man in his twenties who lived in Mosman, the area where most of the killings had taken place. But when Glover attacked another victim outside the local area, the task force headed by Michael Hagan became convinced the attacker was a teenager who lived outside the area.

By November 1989, with the murders continuing unabated, even to the extent that Glover was killing multiple victims within a 24-hour period, the task force was frustrated, confused, and dealing with its own pent-up emotions of failure. But that only made Glover even more elusive than he already was. He was elusive, that is, until the police did the very thing any task force is supposed to do in an investigation, they began cross-checking all of the cases to find commonalities. That was when they realized they were looking for the wrong type of offender. It is almost axiomatic in serial killer task-force investigations that the clues to the identity of the suspect are already in their files. What happened in the Sutcliffe, Bernardo, and Green River cases also happened in the Granny Killer case. When the investigators looked at what they already had in their files, they discovered that witnesses near the crime scenes at some of the attacks had described seeing a middle-aged man who had gray hair, but was otherwise indistinguishable. Descriptions of him, though vague, turned up at so many crime scenes that police thought it worth pursuing. And sure enough, the first victim in the series told police that she had seen a middle-aged gray-haired man only minutes before she was attacked, although she didn't see her attacker. Another victim provided the same description.

Suddenly, police realized why the killer was so elusive. He was so much a part of the scene, so completely camouflaged by his age, hair, and the way he was dressed he simply didn't look like an attacker. The police were looking for the wrong man. But who was the middle-aged man they were really looking for?

What the task force would soon find out was what many task forces learn toward the end of their investigations. They discover that the reason their suspect was so elusive was that he was always in front of them. He was right in plain sight and clearly identifiable in retrospect, had they only known what they were looking for.

In Glover's case, police found out about him when he showed up at a hospital along his pie sales route and, while there, discovered an elderly woman in her bed, identified himself as a doctor, pulled up her nightgown and began fondling her. When the woman pushed the nurse call button, Glover was discovered and fled. Hospital personnel got his license tag number, gave it to the responding police officers, and identified John Glover from his photo. His victim also identified him as her assailant. He was a well-known figure who regularly traveled this route, and now a likely suspect. However, Glover's name did not make it to the Granny Killer Task Force right away, allowing him time to make another kill.

After police contacted Glover in connection with his latest sexual assault, he attempted suicide and left a note saying words to the effect, "no more grannies." Although this might seem like clear and convincing evidence, it wasn't. Because even after the identification of Glover was made by the hospital and his victim and his suicide note made it to Mike Hagan's task force, the police realized they didn't have the solid corroborative evidence to connect him to the serial homicides. All they could do was connect him to the one groping incident. The other potential identifications were too vague to hold up in court, they believed. The Green River Task Force faced much the same quandary, knowing there were solid leads that connected a suspect to some of the murders but also knowing that without biological evidence the case was still too speculative. So the Green River Task Force and the Granny Killer Task Force did the same thing. They put their suspects under heavy surveillance and tried to learn as much as they could about their backgrounds.

Detectives followed Glover everywhere, even to the house of his final victim, Joan Sinclair. They sat outside while Glover entered her house, waited for him to emerge, and when he didn't, they called in for permission to enter the premises. What they found was Joan Sinclair's body soaked in blood and her panties around her neck. They also found John Glover in the bathroom tub, unconscious from an overdose of Valium and liquor and loss of blood from his slashed wrists. He later told them, after he confessed to the granny slayings, that he had tried to commit suicide in a final act of frustration.

Glover's own confession put him away because without it, police would have had to have built a signature pattern from the different crimes or satisfy themselves with a conviction in the Sinclair murder and the hospital assault. But, though Glover pleaded "diminished capacity" at trial—because of a mental illness as he couldn't form the requisite mental state of intent for premeditated murder—the jury found him guilty and he was sentenced to successive life terms.

In the John Glover case, the surveillance and the arrest are almost prototypical of many serial killer cases where uniformed officers identify an assailant but the information doesn't reach the task force for weeks. Even in Green River, the suspect was picked up for solicitation but the information did not immediately get to the task force even after he had been identified as the task force's prime suspect. The Sutcliffe case followed the same pattern in which police repeatedly identified Sutcliffe in connection with the series of murders, but the task force either didn't receive the information or was unable to do anything with it. And in the Sutcliffe case, as here in the Glover case, the suspect was caught with his final victim. Also in the Bundy, Green River, and Sutcliffe cases, the Glover case turned on the police task force's going back into its own files where they discovered that the clues to solving the case were already there. All they had to do was conduct a systematic review of the case files to find those clues.

There is no magic in finding a serial killer, as most departments at the other end of a serial killer case eventually find out. There is only the hard work and the confidence in a department's own investigative work that must supersede the frustration and denial for the department to trust in its own work.

ANGER-RETALIATORY RAPE MURDERER

DYNAMICS

In the anger-retaliatory rape-murder, the rape is planned and the initial murder involves overkill. This is an anger-venting act that expresses symbolic revenge on a female victim, who might be the proxy for the real female who incited the offender's anger. Nettled by poor relationships with women, the aggressor distills his anguish and contempt into an explosive revenge on the victim. Although the assault is not predicated on a fantasy system, it is often precipitated by a criticism or scolding from a woman with power over him. In the attempt to express revenge and retaliation for being disciplined, the aggressive killer will either direct his anger at that woman or redirect his anger to a substitute woman. Because the latter type of scape-goating retaliation does not eliminate the direct source of hate, it is likely that it will be episodically repeated to relieve internal stresses. Dynamically, the rape-homicide is committed in a stylized, violent burst of attack for the purposes of retaliation, getting even, and revenge on women (Keppel and Walter, 1999).

HOMICIDAL PATTERN

The homicidal pattern is characterized by a violent sexual assault and overkill of a victim. Inasmuch as the actual source of the killer's anger is a woman who belittles, humiliates, and rejects the subject, the fatal hostility may not be directed at a mother, wife, or female supervisor but at an unsuspecting substitute victim whom the killer has sought out. In these instances, it is likely that the victim would come from his own age group or older. Often, the substitute victim comes from areas in which the aggressor may live or work. That is, while conducting routine, everyday living, the aggressor may find a potential victim who reminds him of his mother or girlfriend. A chance meeting could occur at a grocery store or through general cruising of a neighborhood. When a potential victim is selected, he will keep in mind the location and living circumstances of the victim. With the anger-retaliatory murderer, the prediction of when the next murder may occur is next to impossible. It is dependent on when another female triggers his anger, and there could be years between murders.

Alternatively, the aggressor tends to act out against the actual victim directly rather than through a substitute when that actual (targeted) victim is a younger person. The selection of this type of victim may be a dismissive female clerk who says "no" and/or a child who threatens to expose inappropriate sexual behaviors. Again, the perpetrator tends to choose victims from familiar areas. Once angered by the intended target, the perpetrator may choose a previously selected substitute victim as a symbolic vehicle for resolving his internal stresses.

In approaching the crime scene, the killer usually walks. However, if necessary, he may drive to the crime scene area and approach the last 200 feet on foot. The anger-retaliatory killer may have some type of ruse to get inside the victim's door, but once the victim is isolated, he confronts her. Armed with a barrage of accusations, he responds to the victim's denial of him by hitting her in the mouth and about the face. As the assault becomes more combative, the aggressor may use weapons of opportunity (knives, statuary, or other objects) to brutalize the victim.

Depending on the aggressor's age, experience, and internal stresses, the rape-assault may be incomplete because of an inability to get an erection. Therefore, semen may not be found at the crime scene. In either case, the subject is intent on sating his anger through percussive acts of assault with fists, blunt objects, or a knife.

Regardless of whether the victim is alive or dead, the assault continues until the subject is emotionally satisfied. As his anger begins to cool, he places the body into a submissive position by placing it on its side away from the door, face down, putting an artifact or cloth across the eyes, or placement in a closet with the door closed. Generally, following the intense expression of anger, the subject tends to leave a disorganized crime scene, and the improvised murder weapon may be found within 15 feet of the body. Just prior to leaving the crime scene, the perpetrator often takes a small trinket or souvenir.

When the subject views the sexual assault and murder as a success, he often leaves the crime scene with a feeling of having been cleansed and renewed. Because the subject has transferred the blame of the murder onto the victim, he does not experience any sense of guilt. Accordingly, he does not own any feelings of wrongdoing. In fact, quite the contrary is true. That is, he can develop a sense of sentimentality over the victim and help search for the victim with tears in his eyes (Keppel and Walter, 1999).

SUSPECT PROFILE

In the anger-retaliatory type, the offender is usually in the mid-to-late-twenties and younger or older than his victims. He is seen as an explosive personality who is impulsive, quick-tempered, and self-centered. In dealing with people, he is not reclusive but a loner in the midst of a crowd. Generally, his social relations are superficial and limited to many drinking buddies. Socially, he is a person who no one really knows. Although a sportsman, he prefers playing team contact sports.

Conflicted over his relationships with women, he may often feel dependent and aggressively resistant to them. When challenged by women, he may use various forms of aggression to get even and degrade them. If he has been married, his marital relationship may have been ill-fated or may be in some phase of estrangement. In the marriage, there has generally been a history of spousal abuse. Rather than dealing with the problems in the marriage, he will often avoid them by seeking extramarital liaisons. For the most part, these relationships are unsatisfactory.

Sexually, he is frustrated and may be impotent. Often, he links eroticized anger with sexual competence. Although he may use Playboy and similar types of magazines for curiosity, he does not use pornographic materials for stimulation.

When his aggressive feelings toward women are linked with impulsive behavior, he may develop a history of committing crimes such as assault and battery, wife beating, felonious assault, and reckless driving. Humiliated by disciplinary violations, he is usually a school dropout who has not lived up to his potential. If he has joined the military services, his unsettled behavior often results in a discharge from service. Consistent with these behaviors, his free-floating anger is the cause of many difficulties with authority. Mentally, his unpredictable behavior may have resulted in his being referred to a mental health worker.

CASE EXAMPLE

The Shoreline District lies north of the city limits of Seattle in unincorporated King County, WA. An apartment complex is on a cul-de-sac in the 19700 block of 22nd Avenue Northeast, in an area called "Ballinger Terrace." The neighborhood consists of a shopping mall on the north, made up of small to mid-size businesses, convenience shops, and stores near the King/Snohomish County line. The immediate area of the murders consists of multifamily dwellings, apartments, and some single-family homes. The Ballinger Terrace area does not have many murders within a year's time. In the last year, the neighborhood experienced the average variety of crimes and one murder of a male victim. But within 30 days, the locale experienced two separate, atypical murders within the same apartment complex.

Robert Lee Parker was convicted of two counts of aggravated first-degree murder. Before trial, members of the King County Prosecutor's Office, Seattle, WA, requested that a crime assessment be completed on the two murders. Their main question was: Were both murders committed by the same person? The analysis did not include any information about Mr. Parker or evidence about why he was connected to either case (Keppel, 2000, 2003).

Renee Powell

Renee Powell relocated from St. Louis to Seattle. As a registered nurse, she was employed by several hospital facilities in the area. Powell was described as a 43-year-old white female, 5' 4-1/2" , small build, and weighing 100 pounds. She had no criminal record and had not been a crime victim in the past.

Powell was last seen alive at approximately 7:30 p.m. on February 24, 1995. Previously, she had driven to a nearby Albertson's Supermarket to purchase some cigarettes, a newspaper, and some ice. Police investigation revealed that upon returning to her apartment at 2228 NE 197th Place, Apartment B, she had sufficient time to make a jar of iced tea. Also, it was discovered that Renee was doing laundry in the building's laundry room, which was adjacent to her lower apartment unit. The apartment structure was a two-story residence containing four units. No one would see Powell again until firemen discovered her charred remains inside her apartment shortly after midnight on February 25.

At about 11:50 p.m., neighbors reported a fire in Powell's apartment. By 12:40 a.m., the firemen had put out the fire and discovered Powell's body. They discovered that she was bound, gagged, and constrained by a ligature. Homicide detectives from the King County Police were called. Investigation revealed that Powell probably heard a noise at the front door of her apartment because the killer had broken her door open. She probably had no time to respond. Powell was discovered face down on the floor of her bedroom with a bookshelf pulled down and lying on top of her body. The killer appeared to have stripped her naked from the waist down and then tore her shirt from her body. Her bra remained fairly intact, pushed up, exposing her breasts. Her left arm was bound with an electrical cord cut from a study lamp later found in her bedroom.

Arson investigators determined that separate and distinct fires had been started around the residence. They did not communicate with each other.

The first fire was started in the master bedroom near the victim's body. The second began in the living room next to the fireplace.

The autopsy examination discovered that Powell suffered two stab wounds: one in the right abdomen and stomach and the other, in her left back in the parasacral muscle. The gag in her mouth was an elastic bra, tied tightly and fastened in the back with a double overhand knot. The medical examiner removed a segment of electrical cord from around the victim's left forearm and outside of the shirt. The loops were tied with a complicated set of overhand knots. The plug end of the cord was present and the other end appeared cut.

The presence of conjunctival petechiae indicated that there was probable asphyxia. The victim's body was more badly burned in the front than in the back. There was no soot found in the throat; therefore, death occurred prior to the fires. Powell had been vaginally raped and semen was preserved as evidence.

Investigation revealed that the killer had stolen items from the apartment, including an overcoat, a dress, a VCR, several bottles of wine, a duffle bag, and some frozen meat.

Barbara Walsh

Barbara Walsh was a 54-year-old white female who lived alone. She had been widowed over 20 years and never remarried. In the weeks prior to her death, she had not developed any significant relationships. Like Renee Powell, Walsh lived in a lower unit of the same apartment complex. Walsh worked as a receptionist at Group Health Hospital.

Thirty days after the murder of Renee Powell, at about 10:30 p.m., a neighbor saw Barbara Walsh returning from the laundry room of their fourplex. Walsh lived at 2202 NE 197th Place, Apartment B, which is about 100 yards northwest of Powell's apartment. Unlike Powell's one-door apartment, Walsh's had a front door and a back sliding door that opened to a common patio and a wooded area. Her sliding door could not be unlocked from the outside, so police investigators surmised that during one of Barbara's trips down to the laundry room, the killer slipped inside.

At about 1:06 a.m. the following morning, neighbors reported smelling smoke and discovered a fire in progress in Walsh's apartment unit. Fire personnel extinguished the fire and discovered the body of Barbara Walsh. They could see that she was face down, bound, and gagged with a ligature. She was found on the floor of her bedroom with her head next to the foot of her bed. She was nude except for her shirt, which was shoved up nearly to her neck. Multiple fires had been set within the apartment. In the bathroom, between the sink cabinetry and a throw rug, a Trojan condom wrapper was located. Having found the knife in Walsh's kitchen, electrical cords from lamps, and her tights from drawers and in her laundry, the killer had prepared himself for his night's work.

The autopsy report stated that Walsh was gagged with three pairs of tights, tan (innermost), white (laid over the tan), and green (laid over the white). The tan and white tights circled circumferentially around the back of the head once. The green tight circled once through the mouth and once around the anterior aspect of the neck at approximately the level of the thyroid prominence. All of the crotch regions of the tights are located anteriorly. The white tight is knotted once in the midline posterior region and once around the green tight, slightly left of midline. Approximately 11 inches away was another knot in the green tights through which a yellow electrical cord was threaded. Located next to the male adapter of the cord, the pathologist found several strands of blue yarn.

Police discovered that similar blue yarn was also tied to the bedstead, as if the victim had been tied to the bed at one point. Of note was a knife found in the kitchen that police believe the killer used on the victim. The knife had a 7-inch blade attached to a 4-inch handle. All items and mater als used by the killer belonged to the victim. Several items were taken from the victim's residence. Those items included a television set, VCR, CD Player, wicker baskets, a box of silverware, Raggedy Anne and Andy figures, miniature red wire old fashioned bicycles, a glass prism, and small polished stones.

On the victim's left wrist was a ligature that was extensively burned and consisted of multiple types of wires. There was a 9-1/2-inch length of black insulated wire, incompletely burnt through and attached by a few strands to a portion of yellow-tan insulated wire. The yellow-tan wire, from a lamp in the residence, was wrapped and knotted circumferentially around her wrist. The knot was located on the lateral aspect. One portion of the wire completely encircled the thumb.

Walsh suffered three stab wounds clustered on the right side of her abdomen. The stab wounds were gaping and extensively charred around the edges. Near this cluster of wounds was a solitary stab wound. All of the stab wounds proceeded from right to left, without appreciable upward or front-to-back deviation.

In summary, the pathologist stated that Walsh died as a result of ligature strangulation by the stocking, which also served as a gag. Additionally, a ligature was present on her left wrist and multiple abdominal stab wounds were identified, which produced injuries insufficient to account for her death. The thermal injuries were incurred after death and no soot was present in her throat. (Keppel, 2000, 2003)

SIGNATURE ANALYSIS

In these sexually perverted murders, the killer's approach to the victims and his selection of the location were preparatory, enabling the killer to carry out his highly personalized fantasies. Thus, evidence left as a direct result of carrying out his fantasy was far more revealing of the killer's nature than his MO.

In testimony at a hearing over the separation of the two murder charges of first-degree murder, the following characteristics were described as features of the killer's signature in the Shoreline murders.

First, the act of binding was present in both murders. The killer used binding materials found at the scenes. Binding materials were not brought to each scene by the killer. The use of electrical cord and the ligatures exceeded the necessary violence to control the victims for rape-murder. The electrical cord binding and loops around both victims were the specific and necessary control devices that the killer had to use at each crime scene. Typically, these types of arm binding are used by killers who prance the victim around (much like a dog on a leash) and poke them with a knife, thus evoking terror and satisfying his anger.

Second, the number of stabbing strokes was necessary for this killer and increased from the first murder to the second murder. The killer stabbed Powell, the first victim, twice and inflicted four stab wounds on Walsh, the second victim.

Third, the disposition of both victims' bodies reflected this killer's personal feelings. The killer had to leave the victims in sexually degrading and submissive positions. Both were essentially nude from the neck down and intentionally placed face down. The killer purposefully left the victims so they would be found.Fourth, the taking of souvenirs enabled this killer to relive the event at some future time. Such thievery was crucial to this killer's needs. Psychologically, the killer regards these victims as "bitches;" therefore, the he justifies his thefts.

Finally, the presence of arson was evidence of another form of violence inflicted by the killer. The arson fires were a product of refinement and learning. There were more fires set at the second murder scene. Setting fires at the crotch of both victims was totally unnecessary but was an act this killer felt compelled to do.

In summary, as this killer proceeded from one victim to the next, his true piqueristic signature evolved. More stab wounds, more percussive activity with the body, and more fires allowed this killer to feel more attached to his victims and vent his anger. These factors led to the conclusion that the two victims were killed by the same person (Keppel, 2000, 2002).

HITS STATISTICAL ANALYSIS

The Homicide Investigation and Tracking System (HITS) in the Washington State Attorney General's Office is a central repository of murder and sexual assault information in the state of Washington. The HITS program is a database with 227 query capabilities (Keppel and Weis, 1993). Prior to a hearing on the separation of charges, a statistical analysis was performed to determine the relative frequency of the signature character-istics in the Powell and Walsh murders.

At the beginning of the analysis, there were 5788 murder cases in the HITS program. The first search revealed that there were 1164 cases in which the body recovery site was the victim's home. Of those cases, there were 90 victims that were discovered bound in some way. Taking those 90 victims, 49 cases were found in which trophies or significant items were removed by the killer(s). In those 49 cases, there were 16 victims who received stabbing or cutting wounds. When those 16 victims were checked, only two victims, Powell and Walsh, were found burned. The rarity of these characteristics was significant to the prosecution (Keppel, 2000, 2003).

CATCHING THE ANGER-RETALIATORY KILLER

Detective follow-up work and crime laboratory analyses further corrob-orated the opinion that these two murders were committed by the same person. Robert Parker lived across the street from the woods that over-looked the apartment complex where Renee Powell and Barbara Walsh lived, only 130 feet from Walsh's home and 150 yards from the home of Powell. Police detectives contacted Parker's residence during the initial canvas, but the residence was in the name of his girlfriend. Parker was con-tacted at the residence, but he provided a false name. Parker was known to go out for long periods alone at night without explanation.

In late October 1996, detectives were contacted by a therapist, who said she was treating a woman by the name of Princess Gray and told police that Princess Gray had information about murders that occurred in the Shoreline area. Gray had been charged and booked for assault and reck-less endangerment and was in King County Jail awaiting trial when she was contacted by detectives on November 1, 1996. In the interview, Gray told detectives that Parker told her two white guys were involved in the first lady's murder and that Parker had stolen Powell's property from them. She said that on the night of the murder, Parker brought home a VCR, eight or nine bottles of wine, and freezer food that included pork chops. He also had a container with $30 to 40 in change. Gray said that on the second case, Parker left and came back with a TV, VCR, and CD player. Parker also brought home some spices.

The detectives asked Gray whether Parker brought home any trinkets. She said "yes, things you set on your table." Detectives subsequently recov-ered most items from Gray's residence and also recovered Powell's duffle bag from Parker's residence at the time of his arrest for the murders. Inside the duffle bag's pocket were polished stones that Walsh was known to collect. Killers frequently remove items belonging to their victims as sou-venirs or for monetary gain (Douglas et al., 1992). Parker's retention of stolen items found in the possession of Princess Gray and himself con-tributed to the evidence against him in these cases.

More specific evidence linking Parker to both murders was discovered. From semen found on Powell's vaginal swabs, investigators requested that DNA analysis be performed and compared to Parker's DNA. It was found to be a match.

In addition in the Walsh case, hair was found on her bathroom counter. The hair was protected from the fire by a towel on top of it. A DNA analysis was performed on the hair and compared to Parker's DNA and another match was discovered (Keppel, 2000, 2003).

ANGER-EXCITATION RAPE MURDERER

DYNAMICS

The planned sexual assault and homicide are designed to inflict pain and terror on the victim for gratification by the perpetrator. The prolonged torture of the victim energizes the killer's fantasies and temporarily satisfies a lust for domination and control. Precipitated by highly specialized fantasies, the perpetrator selects the victim, male or female, and escalates violence through various acquired and learned incremental levels of ritualistic carnage. Dynamically, the approach of the victim, exploitation of naiveté, torture, and mutilation all serve to appease the perpetrator's insatiable appetite for the process of killing.

Unlike other murderers for whom the victim's death is the ultimate object of the crime, for the anger-excitation killer, the luxury of sadism is found in the art and process of killing, not the victim's death. In some instances, the actual death may be anticlimactic. However, in the execution of crimes, the excitement is heightened by the realization of a rehearsed scenario of eroticized anger and power that has been building, perhaps for many years, in his fantasy life until he steps across the line into the reality of murder. Again, sadistic murder is comprised of a series of recognizable deviancies coalesced into a ritualistic satisfaction. Inasmuch as the development of the process requires an investment of acquired skills, energy, and time, the intent becomes one of indulgent luxury rather than the end goal of a dead body (Keppel and Walter, 1999). As two of the cases previously discussed will show, both Peter Sutcliffe and Paul Bernardo exemplify this type of crime, because both offenders indulged themselves in the suffering of their victims and became erotically excited as the amount of torture they inflicted increased.

HOMICIDAL PATTERN

In the anger-excitation rape-homicide, the homicidal pattern is characterized by a prolonged, bizarre, ritualistic assault on the victim, such as the assault Paul Bernardo perpetrated upon Tammy Homolka. Driven by an advanced plan of action—actually part of the excitation—the fantasy of the assault is put into action with an equipped murder kit. Often, the victim may be a stranger who fits his needs for a symbol, such as a nurse, a prostitute, a child, a student, or a matriarch. Also, he may be attracted to victims who meet certain criteria such as long blond hair, specialized shoes, or a tramp image. When preparing to encounter the victim, the organized offender can invoke a disarmingly charming manner and dispel most immediate fears from the victim.

To activate the assault process, the subject will use a con or ruse to dupe the victim from the time of contact until the victim is isolated. At that time, he will begin to display vacillating mood shifts that confuse the victim. He then will drop the mask. He may tell her in a very matter-of-fact, monotone voice, "I'm going to kill you," just to watch the look of terror on the victim's face. When he sees the victim becoming terrorized, he goes into a fantasy, and a methodical love for torture is demonstrated through acts of sexual ritual and experimentation. Here, although showing variant forms of dependency, dread, and degradation, the offender is only limited by imagination. Most commonly, bondage and domination play a significant role in the killing process.

In addition, there may be evidence of antemortem cuttings, bruises, and various forms of incomplete strangulation, body washing, shaving, and burns. Although some offenders may attempt perimortem sex, the evidence of ejaculate in the body is not likely at this stage. After the victim has been bludgeoned and strangled, the likelihood for postmortem experimental sexuality increases. Here, it is most likely that one will find evidence of secondary sexual mechanisms.

The evidence of sexual exploration is revealed by localized brutalization, skin tears, and inserted objects into the body. In addition, he may leave the body in a bizarre state of undress after possibly cutting the clothing off. In some cases, the clothing could be a fetish item that he would take as souvenirs. In some cases, the perpetrators will leave clothing neatly folded alongside the body. In others, they may harvest the body of parts. These parts and souvenirs taken from the crime scene may provide materials for later extravaganzas of masturbation. (Generally, this type of perpetrator divides the murder into phases in which the first part documents the art of killing and the second phase is a later reverie of masturbation with souvenirs.)

Eventually, when the crime has been completed and the perpetrator has been satisfied, he will carefully repack his ropes, knives, and specialized tools of torture into his murder kit for safekeeping. Alert to not leaving any signs at the crime scene, he may move the body to a second location to conceal it. Again, to distance himself from detection, he may bury the body in a shallow grave or dump it in a location familiar to him where he is comfortable. Again, to avoid detection, the organized offender tends to commit offenses distant from his usual activities. Accordingly, when he needs added stimulation, he may attempt to interject himself into the criminal investigation (Keppel and Walter, 1999).

SUSPECT PROFILE

In the anger-excitation type, the age range of the perpetrator is considered somewhat variable. Although most perpetrators commit their first homicide by the age of 35, it is possible that a late bloomer or an undetected perpetrator could do so earlier. Characteristically, the organized offender is often a well-appearing person who is bright and socially facile with others. Based on the ability to appear conventional and law abiding, he can cunningly deceive others. In the case of Paul Bernardo, for example, the detective who interviewed him was so impressed with his demeanor, he was convinced that Bernardo could not be a sex offender. Because the anger-excitation offender has the ability to separate a general lifestyle from his criminal interest, he may enjoy a good marriage or satisfactory long-term relationship with a live-in girlfriend. Sutcliffe, for example, seemed to have had a very conventional marriage.

In his marriage, he may perform as a dutiful and conventional husband. Financially, he is identified as an adequate provider. His work history may be tumultuous until he finds a position with minimum supervision. Sometimes, he may show a penchant for mechanical interest and working with his hands. If so, he may seek employment in the semiskilled trades such as auto mechanics, carpentry, or a specialty factory position. In his daily habits, he is often compulsive and structurally organized. Educationally, he may have two years of college and/or graduated. On serving in the military services, he will be identified as doing well. Often, his military success may have resulted in his being identified as "good officer material."

Based on his exceptional ability to organize, he can successfully segment his criminal interest into a private world of protected rituals. Often, his ritual for paraphernalia and souvenirs is contained in a private chamber of horrors. This specialty place may be a dark closet, room, basement, or hole in the ground. Also, he may use an abandoned barn, cabin, or garage. Inside the specialty area, he will keep the victim's souvenirs, his murder kit, and favored pornographic materials.

Characteristically, the pornographic materials will depict a look of terror and scantily dressed victims. Most often, the literature shows bondage and sadism. Because the specialty area is designed to help the perpetrator manufacture and refine fantasies, it may contain a wide range of masochistic and sadistic clues. Although alcohol is not indicated, it is possible that the perpetrator will use chemical drugs to fuel his fantasies (Keppel and Walter, 1999).

CASE EXAMPLES

Both the Sutcliffe and Bernardo cases are examples of anger-excitation killers who lived normal lifestyles on the surface while they perpetrated their dark sexual torture and homicide fantasies on their victims. In Bernardo's case, his first homicide wasn't even an intended homicide because his victim, Tammy Homolka, died by accident when she aspirated vomit after being heavily anesthetized. Prior to her death, however, Bernardo had her sister, Karla, perform sexual acts on her while he videotaped the event. Yet, belying his sadistic personality, Bernardo was able to play out the role of an aggressive Yuppie successful executive whose true nature was only apparent to those women he had abused and had reported him to the police.

Peter Sutcliffe held a long-term job, had a long-term marriage, and bounced from police interview to police interview deflecting any suspicion that fell upon him from the various surveillance operations that the Ripper task force conducted. Sutcliffe's lifestyle appeared so stable that even when police admitted to doubts about his alibis they still did not follow up to bring him in as a suspect. Only when caught in the act of preparing for his next homicide was Sutcliffe detained and questioned. The level of anger that was driving Sutcliffe and propelling him from crime to crime was so intense, and growing, that police were able to see it grow at the successive crime scenes even though they didn't know what they were looking at.

There are certainly other anger-excitation killers who fit the mold of a Paul Bernardo and a Peter Sutcliffe, but Bernardo and Sutcliffe exemplify the kind of killer who can go back and fort between his own and his victim's world, that he can pass right before the eyes of the police and escape detection. What kinds of methods can apprehend killers such as these? They exist, to be sure, and police can utilize them if they don't let themselves get sidetracked by the demands of the media during a high-profile investigation, or the police command looking to satisfy their superiors with a quick solution to a case that can't be short-circuited.

SUMMARY AND DISCUSSION

As a point of reference, in October 1995, the Michigan Department of Corrections reported a prison population of 41,584 prisoners. At that time, the number of prisoners serving sentences for homicide was 5928 (14%). This figure represented only those prisoners serving homicide sentences at that particular time and didn't account for the total number who had served throughout history. Of the total number of homicide offenders in prison, 2476 or 42% had committed sexually related murders.

Within that aggregate number of homicides, psychologist Richard Walter conducted a survey to determine the frequency for each category among convicted murderers. This was accomplished by assessing each inmate on entry or reviewing the intake files of previously committed inmates to determine their most appropriate rape-murderer category. The findings of the research revealed the following results: power-assertive = 38% (n = 904), power-reassurance = 21% (n = 599), anger-retaliatory = 34% (n = 807), and anger-excitation = 7% (n = 166).

Based on the assumption that most murderers have the capacity for rational thought in a variety of emotional responses, there exists choice, determination, and a foundation for behavior patterns. Given their ability to learn, interpret, and modify behaviors, the characteristics and details of their crimes are formed into specific patterns. When individual idiosyncrasies and levels of social maturity are factored into their violent behavior, the result may be a complex mixture of knowledge, intentions, and behavioral outcomes. Therefore, when an investigator examines a crime scene, the presence or absence of evidence may reveal recognizable patterns that are indicative to that specific offender.

Finally, this chapter has discussed the efficacy of profiling. Profiling, in and of itself, can be high risk, misleading, and simply wrong. However, when profiling is used to refine the crime assessment, the probability of success is greatly enhanced. The crime scene characteristics of power-assertive, power-reassurance, anger retaliatory, and anger-excitation offer the investigator the ability to understand the behavioral parameters of the perpetrator of an unsolved rape-murder series. The efficacy of this approach is validated by police-generated case facts instead of abstract and sometimes disconnected behavioral indicators. Here, the crime scene itself becomes the initiation point for pattern recognition, evidence collection, decision making for follow-up, and strategy planning for interviews with suspects. If the category for a particular rape-murderer is identified correctly, the perpetrator can be his own accuser (Keppel and Walter, 1999).

REFERENCES

Copson, G. (1995). Coals to Newcastle? Part 1: A study of offender profiling (Police Research Group Special Interest Series, Paper 7). London: Home Office Police Department.

Copson, G., Badcock, R., Boon, J., and Britton, P. (1997). Articulating a systematic approach to clinical crime profiling. *Crim. Beh. Mental Health*, March.

Douglas, J. E., Burgess, A. W., Burgess, A. C., and Ressler, R. K. (1992). *Crime Classification Manual*. Lexington, MA: Lexington Books.

Geberth, V. J. (1996). *Practical Homicide Investigation: Tactics, Procedures, and Forensic Techniques* (3rd ed.). Boca Raton, FL: CRC Publishing.

Geberth, V. J., and Turco, R. N. (1997). Antisocial personality disorder, sexual sadism, malignant narcissism, and serial murder. *J. Forensic Sci.* 42(1), 49–60.

Hazelwood, R. R., and Burgess, A. N. (1987). *Practical Aspects of Rape Investigation: A Multidisciplinary Approach*. New York: Elsevier North-Holland.

HITS Murder Form (1995). Homicide Investigation and Tracking System, Washington State Attorney General's Office, revised May 26.

Holmes, R. M., and Holmes, S. T. (1996). *Profiling Violent Crimes: An InvestigativeTtool.* Thousand Oaks, CA: Sage.

Johnson, G. (1994). VICLAS: Violent crime linkage analysis system. *RCMP Gazette,* 56 No. 10.

Keppel, R. D. (1995). Signature murders: A report of several related cases. *J. Forensic Sci.,* 40, 658–662.

Keppel, R. D. (2000). *Investigation of the Serial Offender: Linking Cases Through Modus Operandi and Signature,* Joseph Schlesinger, ed. Boca Raton, FL: CRC Press.

Keppel, R. D. (2003). Serial offenders: Linking cases by modus operandi and signature, Stuart H. James and Jon J. Nordby, eds., *Forensic Science: An Introduction to Scientific and Investigative Techniques,* CRC Press, Boca Raton, FL.

Keppel, R. D., and Birnes, W. J. (1995). *The Riverman: Ted Bundy and I Hunt the Green River Killer.* New York: Pocket Books.

Keppel, R. D., and Birnes W. J. (1997). *Signature Killers.* New York: Pocket Books.

Keppel, R. D., and Walter, R. (1999). Profiling killers: A revised classification model for understanding sexual murder. *J. Offender Ther. Comp. Criminol.,* December, 613(4), 417–437.

Keppel, R. D., and Weis, J. P. (1994). Time and distance as solvability factors in murder cases. *J. Forensic Sci.,* 39, 386–401.

Keppel, R. D., and Weis, J. P. (1993). Improving the Investigation of Violent Crime: The Homicide Investigation and Tracking System, National Institute of Justice Research in Brief, Washington, D.C., August, 1993.

Morneau, R., and Rockwell, R. (1980). *Sex, Motivation, and the Criminal Offender.* Springfield, IL: Charles C Thomas. (2002) TheNewOrleansChannel.com

Tripp, P. (2001)., The Granny Killer. True Crime Files.

VICAP Form (1991). Violent Criminal Apprehension Program, Federal Bureau of Investigation, revised March 22.

Walter, R. (2003). Interview.

Warren, J. I., Hazelwood, R. R., and Dietz, P. E. (1996). The sexually sadistic killer. *J. Forensic Sci.,* 41, 970–974.

7

TAKING CONTROL OF
DENIAL AND DEFEAT

Denial and defeat plague serial killer task force investigations. Like twin demons, they debilitate the task force operations from within by luring task force personnel from senior commanders right on down to clerical assistants away from the reality of the task they're confronting and into a false reality. This false reality, this failure to recognize that the enormity of the task is not an impossibility but a surmountable obstacle, is worse than the job itself. In fact, even inexperienced investigators rarely shrink from the job, but might shrink from the false reality of the impossibility of the job.

Given the reality of denial and defeat, what are the positive, proactive steps a task force can take to overcome these forces, keep reinvigorating the task force investigation, and provide a framework for officers that will instill within them a sense that no matter how long the job takes, the investigation will ultimately succeed? How can task force managers impart a sense of confidence to task force personnel that they can stop a predator who knows how to exploit gaps in law enforcement to avoid detection and assault victims at will? One answer in the United States was the development of a multiagency investigative team approach, which established a set of guidelines and procedures for how task forces should operate.

The Multiagency Investigative Team or MAIT task force recommendations grew out of a conference in 1986 where participants, including myself, discussed the various high-profile serial offender cases they'd worked on. I talked about the Bundy cases, Captain Frank Adamson from the King County Green River Task force talked about the Green River murders, and representatives from around the country talked about some of this country's most celebrated investigations such as the Atlanta child murders, the Night Stalker slayings, The Leonard Lake/Charles Ng cases, the Hillside Strangler, the Vampire Killer, the Zebra killings, John Wayne Gacy, and even the often confusing Henry Lee Lucas confessions and recantations. As in the Bernardo case review which would take place over six years later, the participants in our conference agreed that the successful prosecution of serial predator cases depended on a strong case-management system within which each person in the chain of command knew his responsibility and relied on the system itself to provide support for the investigation.

At that time, 1986, the discipline of task-force-driven serial homicide investigation was still relatively new. From what we had learned about Ted Bundy and Wayne Williams, we knew that serial killers could be cunning predators able to camouflage themselves within their victims' community so successfully they could hide in plain sight for years. We also knew that a substantial part of a serial killer's abilities was to stay cloaked until just before he attacked so the victim seemed to disappear suddenly and without a trace. And, finally, we ultimately came to appreciate the serial killer's knowledge of the weak spots of police investigations.

Bundy knew that back in 1975 police didn't understand the kind of predator he was and because they were so predictable in their response, he could reappear at a crime scene on a bike the morning after he killed Georgeann Hawkins and had abducted her in his VW Beetle, because he figured the police would be looking for a predator who drove a car. Wayne Williams suspected that he was invisible as he secreted out his young victims from neighborhoods where nobody thought to look for him. And over ten years later Jeffrey Dahmer, at loose on the streets of Milwaukee, also thought himself invisible as he picked up young men, offered them a hundred bucks to model for him, and brought them back to his apartment where he killed them. Each predator was consistently successful at eluding police even though, with the exceptions of Dahmer and John Gacy, they were operating just under the radar of a huge manhunt, because each predator had a sense of what the police were looking for and knew how to not to look like a suspect. In the Dahmer and Gacy cases, the killers were camouflaged so well and their victims were so much on the fringes of society that police weren't even aware of the serial killer's presence until the killer's final crime in the series, for which he was actually arrested. Upon the killer's arrest, the police learned the extent of the killer's crimes.

Our challenge at the Multiagency Task Force plenary sessions was to figure out what methodologies would be most effective in stopping the Ted Bundys and Hillside Stranglers of the world. We had to pool our collective experience, organize the case files the participants brought to see the commonalities among the cases, and see just how these killers had slipped through our radar.

The first thing we saw was that each time a serial predator committed crimes in a specific jurisdiction, the police had to begin at square one. When a serial predator struck, the police agency started from scratch and had to determine, first, whether the predator was, in fact, a serial; second, how to convince the police command that it was a serial, third, how to reassure the press and the public that the police were doing everything possible to apprehend the predator; and fourth, how to create a system for managing the incoming data so the police were not overwhelmed by information. Now imagine having to do this every time it looked like a serial predator was at work. One can easily see why departments would put themselves in denial just to avoid the bureaucratic work involved. Better just to catch the predator than to build a complete organization from the ground up before you could even start.

Unfortunately, that's what it ultimately takes to catch a serial killer unless you get very lucky. And luck, at least when it comes to homicide investigations, is often a manufactured far less serendipitous event than people think it is. It's not where you find it; it's how you recognize it, because you've already had it happen.

So rather than having to rely on a department's having to reinvent the wheel, so to speak, every time it wanted to move a serial investigation along, we decided that we could build the prototypical case-management system ourselves and make the recommendations available to any agencies that wanted to use them. Our purpose was not, specifically, to deal with the corporate group psychology that informs the behavior of task force personnel. It was to develop a methodology that would stop a serial predator as quickly as possible while bringing as many cases to resolution as we could. If, in setting up an organizational structure that would facilitate our goal we also ameliorated the day-to-day frustration of working within an insular task force, then so much the better.

ADVANCE PLANNING

Because official and collective organizational denial of the existence of a serial predator operating in one's jurisdiction is one of the single most critical problems impeding an investigation from its very first moments, our first step was to attack that denial head on by recommending the creation of an organizational structure—much like an emergency response system— that would come into being if the department believed it might have a serial predator committing crimes within its jurisdiction. We recognized that this would be a difficult step for many smaller and suburban departments because of the financial resources involved, the commitment of personnel, and the regular demands of routine operations. Yet because of the paralysis that can happen within a department when a serial predator strikes, a paralysis that too many times encourages the department to deny they have a serial predator in the first place, it's better to prepare in advance and acknowledge early. For a small agency, there are a wealth of federal and state resources to draw upon, so an early recognition and acknowledgement need not cripple the day-to-day operations.

Accordingly, one of the first steps in the planning process is to prepare for the appearance of a serial killer in the jurisdiction before the occurrence of the first crime. This is done by creating a set of organizational guidelines for how the agency will handle the investigation. In the case of regional planning and a multiagency approach, liaisons among the departments should be prepared to contribute case information to one another and to overlook territorial concerns that too often inhibit cooperation among agencies with contiguous boundaries.

INVESTIGATING RELATED CASES

When a serial murder is recognized in a jurisdiction one of the first things the agency should do, in addition to investigating the homicide just like it would any other homicide, is to begin a systematic search in its own files and any shared database files, particularly on VICAP, for any related cases. Other cases linked to the instant series have to be identified so that clues in those cases can be used to investigate the current case. After tentatively identifying those jurisdictions with similar pattern cases, representatives of those agencies familiar with the cases should meet to organize the details of their respective case files. Had that been done in the Paul Bernardo case, Justice Campbell recognized in his investigation, there was a realistic chance that further murders might have been prevented in St. Catharine's. When detectives from the neighboring jurisdictions finally got together at the final crime scene, they were able to identify the common characteristics, relate the case to the St. Catharine's series, and ultimately complete the investigation that identified Paul Bernardo.

Similarly in the very recent Samantha Runnion abduction/murder case in Orange County, CA, when the Orange County task force investigating the forcible abduction of the young victim was notified about the discovery of the body of a young girl in a remote location in a national forest, the detectives in the neighboring county opened the crime scene investigation up to the Orange County task force detectives. This waiver of the traditional territorial issues surrounding an agency's crime scene allowed the Orange County Sheriff's Department to get a head start on identifying a potential suspect before the suspect was able to leave the area. It resulted in an arrest within the week the young victim was abducted. Thus the importance of interagency cooperation in sexual homicides, particularly serial sexual homicides, cannot be overemphasized.

Traditionally, as far back as the late 1970s, in such cases at the Atlanta child murders, even agencies belonging to the same task force were reluctant to share information because of territorial concerns. Agencies also expressed command and control issues with respect to homicides discovered within their own jurisdictions. Therefore, the DeKalb County Sheriff might assert jurisdiction over the body of a child found in its jurisdiction while the Atlanta Police Department might assert jurisdiction over a victim fitting the same profile type in its jurisdiction. The detectives might share information on an ad hoc basis, but without a formalized procedure for amalgamating that information into an interagency case file, there is a greater possibility of a lost opportunity than there is the chance of coming up with a clue in homicide A that would help in the solution of homicide B. This is particularly important as it might relate to trace evidence, latent fingerprints, DNA samples, and suspect/victim profiles. Imagine, therefore, what it must be like to be a field investigator assigned to this series and to know that valuable data might be in another agency's crime scene evidence file, but be denied first-hand access to it because of jurisdictional disputes. You know that time is of the essence as the serial killer keeps on finding new victims, but the ability to share information depends on agreements struck between higher-ups at the respective agencies so that even if the information gets to the field investigator level, it might be too late to prevent the next crime. This is what often breeds frustration among personnel.

Even within a particular jurisdiction, I've found that sometimes the detectives in one case may not routinely share information about what might be a related crime with detectives in another case. The Los Angeles County Sheriff's Homicide Division, for example, has a kind of round table each week where detectives run through the cases they're investigating in front of the entire group. Although this is instructive because it airs out cases that might be suffering from stagnation and allows for fresh opinions and observations, it also puts on the table cases that might be related but have not yet been recognized as related. It's possible that a case can be a serial without anyone's recognizing it simply because the victims might have relationships to each other that neither primary investigator has seen. They might live near one another, work at the same location, or take the same bus or train home. The victims, as in the Green River murders, might be prostitutes working the same streets, or, as in the Atlanta child murders, they may be children who live in the same neighborhood. Because the victims' remains might have been discovered at remote dumpsites far away from each other doesn't mean that in life the victims might not have connections with each other that put them into the killer's sights.

Accordingly, both within the same agency or neighboring agencies, investigators have to be prepared to share the commonalities of their cases to find related information.

CONSISTENCY IN PERSONNEL ALLOCATION

Because the day-to-day running of a detective unit involves routine work by investigators on the cases they're pursuing, the refocusing of a department's energies on a serial murder case may require the retasking of personnel to new jobs. In fact, for an agency that's already thinly stretched over a large geographical area, like a typical suburban sheriff's department, a high-profile serial murder case is like a flaming meteor burning through the atmosphere and cratering in the middle of the detectives' bull pen. Cases get shifted around, schedules and shifts are turned upside down, and suddenly the flood of information about the serial case crashes over the banks of the data-management system in place to route information through the proper channels. That's why at our conference on multiagency task force organization we suggested that police agencies put a proto-organization plan in place before, not after, the serial murder case lands on the chief's desk.

In many ways like a call to battle stations, the organization plan—although it may require officers to change the duties they normally undertake—if already in place, is something that does not have to be relearned every time there's a new sexual homicide that may or may not turn out to be part of a serial case. If the task force is multijurisdictional, even though one agency may not have the personnel to fill all the organizational slots, officers can be borrowed from other agencies so that the organization plan works even though individual departments would ordinarily be too understaffed to fill it.

For example, given the commonalities that should be discovered at the related crime scenes, instead of having a different crime-scene team from each agency respond, it's probably better to have one crime-scene team working each scene. That way related information can be identified sooner, there's a common filing and retrieval system, and case managers will know how to find information. If one agency has a media liaison officer then his should be the face the press sees every time there's an announcement instead of a different face for each agency. The press will learn quickly enough, as the pressure mounts for information about a high-profile case, how to play one spokesperson off against another so as to squeeze information out that by rights should be kept from the public, because the killer is a member of the public. Therefore, an experienced media relations officer from one agency should be the same face the media sees from the beginning of the case to the announcement that a suspect has been arrested.

Also, people who do the same jobs every day are used to those jobs. One of the ways the killer jumps ahead of the police is that he's constructively allowed to when personnel are shifted around and have to learn new administrative positions. That takes time and the killer uses that time to distance himself from the police. If the same people are put in place during a multijurisdictional task force, regardless of in whose jurisdiction the case takes place, they already know their jobs and the continuity prevents the police from losing valuable time in getting officers re-adjusted to new circumstances.

Finally, with personnel not having to relearn or adjust to new jobs the frustration people feel when put into uncomfortable situations for long periods of time is minimized. As those of us who worked high-pressure serial cases discovered, duty shifts may last as long as 16 hours with no days off while we're playing catch-up with the killer. In the Green River urders, there were so many bodies turning up during the first year it seemed as though the killer was either the invisible man or that the police couldn't even figure out how to step on their own shadows. The frustration was enormous because the results just weren't coming out of the work. Therefore, to reduce some of the frustration, it's best to keep people in their respective administrative positions.

The other important factor to reduce frustration and a sense of failure when the long hours don't result in instant success is positive reinforcement, even for the most minimal accomplishments. If you look at how most agencies handle many long-term cases, you'll find that departments reward instant results. Cases solved in a matter of days or weeks—and most cases are because of the nature of the homicide and the fact that the assailant knew his victim and committed the crime in front of witnesses—are the norm and most detectives expect that kind of result. Cases that take six months or so to solve are generally slow-tracked because other cases that can be solved more quickly take precedence. After a year, the case gets relegated to a cold file and might get handed off to another detective.

In departments where personnel are shifted through units in order to keep them on their toes, long-term cases routinely get reassigned and even though new investigators are required to review cold cases to see if they can bring any fresh ideas to the investigations, most cold cases languish until a new clue or tip comes in to rejuvenate the investigation. However, in a serial murder task force, there is cold-case frustration from the very first day because often by the time a body is discovered, the victim has been gone long enough for the case to have already become ancient history. Therefore, because the cold-case frustration builds up almost immediately, it's important to keep the motivational level high to prevent early burnout.

COMMUNICATIONS AND MEDIA RELATIONS

A number of task force respondents also addressed this issue at the MAIT Conference and made recommendations based, in part, on the experience of case managers who served on such task forces as Green River and the Atlanta hild urders. One of the key priorities of maintaining personnel motivation and successful pursuit of the predator is a coordinated flow of information. An organized method of communication both within the task force, within the larger agency and other agencies, and to the task force constituencies within the public at large is vital both to the success of the task force and to the amount of support the task force gets from the related agencies. Task force personnel, including investigators, analysts, and managers, have to go back to their own agencies. Their jobs are in the contributing agencies, and thus, the success of the multijurisdictional task force is critical to their own senses of professionalism. The same is true for task forces that are comprised of members within the same departments. Here, too, individuals have to return to their routine units and assignments and look for success as task force members as well.

Accordingly, one of the most important ways to reinforce the performance of task force members, to let people know the joint effort is working even though results are not forthcoming as quickly as everyone wants them to be, is the communication of those successful efforts throughout the task force. Similarly, a coordinated communications effort between the task force to the public at large, if effectively managed by a communications professional, will go a long way to preclude the kinds of media leaks that can destroy the morale of task force members and pit different agencies against one another.

MEDIA LIAISON

Just looking at most governmental advocacy endeavors, one can see how a war of leaks both works to the advantage of one side over the other by helping to advance policy issues while at the same time having a demoralizing effect on the people working inside the organization. Therefore, control of unauthorized statements to the press while guarantying to the press that it will receive information that will not compromise the investigation reinforces morale while it allows the media access it should have.

One way to achieve this goal is to have the media liaison officer prepare nonsensitive case material for release. Even though you're controlling the flow of information to the public, the media will realize that the release of compromising information could impede the investigation, tip the predator off about how close the police are to him, provide publicity-seeking false confessors with information only the killer and the police know, and create an unreasonable sense of false expectations in the public at large. Therefore, information made available to the media should be cleared in a formal review process with a group comprised of members of other agencies prior to release, if at all possible.

Where the release of public information can damage morale and create frustration is the lack of coordination regarding public release of information with other cooperating member agencies. In Atlanta, where even though the related agencies were ostensibly cooperating in the search for the Atlanta child murderer, there were competing, and sometimes conflicting, news releases about the case. This might have enhanced the work of one agency while putting another agency on the spot. If agencies believe they have to compete with one another for a public spotlight, even if it's only to reinforce morale within the agency, the result can become a chaotic release of informationsatisfying the media to a point. But even they will become wise to what's going on. Once the media get wind that there's a lack of coordination and that they're being played by competing agencies, the news story itself can turn negative on the agencies doing the investigation. And that's another way morale can fail on a personnel level.

When discussing media relations and release of information to the press, it's important to understand that one of the primary constituencies of the press is the police command and the elected officials who normally only learn about the investigation from what they read in the newspapers. President Lyndon B. Johnson said that he learned more about the progress of the Vietnam War from reading the *Washington Post* than he learned from his own general staff. Conversely, managers, sheriffs, chiefs of staff, even the district attorney or medical examiner will all have issues that will come to the surface during a high-profile serial murder investigation. And the way the game is played today, those issues will more often than not find their ways into how the media covers the serial murder investigation. So not only will many people at the top of the command chain say they learn more from the stories in the papers and on the evening news than they do from the internal task force briefings, they will also find ways to insert their own agendas into the coverage, either through the task force communications office or directly into the media. If handled correctly, none of this should get in the way of the operation of the task force on a day-to-day basis. In fact, the role of the media in a criminal investigation is very important and can be very useful when their aggressive promotion of a story works to the benefit of the task force.

A case in point exemplifying ways the media and a task force can work together is the recent investigation into the Samantha Runnion murder in Orange County. Because the Orange County Sheriff immediately brought the media in to the investigation as an outlet for the message the police wanted to send, he was able to utilize the media almost as if he were hosting an *America's Most Wanted* segment. Sheriff Carana acknowledged that as a result of his media efforts, tips came in from the public leading to the arrest of the prime suspect in the abduction and homicide of the young child.

The media will investigate the story on its own. It's their job, and they can develop leads and avenues of investigation that police might not otherwise discover because of the relationships that reporters have with sources. Media stories have identified witnesses, located witnesses that police have not been able to find, and even identified victims by getting the story out and picked up by other news services.

The media have also been used by perpetrators themselves to contact police. Ted Kaczynski, the Unabomber, used the media to broadcast his message, and his going public with his manuscript resulted in his identification by his brother and eventual arrest and conviction. Recently, Lucas Helder, the Midwest pipe bomber, sent his letter explaining his actions to a student newspaper, and that revelation allowed police, after communicating with his stepfather, to pick him up after a high-speed chase in Nevada. California's Zodiac killer sent letters directly to reporters, who cooperated with police and agreed not to print descriptions of crime scenes.

INTERNAL COMMUNICATIONS

The sense of openness of communication should also operate within the task force unless there is an overriding need to keep one or more salient facts secret. Secrecy, my colleagues at the MAIT conference agreed, can disrupt morale because officers can perceive a lack of communication or a radio silence as bad news, not just no news. Silence is a misinterpretation, of course, but a misinterpretation that can be avoided. Open lines of communication help personnel keep the faith in the overall goals of the task force investigation, prevent misinformation or rumor creep, and boost morale.

That being said, vital information must still be kept on a need-to-know basis. There are various levels of personnel who don't need to be updated about new leads, tips, or names of witnesses. However, there are managers who may make personnel assignments based on old information or inaccurate information because they've been kept out of the loop. A quick review of the Yorkshire Ripper Investigation Inquiry will demonstrate that more than one interview of the suspect was mishandled in its early stages, because the interviewers didn't know that investigators had visited Sutcliffe on previous occasions. When they learned that other detectives had seen Sutcliffe, they were less than aggressive in their treatment of him and as a result, Sutcliffe believed himself invisible to police and invulnerable. Had police known about Sutcliffe's previous interviews, they might have been able to correlate information so as not to dismiss the interview as simply a mistake in scheduling.

Information should be distributed to task force personnel at regular briefings, but the briefings themselves, most of us at the conference agreed, tended to become extremely time-consuming. In fact, the more time an investigator spends sitting in a meeting room hearing what could probably be learned from a memo, the less time the investigator spends on the street bringing in information to the task force. Impatience and frustration over endless meetings are only aggravated by the lack of a quick solution to the case and the fatigue that officers will inevitably suffer during the first few weeks of double shifts and no days off.

COMMUNICATION CAN MAKE SERENDIPITY HAPPEN

Even if one takes it as an absolute rule that information stays within the task force unless distributed by the officer charged with it communication, it's also a truism that people within the law-enforcement agency but not on the task force can sometimes make the impossible happen by encountering the suspect and remembering a fact or a bit of information that lead to the discovery of the suspect. For example, it was important to members of the Green River Task Force that its lead suspect had been picked up for solicitation of prostitution even while he was under surveillance. The arresting officers didn't know at the time they made the arrest that their suspect was also the lead suspect in the murders of prostitutes along the very same strip where his arrest took place. Similarly, in the William Suff Riverside Strangler case back in the early 1990s, the suspect was arrested in a routine traffic stop for an illegal turn. The traffic officers who pulled him over didn't know they were stopping the suspect of an ongoing series of murders.

Because uniformed patrol offers are on the streets day and night every day of the week, they are often the ones who will encounter the serial predator in the course of their duties. It's important to keep uniformed officers informed, therefore, about developments of the task force, persons of interest, and suspects. Also, because patrol officers might be the very first ones to question a suspect, even though they may not know it—as was the case with the arrest of Ted Bundy in Florida for the theft of the van he was driving—they may be the first officers to whom a suspect may confess even though they are unaware of who the person is and to what he is confessing. As we agreed at the conference, there may have been instances during all our investigations where important information was lost or delayed because it was received by personnel unfamiliar with the serial murder case under investigation by the task force.

CASE REVIEW

A little thought of, but, nonetheless, effective, way of maintaining the morale of personnel on a serial predator task force investigation is to involve officers at all levels of the need for an ongoing review of the information already stored in the task force databanks. As my colleagues agreed, complex, long-term investigations need ongoing case coordination, because not only does it reinforce the mission of the task force and keep investigators focused on their goal, it refocuses investigators back on information that might contain important but missed clues. Invariably, my colleagues and I have discovered that the suspect's name is already in the task force information banks. Somewhere in the files, lurking on a tip sheet or index card, will be the killer's name and the critical piece of information that will connect the suspect with the murders scattered through the files. But how do you find it?

Because investigators are hunters, tracking down the information leading them to the suspect, they don't often have time to be farmers, harvesting the information they already have in the files. From my own experience, I found that Ted Bundy's name was in our files from almost the very beginning—he was a Ted with a VW—who'd been tipped off to us by a number of people, including his fiancée. But it wasn't until we conducted a case review on the Ted Task Force that we found our suspect's name in a field of over three thousand candidates. We didn't know he was our suspect at the time, but we would have as a result of a further culling of names based on the accumulation of tips and leads that put Ted in the top 100, the seventh file to be investigated when he was arrested in Salt Lake City and referred to us. When we ran his file, we believed we had a viable suspect based on his relationship with his presumed first Seattle victim, Lynda Healy.

A case review should include an examination and analysis of all investigative information and activities so that leads, though now cold, are not overlooked and re-examined. The purpose of this review is to see if any links or relationships pop up in the data or, when data is managed by computer files, to make sure it's entered correctly. Now with tools like online databases and even stand-alone database retrieval systems, a mistake in data entry can hide data that, if it had been entered correctly, would have established a link with another piece of data in the file. Work also has to be re-examined on witnesses, interviews, suspects, and evidence. If there is biological evidence from an earlier crime or an earlier case that might have bearing on the present case, a review should be able to locate it. Managers also need to review the casework done by field investigators because, as was discovered in the Sutcliffe case, even notes from repeated interviews might be overlooked because the investigators failed to log certain bits of information with a central repository. A case review, particularly if it's ongoing, will help to catch these errors early before they pile up and impede the investigation to the point were personnel at all levels believe that nothing they do will help because any information gathered is simply falling into a black hole. This can be prevented even late in the game.

THE MODEL

As we have seen, the early serial predator investigations worked under the burden of having to reinvent the wheel every time a new series was thought to be underway in a particular jurisdiction. Because of the administrative and bureaucratic overhead in having to assemble a task force every time it looked like a traditional investigation simply wasn't powerful enough to track the case, the typical response of departments was denial and even more denial until the presence of a serial killer was too obvious to ignore. This is still the typical way of thinking in many jurisdictions, although in larger agencies where there may be three or four ongoing serial cases at the same time, that type of thinking is largely passé.

Our own Multiagency Task Force guidelines recommended that agencies have a working group within the agency that could be summoned to battle stations each time it was thought that a serial predator was at work. In other words, in the background of the agency was almost a shadow group of personnel who would assemble to form the skeleton of a task force to begin a serial murder investigation even before the rest of the task force was assembled. This methodology has worked and agencies have been responding faster to the prospect of a serial predator—in part they've been spurred on by media who announce the presence of a new serial predator at the earliest opportunity—and many times can head the predator off before the case stagnates.

But what is still needed in many agencies is a kind of playbook, a manual which gives task force members and the agencies they work for, a drill or set of instructions to pursue the investigation from its inception to the filing of charges. Just such a manual was developed in the UK for handling a method of homicide investigation applying to serial murder as well as to individual cases. Keppel was one of the consultants and contributors to the development of the manual, which, in its own way, not only detailed an organized procedure for investigating homicide, but put forth a theory of criminal homicide itself. This model and the computerization of homicide investigations among larger and regional departments in the United States has led to a new methodology not only of solving homicides, but of changing the corporate psychology of task forces themselves as they pursue some of the most illusive felons they will ever encounter.

REFERENCE

Brooks, P., et al. (1986). Multi-Agency Investigative Team Manual, conference proceedings.

8

THE PLAYBOOK

When senior law-enforcement commanders in the UK reviewed their most significant task-force driven case, the Yorkshire Ripper, they realized that a multiplicity of errors, false assumptions, reliance on conditions that were not true, and the sheer volume of information they had to contend with were enough to stall the investigation in its tracks. Even though the police had the name of the killer in their files and the evidence necessary to link him to aspects of the crimes, they were unable to utilize what they had. Something within the system itself had gone terribly wrong.

In 1978 in the United States, homicide investigators from federal, state, and local agencies assembled to investigate a series of ongoing abductions and homicides of young African-American boys from the Atlanta area. Their efforts failed to stop the homicides until a group of consultants from outside the area were called upon to review and comment on a plan to surveil the places where the killer was dumping his victims and then catch him in the act. Finally, Wayne Williams was arrested, tried, and convicted for the crimes. Yet, after the case was over, some of the obvious clues, it was revealed, had been in plain sight all along even though nobody knew where to look for them. Again, had anything gone wrong that could have been rectified at the time?

In the early 1990s young gay men were disappearing off the streets of Milwaukee, WI. Even though at least one bartender at a local gay bar believed he knew the reasons behind the abductions and the person responsible, police just didn't seem to be able to get a handle on the case. It was only after one of the killer's potential victims managed to escape from the killer's apartment that the police arrested Jeffrey Dahmer who was tried, convicted, and sentenced to multiple life sentences. He was eventually murdered in prison. Among the many facts revealed during Dahmer's trial was that the killer was actively stalking victims while he was on work release from prison, after his own father had begged the court not to release him.

Similarly, as we have seen, the Canadian law-enforcement authorities were so anxious to learn what had gone wrong in the Bernardo case that they launched a top to bottom review of the entire case to make recommendations that would improve the joint investigative process. What they learned would turn out to support, in a large measure, what the English learned from their review of major cases. The learned there was no standardized guide or model for a homicide investigation which could form the framework for the process investigators needed to follow no matter how complicated the cases.

THE MURDER BOOK MANUAL— A FRAMEWORK FOR INVESTIGATION

For the British, in the wake of the Yorkshire Ripper case, there was a call among senior law-enforcement managers for a set of core requirements; a national standard model for how homicide investigations needed to be conducted. Because high-profile investigations in the UK were generally conducted in the glare of national media, London-based media oftentimes held even remote county constabularies to a national standard. This standard was to be a basic field set of instructions that would supersede the local guidelines, so that cases in different parts of the country could touch off the same requirements.

The model focused on a technology-based research procedure rather than a pure reliance upon the investigator's previous experience and suggested that interactive computer support would yield results quicker allowing for a more thorough investigation rather than relying on traditional sources. Finally, underscoring the importance of forensic science to crime scene investigation during the latter half of the twentieth century, the UK model suggests that with the development of DNA profiling forensic support has never been more critical. In Seattle, the Green River Task Force relied heavily on DNA matching to identify its suspect, waiting for over 15 years until the samples they had in evidence could be used for the comparison testing.

THE INVESTIGATIVE THEORY

Perhaps the most important premise that the UK model holds for investigators is the problem-solving approach that provides an investigator, amidst even the most bewildering of cases, a skeletal frame for processing information. Driven by logic rather than by assumptions based on what may or may not be valid experience, the Murder Investigation Manual's investigative theory approach suggests that, particularly when there are no witnesses the police can interview, the most important starting point for the investigation is the crime scene. This is even more true for serial murder cases than for single homicides because of the high potential for clues left by the killer as his psychological calling card.

"Crime scenes are precious," according to the manual. "At every crime scene the offender leaves messages about himself, indicating what is the motivation and drive for the crime." Because the location of the crime scene, routes to and from the scene and its proximity to potential victim contact sites, and the crime scene forensics all contain indicators to the ultimate identity of the offender, the manual explains: "Investigators must consciously subject themselves to a mental process of reconstructing what has happened." All of this is available to the investigator because, the manual promises that a logical assessment of the crime scene will develop lines of inquiry that will form a basis for prosecuting the investigation. In other words, because the victim and the offender are linked by the locations of their contact, the murder, and the disposal of the body, the elements linking the victim to the offender are present at the crime scene or, in the case of victim abduction and disposal of the body, at different scenes.

For our purposes, the linking of the victim and the offender at one or more scenes means that even though the investigation might be clouded in mystery as crime piles upon crime, the scenes themselves provide the basis to begin the investigation and form the touchstones of the kind of logic that sustains morale over the long term. Logic provides direction. Logic provides a path through the evidence and can even predict the existence of evidence that has not yet been discovered. Logic dictates that the crime ultimately will be solved even if the offender is dead or already incarcerated for another crime. And, as the manual suggests, the logic of the crime scene provides investigators with their first clues to the nature of the offender.

Among questions at crime scenes investigators will have to answer are

- How do the defining parameters and dimensions explain the scene?
- What does the selection of the scene say about the offender?
- How did the victim and offender get to the scene?
- Is there evidence that either the victim or offender knew the scene before the crime? In the case of serial homicide body dumpsites this is important because, as in Green River and the Atlanta child murders, it may indicate that the killer has returned to the scene on numerous occasions and will return again in the future.
- What avenues of ingress or egress were available to the killer?
- How did the killer get the victim to the scene?
- Does the crime scene reveal organization and planning? Was it chosen in advance? Was there evidence of postmortem activity with the victim at the crime scene?
- What does the crime scene say about the victim, his or her relationships to the killer, and the proximity to where the victim lives, works, or recreates?

What the crime says about the victim it also says, and possibly to a greater extent, about the killer. The killer's habits, sexual proclivities, mobility, fears, and potential for future dangerousness are all revealed at the crime scene if the analysts and investigators know how to interpret the forensics and clues they find there. In multiple crime scenes in what an agency believes to be a serial homicide case, the evidence at the scenes also shows the direction or continuum of violence of the killer and the way the killer's modus operandi (MO) is changing so as to experiment with victims or to throw the police off the chase. Maybe, as in the Green River cases, the killer knew the police were staking out one particular location or looking for a particular aspect of body disposal to link the cases. Thus, the killer changes the crime scene, prepares or disposes the body in a different way.

Often the crime scene will tell you a lot about the killer's motive. Is he a revenge killer, taking out his anger on women who are only the replacements for the real source of his anger? Does he turn the victim's head away after he's killed her or cover her eyes with some article of clothing? That might tell an experienced detective that the killer's anger abated after the homicide and now he's awash in shame over what he's done. He covers the victim's eyes or turns her away so she'll stop staring at him. Was the victim robbed? Was the robbery staged to make it look like the real motive? Was she posed in a sexually humiliating position or was her body contorted in some way that seemed to gratify the killer's sense of completion? Was this a lust killing where the killer wanted to have sex with his victim before he killed her? Or was the killer a necrophile who had sex with his victim only after she was dead? Perhaps homicide wasn't the issue; it was only the means to an end.

The most important collection of evidence to be derived from the crime scene where the victim's body is discovered is the victim's body itself. With the determination for the cause of death, time of death, type and extent of attack and resulting injuries, toxicology, and the type of life the victim might have led, homicide experts can possibly extrapolate the nature of the connection between the victim and the offender and how the victim was lured into his trap.

Once the evidence from the crime scene or scenes is thoroughly analyzed and fit into the ongoing patterns of the investigation, including victim profiling, the geographical travel patterns of the killer, and the relationship of victim abduction sites to one another, many task forces will have compiled a base level of information about the killer himself. And based on what we've learned thus far from the Ted Bundy, Wayne Williams, Green River, Peter Sutcliffe, and Paul Bernardo investigations, we also know that the killer's name is probably already in the files and waiting for the fit. Depending upon the types of investigative methodologies and surveillance techniques under way, it is also likely that the killer's name has popped to the surface one or more times.

THE PLANNED METHOD OF INVESTIGATION

Implementing the model, the manual suggests, is more than just following a series of suggestions, which, automatically, would inspire confidence and encourage task force morale. Implementing the model requires the development of a planned method of investigation, constant throughout the task force and related agencies, which relies on various, but related, investigative strategies that need to be constructed at every stage of the process. It begins with a forensic strategy concerning the crime scene and the information obtained from it.

FORENSIC STRATEGY

Forensic strategy requires not only protection of the crime scene and preservation of the integrity of the evidence, but that everything at the crime scene is systematically recorded and filed so that it can be retrieved in a methodical and organized way. The entire scene should be recorded as well as the body *in situ* and all areas around the body. But the manual suggests that the processing of the scene should be done within a systematic order starting with the recording of the entire scene, a scene assessment, blood evidence analysis, recovery of trace evidence, removal of the body, recovery of physical evidence, then a fingerprint examination and follow-up. Once the crime scene has been processed, it's original integrity is forever lost, so the only time the investigators will have to evaluate the scene as close to the point as it was left by the killer is at the time they first secure it. And they will only have one chance.

Different agencies have their own guidelines for how forensic investigations are followed up and the evidence cataloged and stored. Surprisingly, many times neighboring agencies have different methodologies, even though there are state guidelines, emphasized in the various training courses for how forensics should be handled. Agencies within the same states, for the most part, may have similar if not identical procedures. However, agencies from different states may handle things differently. Therefore, in task-force investigations that may stretch across state lines, it's important for the task-force managers to agree on one system for processing information and for managing the forensics so that the same retrieval system will have the same results no matter what agency is seeking information from the database.

SEARCH STRATEGIES

According to the manual, any murder investigation, and particularly serial cases, will present a number of different crime scenes and require that detectives know how to define, search, identify, and catalog information about the crime scene. Within the bureaucracy of a task force, it's important to have a consistent strategy for managing multiple crime scenes or successive crime scenes, because investigators need to be able to have a standard information retrieval methodology that can quickly and easily identify the links that identify related evidence from one crime scene to the next. This will eliminate, on the one hand, potential crime scenes that are not part of the task force cases and corral, on the other hand, crime scenes that are. The most experienced investigators trained in crime signature analysis will even be able to make predictions about an offender's behavior at future crime scenes and place a particular crime scene within a roughly defined timeline, even absent specific information about when the victim disappeared.

First, investigators must know how to define a crime scene, particularly if it is not necessarily a scene in which a victim's body is found or where an actual crime took place. It may be a scene related to the crime, which police identify as a crime scene enabling them to obtain evidence from this. This is probably pursuant to a court order preserving the legal integrity of the evidence should charges be filed and the defense move to suppress evidence that has not been legitimately collected.

But what defines a crime scene? The manual suggests a crime scene can be anything from a suspect's vehicle—such as the Green River killer suspect's pickup truck—the suspect's home, a hospital where a victim was taken, body dump sites, victim pickup, contact—such as the strip along Fraternity Row where Ted Bundy made contact with victim Georganne Hawkins—or murder sites; such as the nearby parking lot Bundy lured her to where he struck her with a tire iron while she knelt down by his car to help him pick up what he had dropped. Crime scenes can also be related tool sheds, garages, and outhouses or anywhere else where the suspect might have been where police have the possibility of recovering any evidence. By applying a consistent and systematic method of defining, searching, retrieving, and cataloging evidence from these crime scenes, investigators can work along lines of progress that yield results even during the darkest and most frustrating hours of the investigation.

SUSPECT STRATEGIES

In well-organized case management, not only do the consistent guidelines instill a sense of morale to the entire unit, they also prepare the case for filing once the suspect is charged. Therefore, at every stage, investigators should keep a focus on the legal requirements of what they're doing. They're not just stopping a serial killer, they're preparing a case to go to the District Attorney (DA). As frustrating as some serial killer investigations can be, even more frustrating and ultimately demoralizing is the knowledge that you bring the killer to the DA only to find out that for one reason or another the case won't hold up to the requirements for prosecution. And you'd rather find that out at the pretrial stage then when a jury comes back with a verdict against you. Therefore, the investigatory methods, the record keeping, the setting forth of the elements of probable cause and the grounds for arrest, the adequacy of the search, and the way all of the evidence is handled provide the basis for substantiating the arrest once the suspect is found.

In the Green River case, the King County Sheriff who 20 years earlier was once the lead detective on the case waited for 15 years to arrest the suspect who came to the task force's attention back in the 1980s. The investigators waited to make absolutely sure that the DNA samples recovered from Gary Ridgway during a 1987 interview matched the offender DNA samples recovered from victims, even though they had amassed significant circumstantial evidence linking Ridgway to the cases. Once the DNA match came back, the investigators had their justification to make the arrest and to provide the prosecutor's office with a case they could confidently file and argue in front of a jury.

The Green River Task Force had been reduced to a single detective by the time the DNA match was made and the Sheriff's Department could make the arrest. After years of weighing circumstantial evidence and conducting surveillance on their suspect, the DNA match provided King County with the biological evidence that they believed gave them probable cause to make the arrest in four of the prostitute murders. The documentation in the affidavit filed in support of the search warrants sets forth the basis for the criminal complaint. It recounts the stories witnesses and complainants gave to police; it establishes the forensic evidence between the suspect and the victims in question; it documents that the witnesses told police of the suspect's familiarity with the various crime scenes; describes the suspect's MO from the perspective of two living witnesses, one of whom was his former wife, and it contains the suspect's own admission that he was "addicted" to prostitutes. Prostitutes were the victims the killer selected in the Green River Murders.

Wherever possible, the manual suggests, the arrest of the suspect should be made with as much planning as possible to reduce the risk of danger to the arresting officers as well the suspect. Homicide suspects are dangerous, and especially dangerous when in the frenzy of an ill-planned police action they believe they can escape. That's why the police should be able to deploy an overwhelming presence to secure the arrest scene, make sure that any suspect vehicles and any evidence at the crime scene is preserved, provide for an interpreter should one be needed, and also have an adult representative on hand for juvenile suspects. The manual suggests that a video record be made of the arrest, but such a step must be taken with extreme discretion because, at least in the United States, that's exactly the kind of video that winds up on a tabloid television show and turns the arrest of a suspect in a serious crime into a circus side show. As the case of the Central Park Jogger in New York attests to, even when a suspect's confession is on video, there's no guarantee that that confession will turn out to be truthful in the end, no matter how incriminating it may have seemed at the time.

INTERVIEWING A SERIAL KILLER

Ted Bundy once told me that there is a moment after a serial killer is first arrested when he may be vulnerable. At that point, if someone is present who knows the crimes he's suspected of, is aware of the offender's post-arrest vulnerability, and can capitalize on the moment, the interviewer may just get a confession that will hold up in court. Bundy said that after he was arrested in Florida after a chase in which he was picked up for driving a stolen van, he was ready to give it up. But the local police didn't know the suspect they'd picked up was sought after in the Chi Omega sorority killings and the brutal murder of 12-year-old Kimberly Leach. Had they known, and had they been able to begin the interview process, Bundy may have confessed right then and there before he crawled back behind his shield of invulnerability and decided to tough it out with prosecutors.

Certainly Gary Ridgway, if he turns out to be found guilty in the murders he is charged with, believed himself to be invulnerable. Paul Bernardo believed it as well, as did Peter Sutcliffe. After having been interviewed over ten times Sutcliffe knew that had the police been able to assemble any incriminating evidence against him he would have been arrested. Sutcliffe even volunteered to police that he'd been interviewed previously, but he did so not because he was especially stupid or feeling especially brave. He did it in a way calculated to make the police interviewers doubt not only their own information but the reliability of their own task force.

It's important to emphasize that if the task force you're working for doesn't even tell you you're re-interviewing the same suspect, how are you supposed to rely on the information assembled by that task force. It can be demoralizing, especially in front of a suspect, and make you doubt the process. It explains the psychology of defeat that can permeate a task force, especially after detectives share information that the managers don't even know who's been interviewed in the same case. Sometimes it may lead to the elimination of a suspect who should not have been eliminated at all.

Therefore, when the manual makes a strong point when it suggests that interviewers need to have training in the kinds of crimes that the suspect is charged with, need to have had experience in interviewing suspects of this type, need to behave suitably so as not to try and verbally force a confession, and need to work as teams so a suspect doesn't drain the resources of any one individual. Interviews need to be planned out in advance. The interviewers need to study the case files as if they're studying for the bar exam or Ph.D. orals. They need to understand what the structure of the interview should be while at the same time staying light on their feet so they can react to changes in the suspect's demeanor and strategy. Interviewers have to have expert support from psychiatrists and, often, a prosecuting attorney. If the interviewer is not as familiar with the crime as he should be and the suspect discovers it, the power of the interview can shift away from the interviewer.

One of the most important insights I got from my interviews with Ted Bundy, while he was playing out his hand on Florida's death row, was Bundy's revelation that for him and others like him an interviewer had to appreciate that some murders were okay. It was an astounding thing for Bundy to have suggested, but the more I thought about it, the more I could see what he meant, even if I didn't agree with it. Bundy explained that when a long-term serial killer suspect is in custody that person has developed a range of defenses that he can hide behind during a police interview. And nothing raises those shields faster than an interviewer who's so judgmental he acts like he's accusing the suspect more than trying to gain information from him. Suspects like Bundy are prepared for this and will even challenge a police interviewer, as Bundy did during his final confessions to Vail, CO, Police Department detective Matt Lindvall about the murder of Julie Cunningham.

Assuming that Matt Lindvall knew the Cunningham family, Bundy was prepared for hostility from the detective who was probing for information about the details of her death, specifically what after-death sexual activities Bundy might have engaged in with her body. These were not subjects Bundy was able to discuss freely, usually speaking about what might have happened in the third person as if he were somehow detached from it. But in the case of his interview with Lindvall, Bundy accused him of wanting to be judgmental and forced Lindvall to tread very carefully around the issues concerning postmortem sexual activities. Bundy never actually admitted to any specific sexual activities during that interview except to say that he and his victim had "private moments" at her burial site. That to me, at least, reinforces the assumption that even though serial killers usually don't know their victims—Bundy's stalking of Lynda Healy notwithstanding—they tend to develop instant and intense relationships with them during the crimerevealing their most intimate feelings and projecting them onto the crime scene. This is why crime scene analysis and crime scene profiling are so vital to an understanding of who the serial killer is and where on the arc of violence he is.

When Bundy and I spoke about Bundy's reactions to police interrogations, he said that for all the serial killers he knew and he's spoken to in the Florida State Penitentiary, nothing shut them down faster than a cop who came on too strong and acted as if he were judging what the suspect told him. He said that for all the killers he'd interviewed, there were some murders they would never talk about, some homicides they were either too embarrassed to discuss or in which there was something about the victim that precluded any discussion. Cops had to appreciate this, he said. Cops also had to appreciate that some murders are simply okay because they fulfilled something for the killer. If an interviewer could understand that, not just through words, but really understand that in a killer's mind some murders really are okay, then he would be able to talk about things no serial killer ever thought he would reveal. And that's the level of interview a good investigator should be able to have with a suspect.

LIVING WITNESSES

Anyone who has ever investigated a serial offender will agree that living witnesses provide some of the best means for identifying a suspect and for testimony likely to convict the defendant. It was our experience with Ted Bundy that his attempted abduction of Carol Da Ronch provided the Utah authorities with the legal grounds for an arrest and for holding him, for the search of his car that revealed the strand of hair from Melissa Smith, and for the search of his apartment that revealed evidence of his likely presence at the ski lodges where the Colorado victims were murdered and at a high school play in Bountiful where police linked him to the murder of Debra Kent. Karla Homolka wound up becoming the witness whose admissions to police identified Paul Bernardo as a killer and rapist and Gary Ridgway's former wife actually led police to sites she and Gary had visited and where police had found the remains of some of the victims in the Green River murders.

Living witnesses provide investigators with some of the most important details of a case, even if they never get a chance to see the killer's face or hear his voice. Other times, when witnesses actually spend time with a killer and either manage to escape or, in the case of Florida killer Bobby Joe Long's 17-year-old victim, manage to talk the killer into letting them go, the details they bring back to the police more often than not result in an arrest. Therefore, investigators need to have a consistent strategy when conducting witness interviews and ways to store the information in such a way that facts can be retrieved and compared with the statements of other witnesses and not get lost in the morass of information that inevitably clogs the pipelines in a complex serial killer task force investigation.

HOW THIS MODEL FRAMEWORK OPERATES IN SERIAL TASK FORCE INVESTIGATIONS

If you were to take the premises as set forth in the manual and multiply them not just by the number of cases in a serial homicide investigation but also multiply them by a factor of five to ten, depending upon how clever the serial killer is, you would have some idea of the complexity of a serial murder investigation. Experienced investigators know that it's not just the number of cases that adds to the difficulty, it's the increased number of personnel, all with the capability of tripping over each other's feet that makes for the difficulty. Also, when you factor in additional agencies, each with its own chain of command and management responsible to a different jurisdiction, you also increase the potential frustration and demoralization factor that can impede each detective's job on the task force.

For example, from my own experience, I saw how the problems built on top of each other in the Atlanta child murders when the Atlanta police, Georgia Bureau of Investigation, De Kalb County Sheriff, and the FBI all crossed paths with their own procedures even though they were ostensibly on the same task force. Made worse by the glare of public scrutiny in a racially charged high-profile case, which seemed to defy solution, the competing tactics and priorities of the different investigative teams blocked what might otherwise have been an obvious solution to the case. It was only after an independent group of consultants was brought in to review the prototypical behavior of the unknown suspect and then recommend a proactive surveillance approach that the strategy to find the killer ultimately worked. The issue here isn't a critique of the Atlanta Child Murders Task Force but an example that even with the best of intentions, the pressure and amount of personnel working a task-force investigation is an exponential factor of the complications addressed in the UK police manual.

The essential problem, as referred to earlier, is that investigations of serial sexually oriented killers, as a unique category of multiple homicide investigations, are more than just a multiplier of routine solo homicide cases. Because serial killers are intent on committing successive homicides, many times they actually engage the police who are tracking them by creating blind alleys and false leads, and are driven by a compulsion in which murder is only one aspect of the crime. As in Bundy's case, his homicides were only a means to an end, which involved his control over the corpses of his victims at private burial sites. As he explained to me and tried to explain to other interviewers, the reason he couldn't explain what he did at his burial sites was that they were intimate moments for him, moments he shared with his victims and didn't want to contaminate by telling others what he did. It was bizarre, certainly revealed an aspect of psychological behavior at the very end of the human spectrum, but it made solving the Bundy murders one of the most complicated tasks any set of investigators ever faced.

Bundy is only one example of how a serial killer can be so focused on acts beyond the murder, or before the murder, that their cases sometimes defy traditional homicide investigation routines if those routines are ends in themselves. And this—an overly blue-sky belief in the routine for routine's sake—is precisely why frustration and almost willful incompetence can build up inside a task force. When the routines, even when they are carried out to the letter, fail to bring timely or even palpable results, investigators can lose faith in the routines, go astray, and the investigation dissolves into entropy. Detectives get so anxious to jump over the administrative obstacles they perceive as blocking them from solutions to the case that they abandon logic that serves them well in single homicide cases. Instead they go after suspects they wishfully believe are the prime suspects in the case. Accordingly, awash in clues and tips that need to be combed for real information, detectives can let their emotions lead them and by the time they return to the white line that runs down the road of logic, the real killer has faded into the background once again.

In serial killer investigations, because many times the killer is getting a sexual thrill from his interactions with police or simply because there are just too many suspects and too many clues, the complexity so defies administrative procedures or even human organizational skills, that it takes a leap into another dimension in order to effect the solution. So, given the fact that the UK Manual for Police Homicide Investigations is probably one of the best playbooks in circulation, serial killer task force investigations still require at least one more step in order to keep personnel focused and the task force from becoming a victim of its own procedures. It is a step, I found out in the year 2000 by conducting interviews and focus groups across the country on behalf of a Bureau of Justice Administration grant, that many police departments still have not taken. Simply put, this step involves the transporting of investigative methodologies, records, and even video and audio transcriptions of interviews into computer files so that a good relational database can alert investigators to links among clues that may prove fruitful in pursuing an unknown suspect. I discovered this myself all the way back in 1975 during the Ted Missing and Murdered Women cases in King County and know for a fact that when used properly, computer-assisted investigative methodologies can often mean the difference between catching the killer before he strikes again or waiting until he makes his crucial mistake that puts him in plan sight.

REFERENCE

Philips, J. D. (Sept. 1998). The Murder Investigation Manual, ACPO Crime Committee, unpublished report.

9

BEST PRACTICES

The single best practice that I consistently recommend to all the task forces with which I have consulted is that a thorough and systematic review of all computer records centering around the various murder sites, murder victims, abduction sites, or body dump sites will result in the identification of the likeliest suspects in the case. There is no mystery behind this. Even the most elusive killer will still have to stop to fill up his gas tank, grab something to eat at a restaurant or truck stop, or stay at a motel. More often than not the suspect will use a credit card resulting in a permanent imprint of his name near one of the key sites in the investigation. If there are a number of sites, particularly for a number of victims, it stands to reason that the suspect's name will keep turning up. Thus, a check of the records from various establishments, gas stations, etc., in the areas of the key sites of the case will almost always turn up a list of names upon whom the task force can focus. And one of these suspects will more than likely turn out to be the prime suspect in the murder series. I first learned this during my days on the Bundy case.

THE TED MISSING AND MURDERED WOMEN CASES

A case in point attesting to the necessity of performing a routine check of every database related to a victim, contact site, murder site, or body dumpsite, was the Ted Bundy investigation. This resulted in the discovery of a prime suspect even as he was being arrested for possession of burglary tools in another state. Back in 1975, when the Ted Task Force found itself buried under a morass of clues and tips and couldn't automatically tell which ones were more valuable than the next, we finally decided that we needed a method of sorting and comparing, a way to sift through information so that the individuals with the greatest numbers of tips and clues associated with their names would rise to the top of the pile so we could investigate them first. What was so interesting—and if I hadn't seen it myself with my own eyes it would have taken me years to reach this conclusion—was that the computer universe ultimately coincided directly with real-world events when both the computer and a Salt Lake City law-enforcement officer came up with the exact same suspect independent of each other.

Because our task force was so overwhelmed with information about thousands of Teds who either looked like our composite drawing, drove VW Beetles, attended the University of Washington, or satisfied one of the hundreds of other criteria for which we were looking, we had no way of organizing the information in a timely fashion that would bring us to the top suspects. In fact, in King County and Seattle it was difficult for any "Ted" in his twenties of medium build, Caucasian with light brown or dark blonde hair, and about 5'10" to even walk the streets or have any social life at all because of the hunt for Ted the killer. There were so many Teds that even though they were marching in to see us to get eliminated from the investigation, we had no way of handling that in a speedy fashion, because there was no database we could use to categorize the hundreds of people coming into the office.

The year was 1975, at least 6 to 7 years before workable desktop personal computers capable of crunching numbers as high as ours would reach the market. For those of us on the front lines trying to find ways of using computers to count and record, we were in the era of dumb terminals–windows into larger mainframes and minis. But King County had a mainframe we could use to organize our database of Teds. Our sergeant, Bob Schmitz, had already begun the process of cross-checking the list of names of suspects snitched off by tips from individuals against another list of suspects who drove VW Beetles. We had so many names on different lists that manually conducting the cross-check would have made the task impossible.

Until 1975, we suspected, no one had ever heard of an independent use of a computer application in a homicide investigation; nor had anyone every heard of a program specifically designed to catch a killer or a serial predator. We actually didn't even know back then what the etiology of a serial predator was, much less how to program a computer to catch one. The System Services Department in King County helped us figure out a way to use their mainframe to match up the different lists of Teds we had already compiled. Up until then it had only been used for maintaining payroll and personnel records. Although this seemed to the police traditionalists in our department as a radical departure from procedure—a version of *2001, A Space Odyssey,*—we thought it might prove to be a viable solution because the tasks we were assigning to the computer were relatively simple.

We gave each list we had compiled an alphabetical letter: A, B, C, etc. Then we entered every name on our list under A in the computer and asked the computer to run a cross-check to come up with the list of names that appeared on the greatest number of independent lists that contained other names besides Ted. This was our way to weigh the lists to identify the likeliest candidates for further investigation. For example, the manifest of our lists was:

A: 3500 suspect names gathered through June 1975
B: 5000 mental patients released between 1964 and 1974
C: 41,000 registered owners of VWs
D: 300 campus vendors at University of Washington.
E: 2162 guests at the Mar Si Motel in Issaquah
F: 4000 classmates of Lynda Healy, (the first victim in the Ted series)
G: 1500 transfer students among all the universities
H: 600 participants in the Rainer Brewery picnic (at Lake Sammamish the day Janice Ott and Denise Nasland disappeared and the first official day of the Ted Missing and Murdered Women cases)

When the alphabet had been exhausted, the coding format continued with AA, AB, AC, etc., until we came to the end of our groupings. By the time a month was over, we had 30 separate lists containing more than 300,000 names. These lists related directly to the activities and surroundings where victims had disappeared (contact sites) and where their bodies were recovered (discovery sites). Our examination of both types of sites proved invaluable in discovering possible sources that would help obtain the names of people associated with those locations. We also analyzed the routes to and from those contact/murder and dumpsites to see what associations we could discover.

In the Susan Rancourt case, for example, we ascertained that Susan disappeared after a meeting at the main library at Central Washington State College on April 17, 1974. After analyzing her disappearance site, we identified several sources of names including:

- Her address book
- Fellow students and instructors
- People who attended the meeting on the night she disappeared
- People registered for library privileges
- Traffic citations issued in the Ellensburg, WA, area for one week prior to her disappearance
- Registered owners of VW Beetles in the Ellensburg area
- Campus vendors
- Transfer students from Central Washington State to other area universities and from other area universities to Central

Susan Rancourt was only one victim. Other victims had similar lists associated with their activities, including Lynda Healy, the first victim we knew about.

Once we had all the lists compiled, we asked the computer to print out each potential suspect's name with the most alphabetical letters behind his name. We expected the computer printout format to be "FIRST NAME LAST NAME: A, C, F, AB," who was one of the lists such as VW Beetle owners, Lynda Healy classmates, and the like. What our critics believed was that this would be an enormous waste of time, a complete folly that would only duplicate on computer printout paper the same exact files we had on index cards. We knew this was exactly what would happen, but with a critical difference; the names would be weighted by alphabetical sequences after the names. We believed the names with the greatest number of letters should appear on the shortest lists.

The process was agonizingly slow at first. Because this took place over a quarter of a century ago in the days before digital desktop scanners or even direct keyboard input, it depended upon keypunch operators creating punch cards that rolled along conveyor belts into their waiting bins to be processed by card readers before entering the computer database. But the results of our experiment bore out our expectations.

Although there were over 1600 names with two letters behind them and over 600 names with three letters behind them—too much for a small group of detectives to investigate—there were, however, only 25 names with four or more letters behind them. This was a manageable list we could get through within a year by compiling everything we could about each name to see why the individuals turned up so many times. We had the sense that we were really onto something, because the number of times a name turned up on different lists meant that he was turning up in the right places at the right times. And because no one appears and disappears without a trace, we thought we might have found a trail on Mylar tape that had not been found on the stacks of index cards filling up our offices.

In other words, we were using a computer to index and cross-reference names already in our database. We had compiled these data from all the possible encounters between a victim and those people who might have crossed her path. This was like the various databases of individuals who might have crossed the victims' paths in the Yorkshire Ripper case, but with a critical difference. We loaded our lists onto a computer and cross-checked them. The Ripper Task Force tried to do this manually, succeeded, but didn't know they had succeeded. Their denial of their own success in coming up with the offender made their task almost impossible, because their own denial contributed to their defeat.

As our computer check crunched out the names of the likeliest suspects, somewhere in Salt Lake City Ted Bundy, behind the wheel of his VW Beetle, was driving the streets and possibly trolling for victims. Bundy would ultimately head into an encounter with a Utah state trooper at approximately the same time as our computer, with the mathematical probability of two persons' having the same fingerprint, identified the name of "Theodore Robert Bundy: AAA, C, FFF, and Q." He was 1 of 25 persons who appeared on four or more lists. He was an A, A, A, because he was in the suspect file three separate times, having been snitched off by people who knew him including his former fiancee and a psychology professor who was also Lynda Healy's advisor. Lynda Healy was possibly Bundy's first murder victim in King County. He was a C because he was a registered owner of a VW Beetle. He was an F, F, F because he was in three of Lynda Healy's psychology classes at the University of Washington,—which meant that he must known the very first victim in the series—and a Q because he was spotted driving a VW and matched a composite. These kinds of cross occurrences don't appear unless there is something very good about this prospective suspect, as the Yorkshire Ripper investigation also bore out. We wouldn't have known this in any kind of timely fashion, if at all, but for the systematic harvesting of tips and clues by the computer.

The computer run, which identified Bundy as a potentially good candidate for a prime suspect, was completed one week prior to a very chilling call from Detective Ben Forbes in Utah. Bundy had been picked up in Salt Lake City for evading an off-duty Utah State Trooper who signaled for him to stop for driving without his headlights. After Bundy finally stopped, a search of his car revealed that he had burglary tools. A presumption of attempted breaking and entering was made because the tools served no other purpose than for breaking and entering.

Bundy was arrested, released on bail, and a couple of days later Detective Ben Forbes from the Salt Lake County Sheriff's Department phoned us to tell us about the arrest. "Why?" asked Officer Kevin O'Shaughnessy, who took the call and wanted to know why the Sheriff's Department was calling about the simple arrest of a former King County resident. "Because you asked for it," Ben Forbes told him and explained that King County Sheriff's Detective Randy Hergesheimer had called the previous year after a conversation with Bundy's fiancé e who was concerned that at about the same time Bundy left for Salt Lake City, the missing and murdered women cases in Seattle stopped. Then she read stories of missing and murdered young women in Utah. The coincidence was just too strong, so she told Detective Randy Hergesheimer of the King County Sheriff's Office about her suspicions concerning Bundy. So when Bundy was picked up with burglary tools in his car in Utah, the Utah authorities called us. And right there, on our own computer lists, was Bundy's name as one of the potentially strongest suspects in our case. The computer gambit worked. Only it wasn't a gambit but a rigorous testing of a theory that the name of the killer was already in the files somewhere, because the killer's name would have to turn up in some proximity with a victim, a murder site, or a victim contact site. All we had to do was get our computer to find it.

At about the same time as the Ted Bundy case was unwinding in Washington State, another serial murder case, The Score Card Killer, was under way in California, Michigan, and Oregon. This would overlap the Bundy and Green River cases in Washington and would also be solved by a comprehensive review of records police had already compiled from the separate murder cases. This would show, yet again, that a well-organized database of clues and tips almost always demonstrates that task force investigations work when the personnel who staff them believe in the process and trust that it's working.

RANDY KRAFT

Between 1970 and 1983, Randy Kraft, who plied the I-5 freeway between Southern California and Oregon, picked up hitchhikers and other victims of opportunity, drugged them, tortured them, asphyxiated them, and then dumped their bodies along freeway off ramps. Convicted of 16 murders in Orange County, CA, he was a suspect in over 60 other murders committed in California, Oregon, and Michigan. He was ultimately captured in May

1983, after he was pulled over by California Highway Patrol officers on the I-5 freeway in Southern California for driving erratically. While confronting Kraft and checking out his van, one of the officers discovered what looked like a man in a drunken stupor slumped over in the passenger seat. This was actually a corpse, a murder victim, apparently strangled to death. After they pulled the body out of the car, the officers found photographs of nude men, also apparent murder victims, on the seat where the murder victim had been positioned. This led police to suspect that Kraft may have been responsible for many more murders. It was an eerie prefiguration of what police would discover in Jeffrey Dahmer's apartment almost ten years later.

Shortly after he was charged in the murder of Terry Gambrel, the passenger found in his car, Kraft's home was searched, more evidence was found, and he was subsequently charged with four more homicides in California.

Before Kraft was arrested, after the Bundy and Wayne Williams cases and while the Green River murders case was heating up, the Oregon police were also investigating what they thought might be a series of murdered men cases. After a case review of these murders, it was suggested to the investigators in Oregon that they draw a 1.5-mile radius around each crime scene to determine any location where a list of names (hotels, gas stations, or car rentals) could be drawn. The theory was that if the killer was a traveler he might have left his name at motels or other establishments nearby or in the area. This was the same principle we followed in the Bundy cases. So the Oregon State Police went further and drew a 1.5-mile radius around the entire I-5 area of all crime scenes and gathered a list a names of anyone within the area three days prior and one day after the murders.

Even though Randy Kraft was captured in California prior to the lists' being compared against each other, the Oregon State Police, in order to review its work, conducted the computer comparison and found out that the Lear Siegler Corporation showed up within the 1 miles of each crime scene. It was the only person or company name to show up in the search six times. Further investigation showed that Randy Kraft was the Lear Siegler employee involved for each occurrence, as he had signed his name on the company credit card receipt. Even after they had a suspect in the murders, the Oregon State Police investigation showed that a computer review of compared lists of occurrences of names of people and companies revealed that Randy Kraft turned up again and again. This was a replay, of sorts, of what we did with the Ted Missing and Murdered Women cases computer run. It showed that the using computers to count the numbers of times specific names show up in a database developed from each crime scene usually turns up the name of a good suspect. It also means that police usually have the name of the suspect in their database the entire time, but they just don't know where to look. For example, in the Kraft investigation, the suspect's name turned up as the needle in the haystack as a result of using this computer matching application. In the Bundy case, Ted's name turned up in a group of 25 using the computer matching program. Ultimately, the premise of the computer matching program we used to identify Ted Bundy as a suspect evolved into the concept for the HITS program in Washington State. For an overview of HITS, see Keppel and Weis (1993).

COMPUTER MATCHING AND THE DC BELTWAY SNIPERS

Flashing forward to Montgomery County, Maryland, in October 2002, one can see that the landscape hadn't changed much, because the name of at least one of the suspects in the DC Beltway sniper shooting case was in one or more databases. This happened because they were staying, living, and eating in close proximity to different crime scenes in the area and leaving their names in motel registration books and on credit card receipts. In other words, the suspects left a trail readily obtainable by computer searches of establishments in the area. Only the police simply didn't know it and didn't even know where to look until the suspect himself deliberately gave them the key clue.

BEST PRACTICES

This short list of best practices task forces should follow will accomplish at least three objectives. First, it will maintain the focus of task force personnel on methods that work over the long term rather than on short-term events that most likely won't work and will divert investigators' attentions away from a meaningful search. Second, it provides personnel with a rationale for believing in the investigative methods of the task force by pointing to a light at the end of the tunnel. It helps defeat the forces of frustration and doubt. Third, and best of all, it usually results in the discovery that the task force knows who the suspect is and where he is. It turns the task force from the process of finding a needle in a haystack to gathering evidence and surveilling the suspect while building a solid case grounded in probable cause that a prosecutor can take before a jury.

VIOLENT CRIME ANALYSIS FOR THE LAST FIVE YEARS

Investigators need to locate similar cases because those cases may contain suspect information that may prove valuable in solving the case at hand. If you're working a series of cases, you want to look at all the cases in your jurisdiction over the past five years to locate the similar cases such as rapes gone bad or where the victim has been released, a murder case, a kidnapping where the victim has escaped, etc. You go back five years to find where the offenders are starting off with their series because it's there that the offenders make most of their mistakes. If they don't follow through with their crimes through beginner's inexperience and a victim has been released or a suspect vehicle has been identified, you may find the name of your suspect. It is for this reason that your suspect is already in your files. The trick is to find it in previous case files of similar cases.

LOOK AT CASES IN OTHER JURISDICTIONS

Police have a tendency to restrict themselves to crimes in their own jurisdictions. Although, with the advent of cross- or multijurisdictional databases, this situation has changed to some degree. Historically a serial killer task force in one jurisdiction resisted looking for similar crimes in other jurisdictions. Because serial killers don't confine their activities to only one jurisdiction, there may be crimes in the records of other police agencies containing information helpful to the task force.

SEARCH FOR LIVING OR SURVIVING VICTIMS

Living victims are sometimes the best witnesses. Unfortunately, police usually don't conduct a thorough enough search for surviving victims, particularly if the victims' names turn up in another crime series that police don't automatically relate to the current crime series. Also, the names of witnesses and living victims who tip off police in the current crime series are sometimes buried in the records. By the time police find the name and interview the person making the report, police realize they've had the name of a suspect all along. Therefore, early in an investigation, along with going back to an analysis of violent crimes over the preceding five years, police should also search for the names of surviving victims or living witnesses to related crimes or to the current crime series and interview them thoroughly for any details that can be used to identify a suspect.

PERIODIC AND COVERT SURVEILLANCE OF SUSPECTS

If the task force has already identified potential suspects based on names which pop to the surface after various investigations, such as those that took place in the Yorkshire Ripper case, it is a good practice to place those potential suspects under some sort of covert surveillance. If a potential suspect consistently revisits areas from where victims disappear or displays familiarity with the roads leading in and out of areas where victims' bodies have been recovered, although not probable cause in itself that a suspect is complicit, it's enough of a lead to encourage police to keep investigating. Sometimes the task force gets lucky and a potential suspect may lead detectives to the evidence of a crime he committed or to the scene of a crime he is about to commit.

SURVEILLANCE OF CONTACT AND BODY RECOVERY SITES

As the Atlanta Child Murders Task Force discovered by surveilling the bridges over the Chattahoochee River, maintaining a vigil over sites where the serial killer is believed to visit on a regular basis may yield positive results. In the Yorkshire Ripper case, police maintained a heavy surveillance over the red light district where the killer picked up his prostitute victims and Peter Sutcliffe's name came up as one of the drivers who had passed through. Although Sutcliffe managed to explain his presence away, it was a police surveillance of the red light district that finally caught Sutcliffe in his car with his next potential victim causing the police to detain him. As a result of that detention, critical evidence was found linking Sutcliffe to the murders.

SECURITY OF INFORMATION

It can't be stressed enough that information gathered by the task force can't be shared with the public because in so doing, it is shared with the killer himself. That doesn't mean simply not sharing sensitive information with the press. It means making sure that the people to whom information is shared within the task force are those for whom the information is necessary. If the information about cases, witnesses, evidence, or potential suspects is not protected and it leaks out to unauthorized individuals, the media, and the public, it can be completely compromised. In many serial murder investigations people come forward to confess and many times these are false confessors. Therefore the police need to keep essential details private, because they need to question these false confessors knowing that they would not know the essential details unless they were at the crime scene.

COMPARE EVIDENCE FROM CASE TO CASE

Many lab procedures only examine physical evidence to be compared from a crime scene to a known arrested offender. They don't routinely examine cases where there are similar pieces of physical evidence unless there is a known offender. Therefore in most of the serial homicide cases that crime labs investigate, they don't know they have a serial offender because that hasn't t been determined yet. Thus, it is more important for investigators to compare physical evidence from case to case within a series systematically, particularly forensic biological evidence and trace evidence such as fibers and hairs, to link crimes within a series. This could possibly turn up witnesses from one case against the offender in a subsequent or previous case within the same series.

APPOINT A MEDIA RELATIONS OFFICER

It is critical that task forces appoint a media relations officer to talk to the press. All communications should go through this officer. No communications should go through anyone else, and the officer should be a critical part of any meetings dealing with the top brass relative to what information gets released. Any deviation from this protocol will subject the task force to a potentially hostile press, degrade the morale of the rank and file to the point where they will rely on the press for their information about the case more than their own superiors, and subject the managers of the task force to a buffeting that will impair their ability to run the investigation. A simple primer on how the press interacts with police task forces and where things can go drastically wrong will exemplify the point.

It's also vital that the task force public information officer keeps a record of all of the information he has given to the media. Most task forces don't know what information the public already has as a result of task force releases to the press. This is important because each major media headline about a serial killer case brings scores of false confessors out of the woodwork, looking for their 15 minutes of fame. This was our experience in the Bundy cases.

So, without a record of ongoing press releases, the task force won't know what's out there for false confessors to read. The police need to know what details have been released to the press so they can use details that haven't been released in their interviews with possible confessors. If a confessor only repeats information that's been released to the public, his credibility may be very low. But if the police know a specific fact that's been withheld from the public and the confessor knows that same fact, it lends credibility to his confession. It's important, therefore, that the police keep records of what information they release so they know what information the public's been given.

THE MEDIA AS A PRESENCE IN THE INVESTIGATION

Because of today's 24-hour news networks, the media will dog every step of a serial killer investigation (Keppel and Birnes, 1995). The DC Beltway

Sniper case is a prime example. Fifteen years ago, Bundy was almost prophetic when he said that the police as a rule say far too much to the press. In fact there's very little the police can say to the press that will help them manage the investigation. The press wants to know when you're going to catch the killer. You want to know that, too. But you can't let the reporters in on what you know. So the police and the press play a game. You tell them you're investigating leads and they ask, "What leads?" You can't tell them that, but you can only say that the investigation is proceeding. Then they ask about your suspects, and you tell them that you really can't discuss suspects. And so it goes.

What the uninitiated police representative has to understand is that the press is not, by its nature, unfriendly, just adversarial. But it can turn unfriendly in an instant. Just look at the proliferation of cable news channels, network channels, local channels, radio, print, tabloid, and foreign press. The pressure to get a story and keep a story alive is enormous. The reporters gathered in front of a courthouse or police station are in desperate competition with each other. A quick look at the way the press behaved in the Jon-Benet Ramsey, Chandra Levy, Robert Blake, and DC Sniper cases is instructive. Because reporters are under constant pressure from their editors and producers to come up with new angles, break a story, get readers, and get ratings, they're going to manipulate whoever is in front of them delivering the latest updates. They're your friends for as long as they feel they're getting something. But that can turn around in a minute.

In the throes of any high-pressure investigation, the police will always feel obligated to toss something to the press to feed their appetite every single day. Although they're boxed into a corner, police officials believe they have to keep feeding the press to keep them on their side. Once they begin to get closed-mouthed about their progress and what new clues they've dug up, the press can turn unfriendly. And an unfriendly press can make the job of any task force in an intransigently unsolvable serial murder investigation all the harder.

Last year, the Washington DC Metro Police faced the same kind of situation in the search for missing Federal Bureau of Prisons intern Chandra Levy. In a case that captured national media attention because of the victim's alleged relationship with former Representative Gary Condit from California and with tabloid newspapers speculating wildly about the congressman's possible implication in the intern's disappearance, the Metro Police went out of their way to make themselves accessible to the media. There were press releases, daily briefings, updates, and an unprecedented level of access granted to the media in the investigation. However, even after the FBI got involved and after public searches in Rock Creek Park where it was believed Chandra Levy was heading on the night she disappeared, there was still no victim.

When a person walking his dog discovered the remains of the victim in the exact spot where the police had searched for weeks, the police suddenly looked inept. Because they had searched the area and failed to find a body and because the body had been found at random, even the friendliest media had to ask what went wrong. The lesson here is not to go out of your way to alienate the media, but to understand that the media is not necessarily friendly. They're adversarial, and when police commanders try to make allies out of them by giving them information that could compromise an investigation, they can lose sight of the ultimate goal of the investigation—to catch the killer.

In fact, providing daily upbeat briefings to the press far from bolsters the rank and file detectives working the case. Instead, they may become frustrated at seeing incorrect information being fed to the media. On the other hand, if police release vital clues to the press, detectives can get even more frustrated because sometimes these clues are the only ways investigators will know if a suspect truly knows something about a homicide that nobody else knows. For example, was Chandra Levy's killer able to stay steps ahead of the police because they told him what they were thinking and where they were looking? We won't know until a suspect reveals what he knows to investigators and that is made public.

There is another member of the public audience reading the newspapers and watching television every day, the killer. Most serial killers are avid followers of their own story. For a sexual thrill killer or lust killer, the psychological high of the murder is reinvigorated by seeing the story in the news, because it allows the killer to reexperience the sexual excitement of the act. The news coverage also provides the killer with real-time intelligence into the investigators' activities as they pursue him. With each new piece of information that's disclosed in a daily briefing or press conference, the killer knows just how close the police are, what they know, and what he has to change about his methodology to throw them off the track. Bundy told us that he carefully followed news reports about his crimes because it told him where we were in the investigation.

An even more pointed example of how a killer will not only monitor what he sees on television about himself but will play to the news conferences is the recent media-driven dialog between the police and the assailant in the DC Beltway sniper case. Here, not only did the shooter(s) get the thrill of dealing directly with the chiefs in the jurisdictions where they attacked their victims, their actions brought in ATF and FBI units, involved the CIA and National Security Agency, had military helicopters and high-tech surveillance aircraft circling the areas in Maryland and Virginia where the shootings took place, and actually reduced Montgomery County Police Chief Charles Moose to tears on camera. But the ultimate experience for the power-motivated snipers had to be the revelation on national television from White House Press Secretary Ari Fleischer that the progress of the case was coming up each morning in the president's daily briefing.

If, for the shooter, recognition and acknowledgement of his ability to demonstrate his power over an entire population was a motivating force—and he did leave a message for police saying, "I am God,"—then is it not farfetched to suggest that the sight of police chiefs appealing for him to surrender, updating the media on the search for a white box truck while the sniper was cruising through the area in a dark blue Chevrolet, and the admission of the president's press secretary that news of the case was handed to the president alongside news of Osama bin Laden and Saddam Hussein was exactly what he was after? None of this was handed to the sniper by design. It was a product of an instant news society which thrives on "up close and personal."

But when police and talking heads actually manage to goad an assailant into his next crime or tell a television audience that the community is lucky the shooter hasn't attacked a school only to see, in response, that the sniper shoots and wounds a student on school grounds, it should be clear that the people in charge are doing too much talking. It should also be clear that having scores of self-anointed experts profiling an assailant on television also tells the assailant exactly what police and other consultants are thinking. As we will see, the sniper, seeking recognition for his own expertise, became so disgusted at the erroneous information the experts where disseminating that he actually gave the police the clue they needed to launch their investigation in earnest. If task force managers have not learned from the mistakes made during the Atlanta child murders or from the Chandra Levy case, maybe they'll learn from the DC Beltway sniper case that you don't investigate a case on national television. The lessons are obvious.

Also, over the course of a long-term task force investigation, the amount of information the police will give to the press will ultimately dwindle. It has to. As a task force investigation grinds on, someone near the top will realize that the detectives are making some progress, even if it's only the elimination of a number of suspects. They will want to protect that information because it will eventually lead somewhere. So the new disclosures of information will stop at some point. Then the press becomes edgy. Reporters find angles on their own. Often they interview victims' families to get a handle on the victims' habits. Where were they last seen? Who were their friends? Were there any witnesses that the police might have overlooked? And sometimes reporters will get lucky and actually stumble into something. Often it winds up in a newspaper story, tipping off the killer that there may be a witness out there who has seen him.

At the same time, of course, when the information flow starts to dwindle, the killer is also in the dark. If the police have information they have not released, it gives them time to follow up on leads and slowly amalgamate the facts—many of which might be already hidden in their files—that will lead them to a prime suspect. In fact, that's what police should be doing rather than worrying about profilers and other outside consultants. They should be going back into their own case files to find where a nexus of leads and tips takes them to the names of potential suspects. When police did this in the Paul Bernardo and Yorkshire Ripper cases, and ultimately in the DC Beltway sniper case, it led to the arrests of suspects and the crimes stopped.

The best example of a case where a faulty media relations program definitely influenced the process of an investigation is the previously mentioned DC Beltway Sniper case. Thus, it's instructive to look at the case in greater detail to examine just how the task force response to the media can impact the way the case is managed.

THE BELTWAY SNIPERS

"For you Mr. Police, 'Call me God,'" the letter read. "Do not release to the press." The letter was left by the assumed DC Beltway snipers near a Ponderosa restaurant in Ashland, VA, on October 19, 2002. It was there that a male victim, 37, from Florida was shot in the DC Beltway sniper shooting spree. "We have tried to contact you to start negotiations, but the incompetence of your forces," the letter continued, naming the agencies that the caller said he tried to contact, including the "task force FBI 'females'," but was frustrated. "These people took of calls for a hoax or joke, so your failure to respond has cost you five lives."

The caller and letter writer, presumably the same person who left the tarot card at one of the sniper shooting sites with the message, "I am God," was seeking to assert his power over the combined forces of two states, the federal government, and four county law-enforcement agencies. "If stopping the killings is more important than catching us now, then you will accept our demand which are [sic] non-negotiable."

The demands were, on the surface, as outrageous as the crimes themselves, demanding that ten million dollars be placed in a specific Bank of America Platinum Visa Account from which the letter writers would have "unlimited" withdrawal privileges at any ATM worldwide. "You will activate the bank account, credit card, and PIN number," the letter demanded. Yet, were they about the money, was this taken from the concocted plot of a Hollywood thriller, or were they about the exercise of power that the snipers were really after?

The series of DC Beltway sniper attacks began on October 2, 2002, at 5:20 p.m. with a single round fired through the plate glass front window of a Michael's Arts and Crafts store in Aspen Hill, MD. A witness thought she heard a pop and moments later saw a bullet hole in the window of the store.

She called police, who filed a report, and had no way of predicting that whoever had fired that shot would strike again, less than an hour later, this time with fatal results.

The first murder victim, 44 minutes later at 6:04 p.m., was James D. Martin. He was killed in the parking lot of a Shopper's Food Warehouse in Silver Spring, MD, only two miles away from where the first shot was fired. Then, with relentless persistence, on the very next day victims 2, 3, 4, 5, and 6 were each killed with a single shot, respectively. The police knew that they had a determined sniper on the loose. In the District of Columbia and counties around the district, traffic almost ground to a halt as police searched for a killer who almost had to be traveling by motor vehicle to have covered so much ground, invisibly, in so little time.

With fears of an al Qaeda attack underway around the nation's capital, a federal task force joining the case, and an FBI profile soon to be handed down, the ad hoc task force of local police where quickly overwhelmed with almost 3000 calls. Charles Moose, Chief of the Montgomery Police, appealed to the public for help. This was a mistake. But it was the appearances on national television of talking heads, pseudopsychological analyses on the weekend talk shows, and wannabe profilers that lit the fuse resulting in a schoolyard shooting.

Charles Moose's appearance heralded other appearances by the police chiefs of other counties where shootings took place as well as Bureau of Alcohol, Tobacco, and Firearms (BATF) superiors. The result was a babble of releases from the heads of the different investigations giving the killer(s) the signal that his actions were reaching the top of the various police commands. And for the type of killer this probably was, it was exactly what he wanted to hear. Clearly, at the very outset of the case and for all cases that result in the media's descending en masse upon the doorstep of the police station, a public information officer, someone specifically trained and designated to talk to the press, should be the only channel of communication between official police sources and the media. And even if the President of the United States is being briefed on the case, that's not information the killer needs to know.

Even after you have a public information officer, what should he do? What information should he release? The short answer is that there is no need to release any information to the press because the crimes themselves are the information. If the only information released in the DC Beltway Sniper case was that the police were looking for a common thread among the cases, that would have been enough. But when the police themselves began releasing specific information about leads, tips, Chevy vans, etc., they told the killer(s) how far away they were from making an arrest.

The bottom line is that police should never have released specific information about the possible offender or a suspect weapon because a savvy killer, knowing the police had identified the weapon, would dump the weapon into Chesapeake Bay as soon as he heard the press release. Police know, or should know, that the suspect watches every news story and reads the paper about his case, because that's his best source of information about what the police know. In the DC Beltway Sniper case it was obvious the suspect was watching television. Because after he was nearly taunted into going after a school child, he set up on the Benjamin Tasker school, wounded a student there, and left his tarot calling card for the police to find. It was a clear case of a killer responding to something he heard on television, goading him into his next shooting.

The shooting at the Benjamin Tasker School should have told police to shut off all communication with the outside world. Their own strategy had backfired, the media had taken away the case from them, and another wound had been inflicted as a result of the media's involvement in the case. Therefore, police should have simply become close-mouthed so the killer wouldn't learn anything more. But the police didn't do that. Instead they asked the killer over the air to communicate with them again. The fact that the killer had called them and had gotten a hang-up is not the media's business. It was a mistake for the police to give that information to the media. It would have been better for the task force to have gotten its act together and wait for the killer to call back. They always do.

THE WRONG PROFILE

As the *Washington Post* put it, "It wasn't, apparently, the work of al Qaeda operatives. It wasn't an angry young white man working alone." (*Washington Post* October 25, 2002). The profile and geoprofile notwithstanding, the sniper wasn't living in Montgomery County, Maryland. In fact, nothing that was said on television or in the press, either by the media profilers or the professional profiles released to the public, was correct. In the words of the *Washington Post*, the profiles were "off the mark" considering the identities and backgrounds of the two suspects, John Mohammed and 17-year-old Lee Malvo, who were arrested. Mohammed wasn't a 30-year-old white man with a part-time job who loved to watch football. He wasn't a resident of Montgomery County. In fact he was a drifter, a sometime homeless man, and was unemployed. On *Larry King, Live,* for example, Jack Levin said, "He has other responsibilities in his life. He may be married. He may be playing with his children, watching football on Sunday, or he may have a part-time job." And if that's who the police were looking for, it's no wonder the sniper slipped right through the net and was invisible on radar.

The profilers-for-hire, some of them ex-FBI or former detectives and others just true-crime writers, were elevated to the status of pundits concocting visions of phantom angry white men who fit the standard profile of a character out of a motion picture. The sniper's white van, also a media concoction, allegedly came from one of the witnesses who told a reporter that she had seen a white box van at the scene of one of the shootings. However, as many people who live in Montgomery County have pointed out, white vans are about as common in that area as Mercedes are along Rodeo Drive in Beverly Hills.

The problem is that these profiles tend to pollute the real investigation and, because they rise to the top of the media frenzy, divert investigators from the real work they should be doing which is digging in their own information for clues not the make-work of chasing down phantom suspects. How many times, for example, did the surveillance cameras at gas stations and ATMs pick up suspicious-looking white vans near crime scenes while, upon closer inspection, a nondescript Chevy Caprice was driving by in the background. In reality, it was the Chevy Caprice, police have charged, that was the shooters' car simply leaving the crime scene in plain sight while SWAT teams converged on any white van that lingered too long near a pay phone or a shopping center. Now, even the media is criticizing its own performance, saying, according to the *Washington Post* that "The media's performance raises a chilling possibility that the suspects might have evaded detection for so long because witnesses were focusing too intently on media-created 'profiles' that didn't come close to the real thing."

It was to be expected that in the microcosm of the 2002 bi-year elections, the preparations for a possible war in the Middle East, the ominous threat of terrorism everywhere in the country, fed, in large measure, by news leaks of FBI warnings of an imminent threat, and the general sense both in the public and in the media that another shoe bomb was about to drop, that there would be a huge rush to amateur analysis when the snipers began their attacks. So the rush to profile was almost inevitable, particularly in the dearth of any real information about the invisible snipers.

There was general astonishment among the profiling community that came out during the Monday-morning quarterbacking after a pair of African-American suspects were arrested. Again, it was my experience during the George Russell investigation in Bellevue, WA, in the early 1990s that when the police realized that Russell was black, they were amazed. Because the kind of profiling being done on television and by the FBI is more speculation than a fact-based inquiry, a lot of that speculation will be based upon the profiler's own prejudgments about who commits crimes and why. These will creep into an official profile and will affect the directions an investigation takes. Therefore, when profilers who have no experience with African-American snipers will blithely characterize the offender as a thirty-something white male, they are ignoring the past 35 years of social change in American society.

Why is this an issue? Because the nature of who can be a serial killer or spree killer is at the very heart of what police have to do in a task force investigation. They have to look at reality without preconditions. In a macabre way, looking at the changing face of a serial killer is like looking at the changing face of America, and George Russell, and possibly John Mohammed and Lee Malvo, are examples of this. Because serial offenders exist at the margins of society, and not in the mainstream, even though they can camouflage themselves in the mainstream of their victim pool, it is at the margins where one sometimes has to look to find the truth about what is taking place in society. America has undergone tremendous social change since the 1960s, statistics will show, particularly when it comes to the permeability of what, in before the 1960s would have been hard and fast racial barriers. Accordingly, if Mohammed and Malvo turn out to be convicted in the DC Beltway sniper attacks, it should be a wake-up call to profiler pundits that whether or not these are the days of "miracles and wonder," they clearly are not the days of Ozzie and Harriet.

Everyone, it was clear, was operating in the dark except the snipers who were simply looking for targets of opportunity regardless of their race or gender. The snipers were not targeting individuals as individuals, but only as members of a community. It was the community that was the target. But because the victims seemed so disparate, fitting no set racial or sexual profile while the killings were so precise, television crime analysts offered diverse opinions about the motives and background of the sniper. The geo-profile, offered by the Police Foundation, attempted to place the predicted location of the killer's residence, but even Charles Moose declined to attach any absolute certainty to the dependability of the profile. The geoprofile operates on a mathematical algorithm, which was based upon previous cases where known killers lived in juxtaposition to their crimes on the assumption that the killer lived in a house or apartment. It was not upon the possibility, here the fact, that the killer or killers were transients moving around the area. Thus the geoprofile couldn't work.

Therefore, it was simply impossible to predict where the killer lived based on the Police Foundation geoprofile even though, had the police made a thorough check of all the area motels and restaurants for the names that turned up the most, they might have found the suspects' names. Yet, in an effort to predict the killer's next move, when one of the media profilers made the thoroughly unprofessional public comment that at least the sniper had not struck at a school, it turned out to be a critical mistake.

On Monday, October 7, in Bowie, MD, shortly after eight in the morning an eighth grader, while getting out of a car at Benjamin Tasker Middle School, was struck in the left side of his chest by a single round. His aunt, who witnessed the shooting, drove him to Bowie Medical Center from where he was taken by MediVac to Washington. Police Chief Moose, saying that it was really "personal" now, wept on camera. Federal officials were warning that the killer would soon pay for what he was doing. And the White House Press Secretary reported the president's concern over what was taking place. If the sniper were on a power trip, driven by the absolute

high of dominating the national news and capturing the president's attention, what he was doing was working. And, ironically, it was revealed by
the media on Tuesday, October 8, that a power trip seemed to be what the
sniper was on when news of the sniper's handwritten message on the tarot
death card, number 13 in the deck, saying, "I am God," hit the front page
headlines.

Were there any other indications that power and the assertion of that
power might have been driving the DC sniper? Certainly his letter to the
police was a demand for the police to acknowledge his power by acceding
to his demands regarding the credit card. His constant phone calls to the
police were also assertions of his power, flaunting it in their faces. And, of
course, his continuing acts of shooting, even during some of the most heightened surveillance in the wake of the 9/11 attacks on the United States, were
assertions of that power. In fact, the lengths he took to continue his shooting spree when more cautious snipers would have backed off, waited, or
gone to far distant locations, were almost irrational assertions of power,
challenging police to find him.

By taking the totality of the media's intrusion into the process of the case
into account, you can't help but feel some sympathy for the frustration of
Montgomery County Police Chief Charles Moose, who, at one point, actually pleaded with the media to step back and let the police do their jobs. If
Chief Moose was trying to hold an investigation together in the spotlight
of media coverage and the media, not just through disclosures of what
should have been confidential information, but by inserting their own profilers into the mix and broadcasting their opinions directly to the sniper, he
certainly had to be at his wits' end as the media made it harder for him to
do his job.

The greatest media intrusion of all, however, had to be John Walsh, the
host of *America's Most Wanted,* inserting himself into the case. After the
task force released a special 800 number for the DC Beltway Sniper call,
after his repeated attempts to reach the task force ended in failure when
the operator refused to take his call, John Walsh went on nationally
televised *Larry King Live* where, instead of supporting the police in their
attempts to encourage the killer to contact them, he gave his own 800
number and asked the killer to call there. Since when do private citizens,
even those with large media audiences, insert themselves into the middle
of a high-tension multivictim homicide investigation to divert the killer
away from law enforcement? But, as ill advised as Walsh's strategy was,
it was a foreseeable response to the police strategy to use the media to
communicate with the killer. The police expected that if they asked the
media to facilitate communication with the killer, the media would go along.
But the media usually won't do that because they don't work for the police.
Just the opposite, the media are, and should be, adversarial. Therefore, it's
a naive strategy to broadcast a phone number for the killer and then expect
the media not to give another number for the killer to call. Therefore, police

departments should not rely on the media to cooperate. And it was naive on Chief Moose's part not to expect that the media, or John Walsh, would usurp his role as the contact for the sniper.

At the same time, however, it's only fair to point out that from the moment Chief Moose went before the cameras to talk about the case, he gave the power-assertive sniper part of what he was looking for at the outset—an affirmation of the killer's power. By continuing to stand before the cameras and provide updates and information, Chief Moose was compromising his own position at the top of the chain of command. Accordingly, what police departments should do, particularly in high-profile cases such as this, is delegate all media relations to a public information officer who controls disclosures, schedules briefings, and becomes the liaison between the media and the police. The role of a professional media relations or public information officer is absolutely critical in headline-breaking events that capture the media's attention (Irvine, 1988).

THE CRIME ASSESSMENT PROFILE OF THE POWER-ASSERTIVE KILLER

In evaluating the profile of a power-assertive killer, we have to look for the indicators of that power assertiveness, the clues that this is the personality the task force is after. We look for not just the continuing level of crime, but the assertion of the ability of the offender to keep on committing crimes right in the faces of the police. We look for the offender's response to events of the media, challenging the police through the statements they release to the media to show they're not only wrong but incompetent or impotent. The killer's invulnerability is as important as the police's inability to stop him. If power was the driver for the sniper, which his message on the tarot card made clear, and it was clear from his behavior that his acts were assertions of that power upon a defenseless community, one has to ask whether the professional profiles of him revealed this. More importantly, if profilers found the sniper to be power driven, why couldn't they put two and two together and figure out that power-driven offenders thrive on media attention and their ability to dominate the media headlines? The answer is that the profilers didn't understand what a power-driven killer is actually after and how that informs all of his actions. Had they been able to figure this out, the profilers would have advised the police to shut down all public disclosures until they could figure out where, in all the clues and tips the police had amassed, the critical information might be that would lead them to the identity of the suspect. In this way, they would have stopped feeding the killer's need for an affirmation of his power and actually pushing him to his next crime. They might have been able to see where the killer was on an arc of violence.

One can see from what the Crime Assessment Profile projects that power-assertive killers move across an arc or continuum of violence. At an early point in their dysfunction, they manage to find an equilibrium where they balance themselves between the emotional drivers that propel them and the socialization requirements that their lifestyles demand. This may put them right at the line separating criminal behavior from noncriminal behavior, and as long as they don't cross it they can stay at an equilibrium. They may stay comfortably within a victim pool and they may even creep up to contemplating an actual event with an actual victim but not perform an actual criminal act. Criminal thoughts are not punishable without the requisite criminal act. And so the potential offender may remain within the boundaries of the law until some event pushes him over the line and he begins committing crimes.

Many potential sexually oriented serial killers begin their careers long before their first actual murder with a series of small crimes, crimes that take them to the edge of their psychosexual thrill. They may begin by becoming peeping toms, passive stalkers, putting themselves in front of potential victims, and fantasizing about an act, simply for the thrill of it, but nothing more. At some point, however, they perform an act, maybe it's nothing more than getting busted for illegal drugs or picked up as a prowler, but that act puts them into the criminal justice system. At that point a fundamental change may take place in the mind of the potential homicidal offender.

In sex offender cases, sometimes the crime series begins with rapes, which become increasingly violent escalating to homicides. Sometimes, as in the case of Paul Bernardo, there was a homicide classified initially as "accidental" that started the series. Then the offender reverts to a series of rapes, which ultimately escalate to homicides. Sometimes, as in the case of Peter Sutcliffe, the homicides themselves become increasingly violent. The point, however, is that a crime scene assessment profile can often point not only to the psychological calling cards of the killer and categorize the killer to reveal to police what his motivations might be, but it also provide a roadmap of actions police might take to avoid pushing the killer into escalating his crimes or challenging the police. It seems clear from an examination of what we know about the DC sniper case that there were indicators about what kind of killers the offenders were and what the police should have done to avoid escalating the situation.

It is not readily apparent in the DC Beltway sniper case that there was any sexual motivation for the series of homicides. Therefore, it is prudent to assume that there is no sexual element here and the suspects currently in custody were not committing sexually-motivated homicides. However, power-assertive crimes need not be sexually motivated to satisfy the categorization requirements of a signature homicide series.

If the indicators show that the sniper attacks were the assertion of power, whether directly from the sniper(s) to the public and community at large or, if the two suspects now in custody are ultimately convicted or confess, which Lee Malvo has reportedly done, then how would such a profile have dictated a police response? First, as is almost axiomatic, the higher the level of the official who is communicating with the sniper via the media, the more successful the sniper's perception of his assertion of power has been. Accordingly, a direct dialog with Chief Moose, particularly a Chief Moose visibly shaken by the shooting at the Tasker Middle School in Maryland, would amount to almost a full satisfaction of the sniper's psychological need to assert his power. The more the police chiefs gathered on camera to discuss the case and indirectly send messages to the sniper, the more the assertion of power was working. Thus, why would the sniper stop his attacks when the attacks were bringing results?

An appropriate crime scene assessment profile would have shown that the victims the sniper was attacking were not the ends in and to themselves. Similarly, the homicides that Bundy committed in Washington, Colorado, and Utah, and possibly in Florida, were not ends in and to themselves. Bundy wanted what he called "private time" with his victims, moments he shared in a macabre relationship with the corpses of the young women he battered and then strangled. For the DC Beltway sniper, each new murder was a way to assert power, not over the individual victim, but over the community at large. Therefore, when the sniper left the letter demanding a payment of millions of dollars to a credit card account from one of his victims, far less important than the amount of money being deposited was the process by which banks and police would follow through. Each stop at an ATM thereafter would be a confirmation of the successful assertion of the sniper's power.

The sniper sought to communicate to police, called 911, berated them in a letter. Ultimately became so frustrated that the police weren't responding to him in the way he wanted that he gave them the single clue that turned their attention toward a crime he admitted committing in Georgia. This indicates that not only was the killer seeking to assert his power, but wanted a confirmation or acknowledgment of that power from the police. Chief Moose eventually gave the killer that confirmation when he apologized for the switchboard operators not picking up on the killer's message and actually repeating the killer's assertion, "our word is our bond."

Effectively, the sniper put his own words in the police chief's mouth. Of course, Chief Moose was playing out a strategy to bring the killers in, but he had to do it by parroting on national television what the killer's wrote and affirming their power over him in front of the world. It took a lot of personal courage for Chief Moose to do that, but it never had to get that far had police made the initial decision to buffer the killer from the police command through the deployment of a public information officer.

The value of a crime assessment profile is that it might just tell the police what the killer might be looking for and provide them an edge, which they would not normally find in the fog of a task force investigation. In this case, knowing what the killer might have been looking for might have enabled police to withhold disclosures that fed him. In other cases the crime assessment profile might focus police attention upon specific types of victims in specific locations. But most importantly, it would enable the task force personnel to believe in the effectiveness of their own investigation and realize that when names came up in the tips and clues as a result of their strategies, these names are worthy of investigation. If the same names come up more than once, they are indeed suspicious. Had the Yorkshire Ripper Task Force personnel believed in their own investigation and not fallen prey to the frustration that weakens trust, they would have known that they had a viable suspect in Peter Sutcliffe and would not have dismissed him as many times as they did.

Therefore, best practices require that: the profile be more than mere speculation or psychological hocus pocus, it focus on the crime and crime scene assessments, police rely on a systematic harvesting of data already in their files, and they believe that their strategies are working even though there are no apparent results. But how does an agency tie their crime assessment profiles and the data they've collected into a strategic system in which they can believe? The answer lies in the way the data is organized and how it can be retrieved. This is at the heart of the best practice recommendation that follows for managing and retrieving computer-based information.

COMPUTER PROGRAMS FOR STORING INFORMATION

As we were taught by our experience with the Ted Bundy cases, even the most rudimentary computer tracking system is better than shoebox filing and desktop random access. What you get is what you find. Today, looking at systems like HITS and TracKERS, which are built on a relational data-base technology allowing storage, filing, and retrieval, investigators can run names, license tag numbers, and car descriptions across scores, if not hundreds of cases, to see whether or not there's a data hit. In a serial killer investigation, the storing of names and tips into a computer database is of enormous help in building a reservoir of information within which all sorts of relationships may exist.

In the Yorkshire Ripper case, the indexing system of information was so cumbersome that when the British re-examined their own procedures, they strongly advocated building a computer database system. However, even in the DC Beltway sniper case where there were top-flight computer systems in place from the various state and federal agencies, including the FBI and BATF, the computer systems couldn't talk to one another so investigators had to run their tips and leads from room to room to look for hits within the databases. It's important to have a computer system for the storage of information, but in a multijurisdictional task force, it's also critical to make sure that the different agencies' computer database systems are compatible.

RECORD AND TRACK DECISIONS THAT ARE MADE

When the procedures that took place in the Yorkshire Ripper case and even in the Ted Bundy investigation are reviewed, it's clear that decisions were made about certain tips and leads by individual investigators or even by managers that weren't recorded in the file. In the Ripper case, even though decisions were made at the all levels, because there was no record of what the decisions were, investigators were almost starting from ground zero because they didn't know what, if any, previous decisions had been made regarding Peter Sutcliffe's file. As we pointed out, this had a devastating impact on the investigation. The lack of records regarding decisions made with respect to Sutcliffe also obscured the very fact that the investigation itself was working. Imagine pursuing a series of cases completely in the dark where the task force's procedures and strategies are working, but because there is no record of the decisions regarding that suspect the leads go into blind alleys. Most importantly, the fact that the investigation itself is succeeding is also obscured by the lack of record keeping. Thus, the recording of decisions made at all levels is a vital strategy that must be pursued.

CASE REVIEW AFTER 30 DAYS

In large municipal departments such as the Los Angeles Police Department or the Orange County Sheriff, robbery homicide investigators have built-in case reviews if a case isn't solved within a specific period of time. These case reviews are also milestones, requiring investigators to update records and save notes to file for the subsequent case review as the investigation moves over to a cold case file. These required reviews are important because they force detectives, or should force detectives, to take another look at all the evidence that's there and make connections they were unable to make because of the either the intensity of the investigation or the pressure of other cases. Case review also means that the reviewer can approach the file with a fresh pair of eyes.

We have found that required case reviews are also critical in serial killer task force investigations. In fact, whenever I'm called into consult on a serial killer case, one of the first questions I ask is whether there is a mandatory case review procedure in place and, if not, I ask that one be imposed. I have found that the review automatically brings facts together, relates clues and tips, and, if nothing else, also helps investigators to go over the names of potential suspects to see whether they've been thoroughly investigated and what decisions were made regarding further pursuit of them as suspects. Sometimes a needle will pop right up out of the haystack as if drawn by a magnet, and the magnet is simply a pair of eyes reviewing all the facts after 30 days to look over all the facts and to go over what decisions were made with respect to those facts.

These are the best practices that I have gleaned from my own cases and consulting on cases across the country. I believe the most important practice would be to catalog everything, including the decisions investigators make, and rely on the records and the good faith efforts of field detectives and the strategies pursued. Most, if not all, investigations usually produce the name of the suspect within the first 30 to 45 days. It's often what happens inside the management procedures and information filing systems of the task force that obfuscates what the investigators learn from their field work. Task forces can work if the task force learns how to simplify its procedures, stay out of its own way, and consistently review all records relating to each of the victims, the murder sites, the contact sites, and any other relevant sites associated with the cases. The suspect's name is already there. All the task force has to do is find it.

REFERENCES

Irvine, R. (1988). *When You Are The Headline,* Chicago: Dow Jones-Irwin.

Keppel, R. D., and Birnes, W. J. (1995). *Riverman,* New York: Pocket Books.

Keppel, R. D., and Birnes, W. J. (1997). *Signature Killers,* New York: Pocket Books.

Keppel, R. D., and Weis, J. P. (1993). Improving the Investigation of Violent Crime: The Homicide Investigation and Tracking System, National Institute of Justice Research in Brief, Washington DC, August 1993.

Washington Post, October 25, 2002.

INDEX